EDWARD EVERETT HALE: THE WRITINGS OF AN ECONOMIC MAVERICK

RESEARCH IN THE HISTORY OF ECONOMIC THOUGHT AND METHODOLOGY

Series Editor: Warren J. Samuels

RESEARCH IN THE HISTORY OF ECONOMIC THOUGHT AND
METHODOLOGY VOLUME 19-B

EDWARD EVERETT HALE: THE WRITINGS OF AN ECONOMIC MAVERICK

EDITED BY

WARREN J. SAMUELS

*Department of Economics, Michigan State University,
East Lansing, MI 48824, USA*

2001

JAI
An Imprint of Elsevier Science

Amsterdam – London – New York – Oxford – Paris – Shannon – Tokyo

ELSEVIER SCIENCE B.V.
Sara Burgerhartstraat 25
P.O. Box 211, 1000 AE Amsterdam, The Netherlands

First edition 2001

Library of Congress Cataloging in Publication Data
A catalog record from the Library of Congress has been applied for.

ISBN: 0-7623-0694-7
ISSN: 0743-4154

♾ The paper used in this publication meets the requirements of ANSI/NISO Z39.48-1992 (Permanence of Paper).
Printed in The Netherlands.

CONTENTS

EDITORS' INTRODUCTION
Ronnie J. Phillips and Douglas Kinnear   *vii*

IN MEMORANDUM: EDWARD EVERETT HALE (1975)
Wendell Gordon, David L. Miller and Daniel C. Morgan, Jr.   *1*

THE ECONOMICS OF EDWARD EVERETT HALE:
AN IMPRESSIONISTIC FRAGMENT
Hans Jensen   *7*

METAPHYSICS, SCIENCE AND VALUE THEORY (1926)
Edward Everett Hale   *27*

THE PROBLEM OF MONETARY STANDARDS (1933)
Edward Everett Hale   *57*

ECONOMIC PATTERN OF A DURABLE PEACE (1942)
Edward Everett Hale   *67*

REVIEW OF THE NEW ECONOMICS (circa 1947)
Edward Everett Hale   *77*

KEYNES: GENERAL THEORY OF EMPLOYMENT, INTEREST
AND MONEY (circa 1948–51)
Edward Everett Hale   *95*

ECON 327: COMPARATIVE ECONOMIC SYSTEMS (1948)
Edward Everett Hale   *105*

ECON 389: MARXIAN AND NEOCLASSICAL ECONOMIC
THEORY (circa 1953)
Edward Everett Hale   *139*

EDITORS' INTRODUCTION

This volume includes writings by and about Edward Everett Hale, long-time economics professor at The University of Texas at Austin. Included in this volume are the memorial statement prepared by his colleagues upon his death, a paper by one of Hale's outstanding students, five previously unpublished papers by Hale, and lecture notes taken by Hale's students in two of his most popular courses. Hale was a teacher, scholar, and administrator and, as the memorial resolution makes clear, was quite willing to stand up to the 'powers that be' whether they were the University of Texas administration or members of the state legislature.

A common theme is discernible in the writings of Hale from his graduate student days through the lectures given at the peak of his career in the 1950s. Hale repeatedly stressed two fundamental points: (1) the work of economists to be useful must have practical implications for the lives of everyday persons; (2) the most important economists are those who help tackle and solve the fundamental economic problems of their times. Thus the truly important economist, in Hale's view, is the antithesis of the ivory tower theorist. For this reason, Hale ranks Marx and Keynes (in that order) as the greatest economists. Marx exposed the fundamental contradiction of capital accumulation that success undermines the conditions for further success; while Keynes re-discovered the contradiction within the mainstream of economics at a time when the socio-economic system of democratic capitalism was in crisis.

One of Hale's fundamental themes is clearly evident in the first Hale paper included here, written in 1926 when Hale had returned to the University of Wisconsin to do further work on his Ph.D. (which he never completed). For Hale, mainstream economics was 'too metaphysical' and of little use to the 'common man'. To be relevant, economics must address the problems of everyday life.

The greatest economic crisis during Hale's lifetime was of course the Great Depression. Concern with the problems of the real world is evident in Hale's paper on the problems of monetary standards, written in 1933 shortly after Roosevelt had taken the U.S. off of the international gold standard. Hale points out that the Gold Standard had somehow been erected into 'a tradition sanctioned by all the weight and authority that attaches to a long established usage'. After all, Hale notes, it was really only after the Gold Standard Act of 1900 that the U.S. was exclusively on a gold standard, and because of the fractional reserve nature of our banking system, gold specie was never an effective constraint on the creation of money by banks. Hale concludes that the gold standard is an institution that we no longer need, if indeed we ever needed it. In place of a currency 'managed' by bankers, Hale foresaw a currency 'managed' by government. Indeed, Hale believed that the eventual outcome of Roosevelt's New Deal for banking would be the operation of banks by the federal government. Hale's prediction came very near to being true when the Reconstruction Finance Corporation owned one-third of the bank capital in the U.S. by the end of 1935. Hale failed to realize that a program of centralization of monetary power in the Board of Governors in Washington, together with federal deposit insurance, would restore control of the banking system to the private sector.

As Hans Jensen notes in his paper on Hale, it was undoubtedly the futility and economic waste of World War I, that had a telling impact on Hale and prompted him to study economics. The onset of World War Two was a global tragedy, both because of the loss of human life, but also because once again humankind had resorted to war to remedy economic ills. How can peace and prosperity coincide? War, Hale writes in a 1942 paper, is a consequence of economic competition between nation-states. To establish a durable peace requires the abolition of the economic causes of war. The solution, Hale felt, lay in the use of domestic monetary and fiscal policies to establish full employment and full-capacity output. In addition, income redistribution would be necessary both to alleviate the disparity between income classes and to provide adequate demand for mass-produced goods. Early on Hale embraced the Keynesian solution to the problem of inadequate aggregate demand.

Hale was a pragmatic Marxist, which, in the period after the publication of Keynes' *General Theory of Employment, Interest, and Money* and the Great Depression, meant that he was a Keynesian. The first paper on Keynesian economics is a lengthy review that Hale wrote of the Seymour Harris-edited volume on *The New Economics*. Some of this review was later used in Hale's famous paper (published posthumously) on 'Some Implications of Keynes' General Theory of Employment, Interest, and Money'. In the review, Hale also makes less-than-subtle attacks on the House Un-American Activities Committee. The final unpublished paper was likely prepared for the edification of those – such as members of the Texas state legislature – who might question exactly what was being taught just a stone's throw from the statehouse. In this paper, Hale sets forth, in a simple and straight-forward way, the principles of the 'new' Keynesian economics.

Hale and his fellow faculty members in the economics department at The University of Texas at Austin were frequently under attack from the legislature for their left-leaning views. There is also little doubt that Hale was very sympathetic to communism and to the socialist experiment in the Soviet Union. This is apparent in the 1937 article Hale published on 'Fascism versus Communism' in the *Southwestern Social Science Quarterly* (now SSQ). In this article Hale sought to compare the principles of fascism and communism to determine what elements, if any, they had in common. Hale concludes that the similarities are superficial, and that fundamentally fascism and communism are very different ideologies. Hale states: 'There is no common ground on which these two can meet. The conflict between them is irrepressible' (Hale 1937, p. 24). He goes on to predict that in the event of another great world war or a world depression, 'revolution of some sort, communist, fascist, or other, probably would be inevitable in Great Britain, France, and the United States' (Hale 1937, p. 24).

Hale expounded on his ideas about capitalism, socialism, and fascism in his famous course on 'Comparative Economic Systems'. Included in the present volume are the notes taken by William C. Frederick during the spring 1948 semester. Though the content of the notes has not been altered, the format has been modified. As originally typed by Frederick, the notes were in Frederick's personal outline style. They have been reorganized here in a more reader-friendly manner, though it must be stressed that they are indeed 'notes', e.g., there are many incomplete sentences in the text.

This volume concludes with Hale's lecture notes on Marx, Jevons, and Marshall. In his courses in the history of economic thought, Hale developed his idea that economics is a reflection of real world problems and that the great economists try to solve these problems. The three economists analyzed in these notes present the extremes and middle ground in terms of assessment of 'great' economists. Marx was in Hale's view the greatest economist, as already noted, because Marx dealt with real world problems and attempted a solution to those problems that would aid the common man. Marx was an activist, and this received high marks from Hale, even if it meant advocating the overthrow of the capitalist system. The other extreme among economists is represented by William Stanley Jevons, who is presented as an economist who did little, if anything, to help the common man but instead developed the theory of marginal utility for its own sake. Hale barely conceals his contempt for Jevons, though he does not accuse Jevons of intellectual dishonesty. Midway between Marx and Jevons is Alfred Marshall, who, not surprisingly, is presented as an early institutionalist economist. These lecture notes can thus be read as a dialogue between Marxism, neoclassicism, and institutionalism. These notes were transcribed by students in the early 1950s. It is noteworthy that many of the students who helped construct these notes went on to become economists, several with a specialty in the history of economic thought. These notes were viewed as important then and retain their importance for economists today.

These introductory notes are necessarily brief and those who desire more information about Hale and the Texas School of Institutional Economics may consult the references listed below, which include the only two papers published by Hale. The papers in the present volume are presented in chronological order as near as could be determined. Typographical errors have been corrected, and modifications of form have been made in some papers. The history-of-thought notes on Marx, Jevons, and Marshall were divided into sections by Roman numerals, most likely indicating the lecture number. However, since the numbering was not always consistent, these have been replaced with section titles that we have added in brackets [ ]. Section titles that were in the original text are not in brackets.

For assistance in the collection of these papers we acknowledge a great debt to William Breit and the late Wendell Gordon, both of whom encouraged and supported our interest in Hale from the beginning. We would also like to thank Rick Tilman for supplying a copy of the Hale paper written for John R. Commons and the Wisconsin Historical Society for permission to publish the paper on 'Metaphysics, Science and Value Theory'. We also thank Dan Morgan for permission to reprint the 'In Memoriam' prepared upon Hale's death in 1975. Hans Jensen, one of Hale's outstanding students and history-of-economic-thought scholar, graciously allowed us to publish his previously unpublished paper on Hale. We are grateful for his support. The comparative system lecture notes were provided by William Frederick and the history-of-thought notes were provided by Hans Jensen and the late Clifton Grubbs. Needless to say, this project would not have been completed without the persistence of Warren Samuels in urging us to prepare these papers for publication. We hope that they will help keep the Texas School alive for generations of economists to come.

Ronnie J. Phillips
and
Douglas Kinnear
Colorado State University

REFERENCES

Hale, E. E. (1937). Fascism vs. Communism. *Southwestern Social Science Quarterly* (June), 15–24.
Hale, E. E. (1976). Some Implications of Keynes' General Theory of Employment, Interest and Money. (With an introduction by R. Phillips). *Review of Radical Political Economics*. (Winter), 30–42.

Phillips, R. J. (1976). E. E. Hale's Analysis of Keynes's *General Theory*. *Review of Radical Political Economics*, Vol. 8, No. 4 (Winter), 30–31.

Phillips, R. J. (1989). Radical Institutionalism and the Texas School of Economics. In: W. Dugger (Ed.), *Radical Institutionalism: Contemporary Voices* (pp. 21–37). Westport, Ct: Greenwood Press.

Phillips, R. J. (1994). The Texas School of Institutional Economics. In: G. M. Hodgson, W. J. Samuels & M. Tool, *The Elgar Companion to Institutional and Evolutionary Economics*. Brookfield, VT: Edward Elgar Publishing.

Phillips, R. J. (1995). E. E. Hale on Economic Theory and the Real World. In: R. J. Phillips, *Economic Mavericks: The Texas Insitutionalists*. Greenwich, CT: JAI Press, Series on Political Economy and Public Policy.

DOCUMENTS AND MINUTES OF THE GENERAL FACULTY

REPORT OF THE MEMORIAL RESOLUTION COMMITTEE FOR EDWARD EVERETT HALE

The Special Committee of the General Faculty to prepare a Memorial Resolution for Edward Everett Hale, Professor Emeritus of Economics, has filed with the Secretary of the General Faculty the following report.

James L. Kinneavy, Secretary,
The General Faculty

IN MEMORIAM: EDWARD EVERETT HALE

Edward Everett Hale was born October 24, 1893, in Hubbard, Texas, the son of Elbert David and Mary Jerline Newton Hale. He attended Hico High School from 1908 to 1912 and The University of Texas from 1913 to 1916 and from 1919 to 1920, receiving a Texas B. A. in 1920. His undergraduate major subjects were English, Latin and History.

He served in the Signal Corps of the United States Army from February 1918 to June of 1919 as a wireless operator.

June 16, 1923, he married Kathryn Louise Jarrett.

From 1921 to 1923 and from 1925 to 1926 he attended Graduate School, majoring in economics and philosophy, at the University of Wisconsin, receiving an M.A. degree in 1923.

He was appointed to The University of Texas faculty in June, 1923, as Assistant Professor, specializing in labor economics and economic theory. He was promoted to Associate Professor in 1926 and to Professor in 1936.

Everett Hale served as Chairman of the Department of Economics from 1929 to 1934 and from 1939 to 1959, a number of years totaling a quarter century.

Edward Everett Hale: The Writings of an Economic Maverick, Volume 19-B, pages 1–6
2001 by Elsevier Science B.V.
ISBN: 0-7623-0694-7

About these years Dickens might have said "These were the worst of times," for they were a period of severe budget austerity combined with strong external pressures on the department. Yet Dickens might also have said "These were the best of times" – largely because of the role of Hale. Faculty and student morale was astonishingly high, perhaps higher than in later years of relative affluence and freedom from attempted restraints on academic thought.

Much of this is explained when one understands Everett Hale's personality as departmental chairman. His operations were reasoned and equitable. He was abreast of what was going on, yet did not 'bug' or interfere. He was meticulous with the 'paper work' (or else was careful to see that he had a secretary who was). He did not *allow* his own ego to stir up storms. Yet in times of crisis and on matters of principle he quietly provided firm leadership.

The Department also experienced some major crises during the Hale years: Legislative effort to fire the fabulous Professor Robert Montgomery during the late 1930s; the 1942 firing by the Regents of three junior members of the Department for defending the Wages and Hours Act at a mass meeting in Dallas; the firing of Homer Rainey as President of the University in considerable measure because of Dr. Rainey's defense of the Department of Economics, legislative efforts in 1951 to get Clarence Ayres fired (efforts that were underwritten in the Texas House by a resolution to which there was only one dissenting vote). During the 1944/45 period of troubles at the time of the firing of Dr. Rainey, Everett Hale made a notable appearance before a legislative committee to present the case of the Department (and the University).

In 1941 the Department had a distinguished British visiting professor, Eric Roll (later Sir Eric). A legislator, perhaps sensing a communist, called Professor Hale: "I have been hearing rumors about Professor Roll. Can you assure us that he would be willing to swear allegiance to the United States government?" "No," Hale replied, "I don't believe I could."

Desegregation was late in coming to the University. Even after they acquired legal permission to enter the UT-Graduate School Blacks did not generally regard their welcome as warm. But the Department of Economics under Hale's leadership was different: during the first half of the 1950s its one black graduate acquisition was treated like everyone else. A University administrator (not of high rank) got wind of this fact and telephoned Chairman Hale to inquire whether it was really true that (so-and-so) of his department was a Negro? The administrator received the polite Hale reply: "I'm sorry, I can't tell you; I forgot to ask him." But that kind of performance has never been highly rewarded by University of Texas administrations.

In 1959 Everett Hale turned over the chairmanship to Benjamin Higgins. From that point on he never attempted to manage the Department or even to meddle.

Over four decades Professor Hale taught a wide variety of courses. Among them were: Value and Distribution, Modern Economic Reform, Labor Problems, Foreign Labor Movements (Labor Movements), Trade Unionism and Labor Problems, Classical Economic Theory (Development of Economic Thought from 1776–1848), Neo-Classical Economic Theory (Development of Economic Thought from 1848–1900), Economic Trends, Comparative Economic Systems, Systems of Economic Thought, Contemporary Economic Theory, Theories of Depression (Theories of Economic Fluctuations), Systems of Economic Thought, Income and Employment (this being the name in the later years of the masterful course on Keynesian theory), and countless offerings of the elementary course under various titles.

But Everett Hale was not simply a teacher with broad interests, he was a great pedagogue. Thousands of his former students would attest to this fact today. His exposition was always clear and his logic was sound. In some of his courses he employed the Socratic method, in some he lectured. Somehow the technique always seemed appropriate for the subject. The Hale course in comparative economic systems was consistently one of the campus's most popular. And this was not because the man was an easy grader. As this is written local and national administrators are giving a lot of attention to 'grade inflation'. No such phenomenon would occur if professors were following Hale's example. As a matter of fact Everett Hale served as the index professor around the Economics Department. For the very stiff grading professor the students would say "Man, he's hard as Hale!" Nevertheless, the students loved his courses, because they learned their subject matter from this man.

In his lecture courses Hale brought large index cards to class. So much was verbalized from those cards that his students began to puzzle. Could it be that Hale knew so much that he merely brought those cards to class for purposes of modesty or else to feign authenticity? Believe it or not, the rumor spread that one student had actually seen those cards, and they were blank! The likelihood of blank cards began to be debated furiously, till wagers were laid on whether the cards really had notes on them.

In 1949, he wrote, but never submitted for publication, an article entitled: *Some Implications of Keynes' General Theory of Employment, Interest and Money*. It received a long-standing ovation when he read it at a departmental supper seminar. And in the years that followed it was reproduced for use as collateral reading in various national income theory courses over the country.

During the 1940s and 1950s he may well have been on more Ph.D. dissertation committees than any man in the history of the University. There was one stage when he was on something like a hundred such committees.

He was the supervising professor on the following thesis and dissertation committees:

Ph.D.:

1960 Mario Belotti: 'The Importance of Keynesian 'Dirigisme' and Christian Socialism in Postwar Italian Economic Policies'

1937 John O. Gragg: 'The Theory of Saving in English Classical Political Economy'

1944 Richard Johnson: 'The Legal Reserve Life Insurance Industry in the U. S.: An Appraisal of its Operations and Proposals for Reform'

1958 Irving O. Linger: 'The Role of Clearing under the Federal Reserve System'

1958 Dudley Luckett: 'The Interest Rate Pattern: A Theoretical and Empirical Study'

1931 Norman S. Spencer: 'Dynamic Theory of Interest: A Differential Analysis'

1955 Robert Voertman: 'Market Expansion and Economic Development'.

M.A.:

Mrs. Marjorie S. Brookshire, Gerald A. Brown, Austin L. Crouch, Allen Early, Jr., Annie Mae Engel, John O. Gragg, Mrs. Anne Davis Clark Gulo, John M. King, Calvin S. Lemke, Joseph L. Love., Nelson D. McClung, Anne McGarry, James W. McKie, Ernst S. Maas, Laura F. Nixon, Louis M. O'Quinn, William Bell Templer, Robert F. Voertman, Malcolm E. Wallace, Harry Williams, Jr.

Professor Hale served as a member of the Executive Committee of the University's Institute of Public Affairs during much of the 1950s.

In addition to his teaching and administrative work at the University, Professor Hale engaged in a major amount of labor arbitration. In several cases he was appointed as arbitrator by the Federal Mediation and Conciliation Service. A great many of his awards were published in Labor Arbitration Awards, Bureau of National Affairs., Washington, D. C., and in Employee Relations and Arbitration Service and in American Labor Arbitration Awards., both of the latter being Prentice–Hall, New York, publications.

Companies and unions for which he served as arbitrator in labor disputes include: Consolidated Vultee Aircraft Corp., Butane Equipment Co., Texas–New Mexico Pipeline Co., Republic Oil Refining Co., Atlantic Refining Co., Carbide & Carbon Chemicals Co., Carey Salt Co., Columbia Southern Chemical Co., Corn Products Refining Co., Ethyl Corp., General Refractories Co., Lone Star Steel Co., Magnolia Petroleum Co., Morton Salt Co., Pan-American Refining Co.,

Pan-American Corp., Phillips Chemical Co., Sinclair Refining Co., The Texas Co., Mineworkers, Brick & Clay Workers, Transport Workers, Chemical Workers, Brewery Workers, Machinists, Boilermakers, Oil Workers, and Steelworkers.

Other non-University activities over the years included: Labor Compliance Officer with the Dallas Office of the National Recovery Administration in 1934–35; Director, Division of Employment of the Works Progress Administration in San Antonio in 1935–36; public member of several Industry Committees of the United States Department of Labor between 1940 and 1942; State Price Executive, Office of Price Administration, Summer of 1942; Member of the Board of Directors of the San Antonio branch of the Federal Reserve Bank of Dallas from 1948 to 1953; consultant to the Stanolind Oil and Gas Company of Tulsa in 1952.

Professor Hale was listed in Who's Who in America, the Directory of American Scholars, and American Men of Science. He was a member of the American Economic Association, the Southwestern Social Science Association, and the American Association of University Professors. From 1945 to 1948, he was Chairman of the Subcommittee on Elementary Courses in Economics of the American Economic Association.

Professor Hale resigned as Chairman in 1959 and as a full-time teaching member of the Department in 1962. He was Emeritus Professor of Economics from 1962 until his death, February 3, 1975 at St. David's Hospital in Austin. He is survived by his wife Kathryn Hale, who lives at 7408 Cooper Lane in Austin. They have no children. He is survived also by a niece, Kathryn Hill of Brady and a nephew, Robert Hale of Jacksonville, Florida.

It should be said with emphasis that Professor Hale was a major influence in and on the Department of Economics at The University of Texas for four decades. He understood not only what a good department should be, but also what academic freedom and responsibility means when applied to a university community. He was a direct participant with other University staff members who were continually struggling to improve the University and to make it respectable throughout the country. If there is a sense in which the University has been saved from the onslaught of pressure groups whose ideas would lead to provincialism, mediocrity and stagnation, we can be assured that Professor Hale was one who helped in the saving.

As a person he was always courteous, honest, forthright and courageous in expressing his views. He was highly respected by members of the University and by business and labor associations with which he worked. He was conscientiously devoted to his work.

Prepared by a special committee consisting of Professors Wendell Gordon (chairman), David L. Miller, and Daniel C. Morgan, Jr.

Distributed to members of the General Faculty on July 16, 1975

THE ECONOMICS OF
EDWARD EVERETT HALE:
AN IMPRESSIONISTIC FRAGMENT

Hans Jensen

INTRODUCTION

This chapter consists of impressionistic observations about the economics of my old teacher, the late Edward Everett Hale, erstwhile Professor of Economics in The University of Texas at Austin.[1] It is, therefore, written from my perspective as a graduate student in economics at Austin in the early 1950s. These were years in which the Texas Department of Economics was still judged by some observers to be 'the most interesting in the country' (Galbraith 1981, p. 24n). The department was unique because of the unorthodox teachings of Ruth A. Allen, Clarence E. Ayres, Hale, Robert H. Montgomery, Clarence A. Wiley, and a small number of younger faculty members with heterodox views and leanings.

By virtue of his extensive, and controversial, literary production, Ayres was the most well known of the five 'big guns' of the Department of Economics on the Austin campus. Consequently, outsiders tended to identify the 'Texas school' (Ayres in Breit & Culbertson, 1976, p. 11) with Ayresian institutionalism. Ayres was the first one to point out, however, that the Texas school was a house with many dwellings. For example, he observed on several occasions that important and valuable comments, propositions and proposals had 'been

Edward Everett Hale: The Writings of an Economic Maverick, Volume 19-B, pages 7–26.
Copyright © 2001 by Elsevier Science B.V.
All rights of reproduction in any form reserved.
ISBN: 0-7623-0694-7

made most clearly and forcibly by Professor E.E. Hale . . . unfortunately never in print' (Ayres, 1944, p. 276n).

As a result of this lack of a Haleian publications record, the sources for the present chapter do not meet the conventional standards of scholarship in doctrinal history. With the exception of one posthumously published paper (Hale, 1976), which he wrote in 1949, none of my sources has come from Hale's pen, or even been authorized by him. Instead, they have come from the pencils of graduate students, including myself, who recorded Hale's lectures in the form of handwritten notes. Some of these were ultimately transcribed and mimeographed by enterprising students for circulation among their peers.

In my use and interpretation of these notes, I have frequently relied on personal recollections of conversations with Hale in the first half of the decade of the 1950s and on letters exchanged with him between 1956 and 1973. Needless to say, such an approach to the employment of secondhand sources, not to speak of this very employment itself, is fraught with danger. Hence what follows should not be construed to be an accurate rendering of what Hale 'really meant'.

WHY DID HALE BECOME AN ECONOMIST?

Why did Hale become an economist? In general, why do people become economists? Aside from certain frivolous motives, on which I shall not comment, there appear to be two basic sets of causal circumstances that induce individuals to select the practice of economics as a career.

In the first place, there are a large number of economists who have been programmed, as it were, to be interested in the purely technical or analytic aspects of mainstream economics. During their undergraduate and post-graduate days, these individuals became conditioned to gain satisfaction from the 'solution of all sorts of complex . . . mathematical puzzles' (Kuhn, 1970, p. 36). That is to say, 'colleges train aspiring young economists to use this language (of mathematics); graduate schools require its knowledge' and departments of economics 'reward its use' (Leontief, 1971, p. 2). The result is that economists so rewarded are habitually and single–mindedly in continuous 'pursuit of ever increasing rigor' in their research and teaching, even if their 'theoretical exercises . . . rest on assumptions that fly in the face of facts' (Gordon, 1976, pp. 1, 5).

But there is another, and apparently shrinking, group of persons who were originally attracted to economics because 'they wished to solve live economic problems and felt a need to master the weapons provided by the science which deals with these problems' (Stigler, 1965, p. 56). They did not scuttle their initial concerns, however, once they achieved such a mastery. On the contrary, they continued, and continue, to 'ask the really big questions about the economic aspects of society – questions which, because they are big, must be concerned with . . . the institutional fabric'. Hence their 'credo' is 'relevance with as much rigor as possible', rather than 'rigor regardless of relevance' (Gordon, 1976, pp. 10, 12). It is not surprising, therefore, that several of these practitioners of normative economics accept Alfred Marshall's dictum that 'almost every existing institution must be changed' (Marshall, 1975, p. 341).

Hale belonged to the group of concerned economists who were, and are, preoccupied with the relevance of their discipline. He belonged to this coterie by virtue of the circumstances that induced him to study and practice economics.

When he returned to The University of Texas to resume his undergraduate studies after his discharge from the Army in 1919, Hale did so as a troubled person. He once told me that he had become convinced by that time that the First World War, and its protraction for four years, had economic causes and roots. He was therefore of the opinion that the discipline of economics might contribute to the prevention of a reenactment of the Great War. He felt so, he said, because sane policies had to be based on economic literacy as a means to the fostering of an understanding of the relationships among war, peace, politics, and economic phenomena.

Although he was by no means certain that the study, practice and teaching of economics would actually promote peace, Hale believed that these activities, properly conceived and executed, offered the best hope in this respect. Consequently, upon his completion of the requirements for a Bachelor's degree in the humanities in 1920, he decided to embark upon a program of graduate studies in economics. With this objective in mind, he sought, and was granted, admission to the Graduate School of the University of Wisconsin, which he entered in 1921.

Given his predilections and motivations, Wisconsin was a logical choice for Hale. In the early 1920s, the Madison Department of Economics was being shaped in the mold of John R. Commons' 'institutional economics of collective action' (Commons, 1964, p. 62). The department was therefore characterized by an openly displayed commitment and devotion to 'social and institutional reforms' (Harter, 1962, p. 6) which appealed to the young Hale.

THE WISCONSIN LEGACY

As a practitioner of economics, Hale was deeply influenced by his experience at the University of Wisconsin. This experience did not make him a follower of Commons, however; at least not in the conventional sense of the term. Instead of accepting the whole cloth of Commons' institutional economics, Hale selected a limited number of strands in that fabric and interlaced them anew in such a manner that a peculiarly Haleian type of economics emerged in the process.

From the point of view of its impact upon the economics of Hale, the most important strand selected by him was in the nature of an historical approach which involved a synthesis of doctrinal history and socioeconomic history. This aspect of the Wisconsin school is displayed prominently in the first volume of Commons' *Institutional Economics* where he observed that "institutional economics consists partly in going back through the court decisions of several hundred years" for the purpose of laying bare those processes in which "collective action . . . takes over, by means of these decisions, the custom of business and labor . . . ". Obviously, an analysis of this kind must be carried out within a frame of reference. Commons selected "the history of economic thought" as his framework. Consequently, his historical "interpretation also consists in going back through the writings of economists from John Locke to the Twentieth Century . . .". By means of this method, he was able "to give to collective action, in all its varieties, its due place throughout economic theory." But although collective action 'has always been there', i.e., in economics, Commons argued that it was not until the "middle of the Nineteenth Century" that real "beginnings (were) laid for institutional economics" by such "heterodox economists . . . as Marx, Proudhon, Carey, Bastiat, (and) MacLeod" (Commons, 1959, Vol. 1, p. 5; 1964, p. 59i and 1959, Vol. 1, p. 5).

A second strand selected by Hale consisted of a concern with, and an attempted explanation of, the 'causes of . . . unemployment' (Commons, 1959, Vol. 2, p. 550). This preoccupation, which was deeply embedded in the economics of Commons, also came to occupy a central place in the economics of the mature Hale. Moreover, the way in which Hale combined this strand with the aforementioned intertwined theories of doctrinal history and socioeconomic history was also conditioned to a certain extent by Commons' approach, especially by his view of the nature and functions of institutions and clusters of institutions.

As Commons saw it, institutions function, and sometimes malfunction, by virtue of being the depositories, guardians and executors of society's 'working rules' which consist of an amalgam of 'customs, precedents, statutes, and habitual assumptions' (Commons, 1959, Vol. 2, pp. 705, 706). Institutions do not function atomistically, however. On the contrary, their operations are coordinated and synchronized in consequence of the fact that they form 'institutional structures' (Harter, 1962, p. 212). Hence it is from such structures that the working rules emanate. As a result, when individuals are told by these rules what they 'can, cannot, must, must not, may, or may not do', their resultant 'economic behavior' is structured rather than random (Commons, 1959, Vol. 1, p. 71).

This notion, or concept, of structure was to play a fundamental role in Hale's future economic thinking. It was also a concept which stimulated his interest in the fields of labor economics and comparative economic systems;[2] subdisciplines which Commons and his colleagues viewed as integral parts of the entire corpus of institutional economics (Commons, 1959, Vol. 2, pp. 876–903).

HALE'S HISTORICAL VIEW OF ECONOMICS

By the early 1950s, Hale's economics had crystallized and achieved the status of an oral tradition which, by then, had become an influential and recognized component of the Texas school of economics. Based on the initial impressions and influences which he had received at the University of Wisconsin, Hale's mature economics was grounded in history and the result of many years of study of, and reflections on, the works of those scholars whom he called the 'great' economists' (Hale, 1952, Lecture 1).[3] As he saw it, however, the greatness of an economist is synonymous with his success. Hale put it in this way:

> The history of economic thought is only concerned with the successful economic thinkers and writers. This criterion, success, is determined not by originality or priority of the economist concerned. Success is dependent on the influence of the thinker (or the writer) on his contemporaries and on future generations. Influence, that is, on public policy, legislation, and on molding the economic climate of present and future generations, and on the founding of socioeconomic movements, and influence on other writers and thinkers (Hale 1952, Lecture 1).

Hence as far as success in economics is concerned, it 'is influence, not originality, that counts'. For example, Richard Cantillon and Hermann H. Gossen were highly original writers, but 'Cantillon was unknown to his own generation' and 'Gossen commanded no attention whatsoever' when his work in economics was published in 1854. Such writers have therefore 'remained unknown to most people ever since' their first, only and unsuccessful forays into economics (Hale, 1952, Lecture 1; 1953, Lecture 3; 1954, Lecture 17, and 1953, Lecture 3). Some of the truly successful economists of the past were more successful than others, however. The "greatest, or most successful, writers," said Hale, were those economists who "influence(d) both reality ... and thought." And Hale had no difficulty in identifying these masters, as he fondly dubbed them: 'Adam Smith, Ricardo, Stuart Mill, Karl Marx and Keynes shaped both reality and the development of thought', as did 'Malthus'. Among these, Hale awarded Marx the top prize for influence: 'Marx had a tremendous influence both on socioeconomic movements and on thought ... The influence of Marx may be said to have been greater than (that of) anybody else in the world of economics, his influence has seemingly been greater than both the influence of Adam Smith and Ricardo' (Hale, 1952, Lectures 1, 2). In Hale's opinion, Keynes came in as a close number two. "In our own time," observed Hale, "John Maynard Keynes has had a tremendous influence on both theory and policy". Consequently, his *General Theory* "will (not only) be ranked with the *Wealth of Nations* and Ricardo's *Principles*," its influence will also be judged to be of Marxian proportions because it afforded "the only alternative to Marx and Marxism" in the 1930s (Hale, 1953, Lecture 3; and 1952, Lecture 1).

In Hale's frame of reference, the architects of the neoclassical body of doctrine were less successful than were the classicists, Marx, and Keynes. For example, the founders of the "psychological, marginal utility school (Jevons, Menger, Walras) . . . have only had influence on thought and hardly any influence on policy or (socioeconomic) movements." Thus although the members of this trio were 'great' economists, they were not so great as Smith et al. because the trio "influenced (only) economic thought . . . (and) not reality" (Hale, 1953, Lecture 3; and 1952, Lecture 1).

Hale consigned the fourth designer of the neoclassical paradigm, Alfred Marshall, to a halfway house between the true masters and the merely great. According to Hale, "knowledge for its own sake, (or satisfaction of) idle curiosity, has never been the motivation . . . for Marshall." On the contrary, he was "deeply concerned with the problems of Great Britain of his day" and "wanted to use knowledge to throw light on practical problems and issues". This concern with the 'evils of society' prompted Marshall to accept appointments on Royal Commissions and to appear as an expert witness before Parliamentary Committees and other investigatory bodies. Marshall was therefore in a position to "tell the lawmakers" about the 'means . . . (to) be used to reach . . . preconceived goals" (Hale, 1954, Lecture 28). Hence Hale acknowledged that Marshall had more influence on reality than did Jevons, Menger and Walras; but as he (Hale) saw it, it was an influence that was much less conspicuous and discernible than was that of Smith, Ricardo, Marx and Keynes.

Given his concept and definition of success in economics, it is not surprising that it was the contributions of the great economists that constituted the bulk of the subject matters which Hale taught in his most famous courses: Classical Economic Theory, Neoclassical Economic Theory, and Income and Employment. In other words, Hale was primarily concerned with the works of those economists who had blazed new doctrinal trails. And it was the thoughts of the masters among the innovators, especially Smith, Marx, and Keynes, that influenced Hale's thinking, rather than the works of those economists who engaged in 'normal research' with a view to a 'further articulation' (Kuhn, 1970, pp. 36, 24) of the purely analytic apparata ensconced in the innovators' bodies of doctrine.

Hale himself was an articulator *par excellence*, namely of the economics of the masters. He was not, however, an articulator *a la* the typical practitioner of 'normal (economic) science'. In economics, as elsewhere, the 'areas investigated by normal science are . . . minuscule; the enterprise (of normal research) . . . has drastically restricted vision' (Kuhn, p. 24). Hale's outlook and approach were different. He shared the bold vision of the masters, and he articulated their concerns, their images of the economic order and its problems, the sources and foundations of their formal analyses, and the methods of their theoretical inquiries. The result of this effort was a distinct body of Haleian economics which was a unique blend of doctrinal history and analysis of actual socioeconomic problems and processes. In short, Hale's economics was doctrine–history cum political economics.[4] It was therefore logical for him to insist that economics must deal with the economic problems of the world in which human beings actually live. He put it in this way:

> Economics is a hypothetical science. The assumptions on which theories are built must be realistic, or must seem realistic in their time. A theory has only meaning to the extent and degree its assumptions are accepted as realistic. Only if this is the case can theories throw light on economic conditions at their time (Hale 1953, Lecture 2).

Hale's notion that the practitioners of economics must hypothesize about real-world phenomena and problems was an outgrowth of his Wisconsin-based sociology of knowledge according to which, to use Werner Stark's words, there is a close and definite "interconnection between human thought and social life" (Stark, 1958, p. 11). Hence the main feature of this particular sociology, which Hale formulated between ca. 1926 and ca. 1950, consisted of a relativistic interpretation of the history of economics. Due to his reluctance to publish any of his ideas, Hale's conceptual framework for the study of doctrinal history was not available to his students in printed form, however. In order to remedy this situation, at least partially, he included in his lists of readings such works as Wesley C. Mitchell's *Lecture Notes on Types of Economic Theory*, Harvey W. Peck's *Economic Thought and its Institutional Background*, and Ferdinand Zweig's *Economic Ideas: A Study of Historical Perspectives*. Each of these works, in its own special way, is cast in the mold of a 'relativistic approach' to the study of the history of economics (Peck, 1935, p. 367).

HALE'S INTERPRETATION OF DOCTRINAL HISTORY

After a careful and extensive reading of the major contributions to the economic literature, Hale was convinced that economic 'theories do not develop in a vacuum'. On the contrary, as he saw it, any given theory is formulated 'under particular circumstances and conditions and these conditions shape or influence the type of theory which is developed'. In other words, it was Hale's 'thesis . . .

that economic theory is an intellectual reaction to reality'. Hence in order to 'understand any particular theory, we must know the issues and problems of the age in which the theory was developed' (Hale, n.d., Lecture. 3; and 1953, Lecture 6). These notions and concepts, Hale summed up as follows in his introductory lectures in Classical Economic Theory in the Fall Semester of 1952.

> The theme of this course is that the development within the science of economics has been a series of responses to changing economic conditions in the economy and in society. The successful writers and thinkers are those who are concerned with the problems of their own time. They propose means for the solution of the problems in reality. . . . Economic ideas are the result of reality. They are generalizations of problems in society . . . (Consequently, a) change in the institutional structure of society will cause a change in economic theory (Hale, 1952, Lectures 2, 4).

According to Hale, "all economic theory is illustrative of that fact". Mercantilism "grew out of the commercial revolution," Physiocracy was born of "an agricultural revolution," and "classical political economy developed in England after the so-called Industrial Revolution" and the "rise of the industrial system" of that country; and "Keynesian theory is the result of the Great Depression of the 1930s" (Hale, n.d., Lecture 3) Hale admitted, however, that the "thesis that economic theory is an intellectual reflection of real problems" is somewhat "thin in the case of Jevons" and his intellectual compatriots; "but it is present," he said (Hale, 1954, Lectures. 14, 28).

In the first place, the emergence of the new economics of the late nineteenth century was stimulated by a change in the nature of unsolved economic problems. In the classical period, the 'problem seemed to be production' and there appeared to be 'no trouble with markets' and demand. At the end of the nineteenth century, on the other hand, 'markets were not considered unlimited anymore'. Consequently, the 'conditions of demand became more significant . . . than the problems of supply'. Secondly, in viewing the contemporary economic landscape, it appeared to some economists, in particular Marshall, that 'the cost theory of the classicists was inadequate' as an explanation of what was actually occurring on the supply side of the economy. Thirdly, the economic problems of the time seemed not to be very 'serious'. As a result, economic issues and problems ceased to be debated to any large extent in society at large. It meant that 'economics . . . retired into the academic halls' where it was left in the hands of 'learned professors' who spun 'out their subtle theories by heavy use of mathematics'. This was a logical development inasmuch 'as they did not have (any) great problems to occupy their minds'. It could therefore be argued, said Hale, that neoclassical economics was "a reflection in a negative sort of way," namely a reflection of the absence of serious economic problems (Hale, 1954, Lectures 15, 14; 1952, Lecture 3; and 1954, Lecture 14).

But when the countries of the West were 'hit' by the Great Depression of the 1930's, 'economics was (again) placed in the turbulent life of the market place (and) drawn out from the academic halls to the wild life of the town square'. The result was, of course, the appearance of *The General Theory* by Keynes. Thus Keynes' success as a paradigm builder was a latter–day confirmation of Hale's thesis that 'all economic theories are relative to time, place and circumstance and (therefore) . . . not absolute truths' (Hale, 1954, Lecture 14, and n.d., Lecture 3).

But what motivates an individual, or group of individuals, to undertake the task of fashioning a new economic theory? That is, why did each of the so-called great economists respond in a novel fashion to a discernible change in the socioeconomic actuality?

Hale obtained the beginning of an answer to that question when he was a graduate student at the University of Wisconsin. For instance, Commons observed that Francois "Quesnay was the original agricultural economist" and that his *Tableau économique* represents the eternal "view of . . . farmers who complain that the middlemen, manufacturers, and urban residents take so much from their product" that they are impoverished "and must eventually abandon their farms and move to the cities." Quesnay was therefore in favor of policies leading to the emergence of an economic order in which the "artificial or collective scarcity of Mercantilism is eliminated." According to Commons, Quesnay took this position in consequence of his particular use of the concept of 'Natural Order'. Thus, said Commons, "where Locke had looked on natural law as justifying manufacturers and merchants against kings and landlords, Quesnay saw it justifying kings and landlords against merchants and manufacturers". Moreover, as Commons saw it, "Adam Smith took over bodily this branch of Quesnay's Natural Order (i.e., natural law), but used it to justify the capitalists instead of the landlords or monarch." Commons concluded, therefore, that whereas Locke, Quesnay and Smith agreed upon the concepts to be used in economic analysis, they "differed respecting the beneficiaries" for whose sake economic policies and reforms were to be instituted (Commons 1959, Vol. 1, pp. 130, 133, 135, 138, 135, 138).

Hale's continuous study of, and reflections on, the economics of the innovators provided him with what he considered to be empirical evidence of the basic correctness of the Wisconsin thesis of strong interconnections between class interests, on the one hand, and the contents of economic doctrines, on the other. Thus he accepted Marx's proposition that classical political economy was "a rationalization of the interests of the capitalist class." Hale observed, for example, that Smith "developed a theory which supported the interests of the middle class" at a point in time when "the middle class was ready to accept political power" in England (Hale, 1953, Lectures 4, 6). Moreover, Hale commented approvingly in 1953 that "Peck (1935) generalized this statement (by Marx about classicism) to include all economic theories" (Hale, 1953, Lecture 5). There is, therefore, substantial evidence to the effect that Hale agreed with Peck and Zweig that economic theories are "rationalizations of various economic interests" so that "a particular economic theory is a rationalization of . . . the interests" of a given 'class' (Zweig, 1950, p. 13. Peck, 1935, p. 77). Hale elaborated on this proposition as follows.

> (F)rom that point of view) . . . Mercantilism would be a rationalization of the interests of a ris-
> ing merchant class . . . French physiocracy . . . would be a rationalization of the interests of a
> rising class of capitalistic farmers or the capitalist farming class. English classical political
> economy . . . would be essentially a generalization and a defense of economic and other poli-
> cies favorable to a rising class of industrial capitalists . . . (And) Marxian theories (would be a
> generalization of the interests of) a class-conscious proletariat . . .(Hale, n.d., Lectures 4–5).

According to Hale, neoclassical economics was also class conscious, but in a way that was different from the manner in which early classicism was class oriented. With the advent of neoclassicism, said Hale, economics "ceased to be a criticism of (the) economic practice" of an established class "as it had been in the time of Adam Smith." Instead, economics "became a defense of the existing order." But in spite of the fact that the new economics was conserving, or conservative, whereas the old doctrine was subversive, the former was just as 'normative' as the latter, of course (Hale, 1952, Lecture 3; and n.d. Lecture 5).

Finally, Hale made the following comments concerning the ideological contents of the economics of Keynes:

> Now, Keynes' theory is the same thing. I think there can be no question that Keynes was
> interested in working out and in rationalizing certain economic problems, certain economic
> policies which he considered essential to the maintenance and continuation of the capital-
> istic system; that is, he develop(ed) a theory which furnished the basis for a set of policies
> which he thought would save capitalism, a system which had been most grievously impaired
> by World War I and the depression of the 1930s (Hale, n.d., Lecture 7).

As a doctrine-historian, Hale could therefore not 'help but notice the bias and prejudice present in the (works of even the) greatest of the economic thinkers. None of them escaped his society and thus did not attain complete objectivity'. This does not mean, however, that Hale viewed Keynes, or any of the other architects of doctrines, as a 'propagandist'. Each of these writers 'thought (that) his theory was true'. In other words, as far as 'the great figures in the history of thought' are concerned, Hale did not question 'their sincerity and (belief in their own) objectivity and (devotion to the) pursuit of truth' (Hale, 1953, Lecture 5; and n.d., Lectures 7, 7–8).[5]

The innovating economists engaged in such pursuits with the aid of certain analytic instruments which Hale labeled 'scientific elements'. It was from such elements that the great economists constructed those 'economic laws' which they employed in order to 'describe what is' and for the purpose of predicting what might happen in the economic order under certain, given conditions. And, argued Hale, the integrity of the scientific elements was not compromised by the fact that they were embedded in purely 'fictional elements'. In Hale's opinion, it "would be very difficult to get along in this world if we did not make use of some fictions." The innovating economists, in particular, would have been intellectually paralyzed if they had not resorted to fiction. Hence they did so, of course, and their "fictions . . . comprise the philosophic rationalizations, the fundamental preconceptions or assumptions underlying the (entire) system of thought" which they erected. Among these theory-supporting foundations, Hale assigned special prominence and importance to the concepts of 'natural order, . . . natural rights' and 'natural laws' in classical economics; to the 'labor theory of value' in early classical economics and in the economics of Marx; and to the concept of the 'economic man' in classical and neoclassical economics (Hale, n.d., Lecture 10; 1954, Lecture 14; and n.d., Lectures 10, 12, 10, 12, 14, 13).

It may therefore be argued that Hale employed a Schumpeteresque notion according to which the great economists had built their models and theories on a 'preanalytic' or 'prescientific' foundation (Schumpeter, 1954, p. 42; and 1949, p. 350). In other words, as Hale saw it, the scientific elements of a given body of doctrine consist of those analytic tools which the innovators constructed in order to explain and predict how certain preconceived goals could be achieved. Thus he observed that the fictional assumptions "are used to justify certain policies." But, said Hale, the details and particulars of these recommended policies were derived by the successful economists from the conclusions which they reached on the basis of their formal analyses. The variables selected for analysis, and hence the outcome of such analysis, depended, however, on the entire mix of 'fictions' employed by a given writer. For example, Hale observed that the "labor theory of value . . . was developed and used by John Locke to justify the institution of private property, and about 150 years later it was used by Karl Marx to condemn the institution of private property" (Hale, n.d., Lectures 12, 10, 14).

It may be concluded, therefore, that Hale was a true relativist in his interpretation of the history of economics. It meant, of course, that he slighted the contributions of the 'puzzle–solving' practitioners of normal economic science (Kuhn, 1970, p. 35). He did so largely for two closely related reasons. In the first place, when economists turn from the solution of real world problems to the solution of puzzles, Hale felt that their discipline is reduced to a game to be conducted for its own sake. Secondly, he was of the opinion that increasing professionalization and mathematicalization of normal economic science are synonymous with expanding intellectual conservatism which presents growing barriers to the acceptance of potentially promising new departures in economics. Hence, in his opinion, to the extent that intellectual conservatism is dominant in the profession, to the same extent will its practitioners be incapable of dealing with new socioeconomic problems. Thus, although he may never have said so, I have a feeling that Hale would have agreed with Mitchell that the "passing on of ideas from one to another and their development by successive genera- tions as an intellectual stunt has been ... a secondary rather than a primary factor" in the formulation of new approaches to the study of socioeconomic problems and phenomena (Mitchell, 1967, p. 99)

Hale's contributions to the Texas school were not confined, however, to the infusion of a corpus of relativistic doctrine history into a curriculum that was influenced by the institutionalism and instrumentalism of Thorstein Veblen, John Dewey and Ayres. As pointed out above, Hale also developed his own rather distinct political economics of capitalism which was intimately intertwined with his interpretation of the history of economics. That was so by virtue of the fact that both approaches rested on a common foundation. This base consisted of a thesis, or a theory, according to which it is 'the institutional structure of society' that determines the economic problems of society and, therefore, also those economic theories which the successful economists formulated 'in an attempt to solve (these) problems' (Hale, 1952, Lecture 4, and 1976, p. 34).

In basing his economics on this type of foundation, Hale in effect placed himself within, and contributed to, a tradition that reached its apogee in 1958 with the publication of Claude Levi–Strauss' book on *Structural Anthropology*.[6] I am, of course, referring to the intellectual movement known as structuralism.[7]

A CONJECTURAL VIEW OF HALE'S 'STRUCTURAL ECONOMICS'

The term structuralism refers to a viewpoint, a view, an approach and a method of inquiry which leads its practitioners to concentrate their attention on subsur- face phenomena in those subject matters that are studied in a number of disciplines in the humanities and in the behavioral, cultural and social sciences. The investigators in question take this approach in order to lay bare 'the rela- tions among (the said) phenomena' with a view to specifying the structural 'system' into which 'these relations (may) enter'. In so doing, however, the structuralists are not so much concerned with 'the nature of the (underlying) phenomena themselves' as they are with the consequences and effects of such systemic elements (Jacobson, 1963, p. x.; Levi–Strauss, 1963, p. 279; Jacobson, 1963, p. x). That is to say, the structuralists make their inquiries into the nature and character of subsurface systems because they are convinced 'that surface events and phenomena are to be explained by structures, data, and phenomena below the surface' (De George & De George, 1972, p. xii). As far as capitalism is concerned, Hale shared this conviction.

Thus in his frame of reference, the surface phenomena consist of employment and unemployment, income and its distribution, buying and selling, consumption and saving, investment and disinvestment, borrowing and lending, prices, wages, profits, and so on. As Hale saw it, these processes and variables are influenced and conditioned by underlying institutional elements which are bound together in an 'economic structure ... through which goods ... get produced' and which, in toto, constitutes the 'capitalist system' with which he was concerned (Hale, 1954, Lecture 14).

The manner in which Hale conceived of this structure, and the socioeconomic problems which it caused, may be inferred from some observations which he made concerning the particular "types of theory in which we," i.e., Hale's 'generation', are "positively interested today" (Hale, 1953, Lecture 2). In his comments on this topic, Hale selected as his point of departure a pronouncement by Zweig according to which the "history of economic thought ... needs to be rewritten for every generation." That is partly due to the fact that every "generation is interested in different parts of the ... material presented by historical experience." "For example," said Zweig, "the present generation is interested above all else in the rich material presented by the mercantilist epoch" (Zweig, 1950, p. 1). Hale's elaboration on this proposition reads as follows:

> Today we have a positive interest in mercantilism because our economic problems have a close similarity to the problems of the mercantilist writers. Therefore we think that we understand better the issues with which the mercantilists were concerned. The mercantilists practiced economic control and economic planning. These are the issues today. Those people who advocate economic control and planning are the grandchildren of the mercantilists. The most striking revival of mercantilism is (found in) the theories of J.M. Keynes. The Keynes of *The General Theory* is a neo-mercantilist (Hale, 1953, Lecture 2).

Thus, Hale was of the opinion, as was Keynes, that "we can learn from the mercantilists in order to improve our economy." The need for governmental action had arisen, according to Hale, because of the impact of an historical process of interaction between technological advancement and *laissez-faire* policies. In combination, these two forces called forth an economic 'structure' that fostered what Hale referred to as a "basic contradiction in the capitalist economy". Inasmuch as it is "the structure ... of society" that "shapes people's social and economic behavior," the fundamental contradiction is actualized in the motivations and behavior of the members of society's economically powerful classes (Hale, 1953, Lecture 2; and 1954, Lectures 5, 13, 5). Hale put it this way:

> Although it is true that the capitalist economy (like any other economy) exists ultimately to produce goods and services for consumption, that is not the immediate objective of those who control the economic process. Rather, they are interested in making profit. Therefore, the active variable in a capitalist economy is not the volume of consumption, but the level of investment, because it is through investment that profits are realized and investment is itself the process of accumulating capital or profits (Hale, 1954, Lecture 13).

Thus, as Hale saw it, the fundamental contradiction in capitalism is this: 'the process of capital accumulation at one and the same time restricts consumer demand and increases the capacity to produce consumer goods'. It means that the process of accumulation is 'self–defeating' (Hale, 1954, Lecture 13). One of the reasons for Hale's frequently expressed admiration for Keynes was that the latter recognized, and admitted, the existence of such a contradiction. "Keynes," said Hale, "finds precisely the same contradiction" to be at work in the capitalist order (Hale, 1954, Lecture 13). There is ample evidence to that effect in Keynes' writings. He observed, for example, that it was not natural for a population, of whom so few enjoyed the comforts of life, to accumulate so hugely. Keynes was therefore led to the "conclusion that in contemporary conditions the growth of wealth, so far from being dependent on the abstinence of the rich, as is commonly supposed, is more likely to be impeded by it." Actually, the process of growth had been impeded to such an extent that "the existing (economic) system has broken down," as he remarked in *The General Theory* (Keynes, 1971, p. 13; and 1936, pp. 373, 379). According to Hale, Keynes took this position because he (Keynes) had become aware that historical developments in the economy's underlying structure had caused the private sector to descend to a "resting-place below full employment" where it was grounded so firmly that it was fated to remain in a "chronic condition of subnormal activity without any marked tendency either towards recovery or towards complete collapse." Thus Hale was confident that Keynes had come to realize that it was due to a twisting of the structure of the economy that its institutions malfunctioned. The result was a dismal paradox, namely "the paradox of poverty in the midst of plenty," as Keynes labeled it (Keynes, 1936, pp. 304, 249, 30).

HALE'S CONSEQUENTIALIST STRUCTURALISM[8]

As evidence of his agreement with Keynes concerning the structure and contradictions of capitalism, Hale quoted with approval (Hale, 1976, p. 35) the former's observation in *The General Theory* that the "outstanding faults of the economic society in which we live are its failure to provide for full employment and its arbitrary and inequitable distribution of wealth and incomes". Hale criticized Keynes, however, for not being consequential in his conclusions. Keynes claimed, for instance, that his general "theory is moderately conservative in its implications" because it merely "indicate(s)" that the 'Manchester System' should be modified just enough to provide the kind of "environment which the free play of economic forces requires if it is to realize the full potentialities of production" (Keynes, 1936, pp. 372, 377, 379)

But, said Hale, in reaching this kind of conclusion, "Keynes did not solve the basic contradiction in the capitalist economy". Or more to the point, Hale maintained that Keynes did not draw the full and logical consequences of his own arguments when he (Keynes) insisted that "the basic contradiction in the capitalist economy could be solved without total institutional change." In other words, Hale was of the opinion that Keynes' own concept, description, theory and analysis of the capitalist order did not support his contention that the "faults of the capitalist economy . . . could be corrected or removed by measures that would not impair the basic institutions of the system or injure any of its vital organs" (Hale, 1954, Lecture 13; and 1976, p. 35). It is, therefore, fairly evident that Hale reached un-Keynesian conclusions from an analysis that rested on Keynesesque premises. The nature and character of these conclusions are implied in his discussion of what he considered to be Keynes' erroneous, unwarranted and illogical inferences. Hale introduced that discussion with the following summary of Keynes' conclusions and recommendations:

> It is financial capital that is the villain (in *The General Theory*), not industrial capital . . . (Keynes') sharpest barbs are reserved for the *rentier*, the idle and functionless receiver of property income, and the speculator, who, he says, has made the capital development of the country a 'by-product of a casino'. Keynes would eliminate the rentier by reducing the rate of interest to zero. Such a measure . . . would (also) cause investment to increase to the point at which the marginal efficiency of capital, the expected return over cost, would fall to zero – that is to say, capital goods would cease to be scarce. He would make up for the deficiency of private investment and eliminate the speculator as the guiding force in investment by what he calls the 'socialization of investment' . . . (By this) he seems to mean a wide expansion of public investment and sweeping public controls of private investment (Hale, 1976, p. 35).

As Hale pointed out, these measures, together with "progressive taxation and regressive expenditures," constitute the bulk of those governmental actions which Keynes suggested for the purpose of "correcting the faults of capitalism". Socialism, "or the collective ownership of the means of production," Keynes insisted, "is unnecessary" (Hale, 1976, p. 35). As far as Keynes' intentions were concerned, Hale did not doubt that it was his goal to "buttress political liberalism with a new economic program and to fortify this economic program with a new political economy," as argued by Dudley Dillard (Hale, 1976, p. 35; Dillard, 1948, p. 318). But as already indicated, Hale maintained that Keynes could believe "that his new economic program fortified by his new political economy would buttress political liberalism and capitalism only because he failed to draw the logical conclusions of his (own) theory." And Hale found that these "conclusions are startling, to say the least" (Hale, 1976, p. 35). That is so, he maintained,

> (because) the reduction of the rate of interest to zero surely could not be effected short of complete nationalization or socialization of the banking system, and the banking or credit system is the very heart of capitalism. Further, on Keynes' assumption that investment will be pushed to the point at which the marginal efficiency of capital equals the rate of interest, a zero rate of interest would lead, as he notes, to a zero marginal efficiency of capital – that is to say, to the disappearance of property as such (Hale, 1976, pp. 35–36).

But "this is not all," according to Hale (Hale, 1976, p. 36). Thus Keynes pointed out that one of "the more obvious and outrageous defects of the economic system" manifests itself in the fact that "the richer the community, the wider will tend to be the gap between its actual and its potential production." He admitted, however that it is highly unlikely that this gap will be filled by private investors because, "owing to its accumulation of capital being already" large, the advanced capitalist society's "opportunities for further investment" are strictly limited (Keynes, 1936, p. 31). "Hence," said Hale, "public investment will be necessary to compensate for (the) deficiency of private investment" (Hale, 1976, p. 36). And he continued:

> This is in part what constitutes his (i.e., Keynes') 'socialization of investment'. Yet it must be obvious that public investment would in time inevitably and necessarily result in government ownership of all industrial capital and all industries, that is, would result in the destruction of whatever may be left of the institution of private property after its income–yielding power to private owners has been destroyed. For a while government could invest in farm-to-market roads, in schoolhouses, in parks and playgrounds, and in leaf raking. But after all the farm-to-market roads (and so on) have got constructed ... government would have to find something else in which to invest. Nothing else could be found except in those fields which previously had been posted and held for private investment only ... And thus not only would finance capital get socialized, but industrial capital as well (Hale, 1976, p. 36).

Thus "Keynes tried to remedy capitalism, but his remedies tear capitalism down inch by inch, whereas Marx levels the axe in one powerful blow." That is to say, regardless of Keynes' own preference for a modified capitalist society, "(a)bolition of capitalism is the logical consequence of Keynes' (own) theory," as Hale put it (Hale, 1954, Lectures 13, 5). But why did Keynes fail to draw this conclusion? Why did he have a blind spot in his vision? Hale answered that question in a manner that clearly reveals his own concept and view of the structure, problems and operations of the capitalist economy. According to Hale,

> Keynes' blindness at bottom results from his failure or refusal to recognize that he had hit upon the contradiction in the process of capital accumulation which Marx had so clearly pictured three quarters of a century earlier. For capital accumulation is a self-limiting and a self-destructive process. The very process of accumulation destroys the profitability of further accumulation. This has always been true. The economic heretics such as Malthus and Marx and Hobson recognized it, but all others failed to do so (Hale, 1976, p. 37).

Of course, Hale included himself in that small band of economists who recognized the truth of this principle; a principle which he viewed in terms of a law of capitalism that is rooted in the very structure of that socioeconomic system.

CONCLUSION

What conclusion is one justified in drawing concerning the economics of Hale? I think that I may fairly postulate that he conceived of the capitalist order in the manner of a system that is so structured that it is incapable of surviving on its own power. He was confident, however, that the underlying structure could be corrected through institutional adjustments. In other words, instead of conceiving of institutional change in catastrophic terms, like Marx, or in technological terms, like the Texas institutionalists, Hale held the Commonsesque opinion that structural change *could* be effected through institutional engineering.

But unlike Joseph A. Schumpeter, who was convinced that "centralist socialism is . . . a likely heir apparent" to capitalism (Schumpeter, 1950, p. 417), Hale did not assume that it was inevitable that a centrally controlled economy would replace the existing economic order; at least he did not believe that it was likely that a democratically engineered and controlled political economy would come into being. Thus although he argued that the "Keynesian revolution" is found in the circumstance that "the logical conclusions of the *General Theory* . . . are . . . in plain sight for all to see" (Hale, 1976, p. 38), Hale doubted that any meaningful reforms would be formulated on the basis of these conclusions. He had such doubts because he did not share the Smithian, Millian, Marxian, Marshallian and Keynesian faith in the possibility of a continued improvement of human nature and intelligence. Hale was therefore unable to accept Keynes' optimistic notion that the "economic problem," i.e., the problem of "want and poverty and the economic struggle between classes and nations," would be "solved, or be at least within sight of solution, within a hundred years," or *circa* 2030 A.D. (Keynes, 1972, pp. xviii, 326).

Instead, Hale feared that the politically powerful members of society would employ an ancient device in an effort to make the economy perform tolerably well. He put it in this way: "We seem in this modern age to be reduced to only one expedient surely available (and surely adequate) to make possible profit making and further private capital accumulation on a scale adequate to the maintenance of reasonably full employment. That expedient is war and preparation for war." And Hale concluded: "It is, of course, the one upon which we are now placing, and for some time past have placed sole reliance" (Hale, 1976, p. 37).

NOTES

1. E.E. Hale was born on October 24, 1893. He was awarded the degree of Bachelor of Arts by The University of Texas in 1920. As an undergraduate student, his major fields of study were English, Latin and history. He entered the graduate school of the University of Wisconsin in 1921 which granted him the degree of Master of Arts in 1923. For this degree, Hale offered economics and philosophy as his areas of concentration and he continued to pursue graduate studies in these fields at the University of Wisconsin in 1925–1926. He was appointed to the economics faculty of The University of Texas in 1923 and he continued to serve on that faculty until his retirement in 1962. He occupied the position of Chairman of the Department of Economics in the period 1929–1934 and again from 1939 to 1958. Hale died on February 3, 1975 (Gordon, Miller & Morgan, *this volume*).

2. Thus at The University of Texas, he taught courses dealing with labor movements, labor problems, and contemporary economic problems in addition to those courses for which he became most famous: history of economics, income and employment, and comparative economic systems (cf., Gordon, Miller & Morgan, *this volume*).

3. References to Hale's lectures will be given in terms of the number of the course, the year the lectures were given, and the number of the lecture. Thus the above reference is to Economics 388, Fall 1952, Lecture No. 1. Full bibliographical entries are found in the list of references below.

4. I use the term political economics in Adolph Lowe's sense of a body of doctrine designed to serve as an 'instrument' for 'active interference' in society's political economy' (Lowe, 1977, p. 91).

5. Hale was not 'so sure' about some of the 'minor figures' in the history of economics. Thus he was somewhat 'dubious about Nassau Senior' and thought that 'he was a propagandist'. Hale also had some doubts about the intellectual honesty of Eugen von Böhm-Bawerk, especially in the latter's critical works on the economics of Karl Marx. But inasmuch as 'we do not know whether Böhm-Bawerk misunderstood Marx, or (whether) he intentionally misrepresented him, we are not justified in labeling him (Böhm-Bawerk) as intellectually dishonest'. Hale therefore did 'not think that he (Böhm-Bawerk) was dishonest' (Hale, n.d., Lecture 8; and 1954, Lecture 14).

6. This book, published in French in 1958, consists of a collection of essays and papers written by Levi-Strauss between 1944 and 1957. Its wide acceptance and acclaim outside the disciplines of anthropology and sociology were stimulated by Levi–Strauss' earlier work of 1955, entitled *Tristes Tropiques*. In 1973, Levi-Strauss published *Structural Anthropology*: Volume II which 'brings together texts which were written before and after the publication of the first' volume of *Structural Anthropology* Levi-Strauss, 1976, p. vii).

7. Although Levi-Strauss is often hailed as the 'Father of Structuralism' (Kurzweil, 1980, p. 13), this particular approach has ancient roots. 'Among the precursors of the movement, three figures stand out clearly both for having foreshadowed and for having directly influenced the major structuralists of today. The three are Karl Marx, Sigmund Freud, and Ferdinand de Saussure' (De George & De George, 1972, p. xii).

8. I have borrowed the term 'consequentialist' from R.B. Braithwaite who used it as a label for a way of thinking according to which "the rightness of an action derives from the character of its consequences" (Braithwaite, 1975, p. 243). What I mean by Hale's consequentialist structuralism is that he argued that the efficacy and correctness of an investigator's policy recommendations are measured by, or a function of, the correctness of the conclusions which the said investigator derives logically from her/his own image, or concept, of the economic structure and the institutions that are embedded therein. In other words, a scholar must take the consequences of her/his concepts of the structure and problems of the economic order.

REFERENCES

Ayres, C. E. (1944). *The Theory of Economic Progress*. Chapel Hill: The University of North Carolina Press.

Braithwaite, R. B. (1975). Keynes as a philosopher. In: M. Keynes (Ed.), *Essays on John Maynard Keynes* (pp. 237–246). London; New York: Cambridge University Press.

Breit, W., & Culbertson, W. P. Jr. (1976). Clarence Edwin Ayres: An Intellectual Portrait. In: W. Breit and W. P. Culbertson (Eds.), *Science and Ceremony: The Institutional Economics of C.E. Ayres* (pp. 3–22). Austin: The University of Texas Press.

Commons, J. R. (1959). *Institutional Economics*. Madison: The University of Wisconsin Press. Vol. 1 and Vol. 2.

Commons, J. R. (1964). *Myself*. Madison: The University of Wisconsin Press.

De George, R., & De George, F. M. (Eds.). (1972). *The Structuralists: From Marx to Levi–Strauss*. Anchor Books. Garden City, N.Y.: Doubleday & Co.

Dillard, D. (1948). *The Economics of John Maynard Keynes*. Englewood Cliffs, N.J.: Prentice–Hall.

Galbraith, J. K. (1981). *A Life in our Times: Memoirs*. Boston: Houghton Mifflin Co.

Gordon, R. A. (1976). Rigor and Relevance in a Changing Institutional Setting. *The American Economic Review* 66 (March), 1–14.

Gordon, W., Miller, D. L., & Morgan, D. C. Jr. (1975). *In Memoriam: Edward Everett Hale*, this volume, 1–6.

Hale, E. E. (1976) (1949). Some Implications of Keynes General Theory of Employment, Interest and Money. *Review of Radical Political Economics, 8* (Winter), 30–41. (Published posthumously with an introduction by Ron Phillips.)

Hale, E. E. (1952). Lectures in Economics 388: Classical Economic Theory, recorded and transcribed by the author (Fall semester).

Hale, E. E. (1953). Lectures in Economics 388: Classical Economic Theory, recorded and transcribed by the author (Fall semester).

Hale, E. E. N.d. Lectures in Economics 388: Classical Economic Theory, recorded, pooled and transcribed by unidentified graduate students.

Hale, E. E. (1954). Lectures in Economics 389: Marxian and Neoclassical Economic Theory, recorded and transcribed by the author (Spring Semester).

Harter, Lafayette G., Jr. (1962). *John R. Commons: his assault on laissez faire*. Corvallis: Oregon State University Press.

.Jacobson, C. (1963). Translator's Preface. *In Structural Anthropology*, by C. Levi–Strauss (pp. ix–xvi). New York: Basic Books.

Keynes, J. M. (1936). *The General Theory of Employment Interest and Money*. New York: Harcourt, Brace & Co.

Keynes, J. M. (1971). The Economic Consequences of the Peace. Vol. II of *The Collected writings of John Maynard Keynes*. London: Macmillan & Co.

Keynes, J. M. (1972). Essays in Persuasion. Vol. IX of *The Collected Writings of John Maynard Keynes*. London: The Macmillan Press.

Kuhn, T. S. (1970). *The Structure of Scientific Revolutions*, 2nd ed. Chicago: The University of Chicago Press.

Kurzweil, E. (1980). *The Age of Structuralism: Levi–Strauss to Foucault*. New York: Columbia University Press.

Leontief, W. (1971). Theoretical Assumptions and Nonobserved Facts. *The American Economic Review 61* (March), 1–7.

Levi–Strauss, C. (1963). *Structural Anthropology*. New York: Basic Books.

Levi–Strauss, C. (1973). *Tristes Tropiques*. London: Jonathan Cape.

Levi–Strauss, C. (1976). *Structural Anthropology*: Volume II. New York: Basic Books.

Lowe, A. (1977). *On Economic Knowledge: Toward a Science of Political Economics*. English. ed. White Plains, N.Y.: M.E. Sharpe.

Marshall, A. (1975). How far do Remediable Causes Influence Prejudicially (a) the Continuity of Employment (b) the Rates of Wages? In: J. K. Whitaker, (Ed.). *The Early Economic Writings of Alfred Marshall, 1867–1890* (Vol. 2. pp. 341–34). New York: The Free Press of Macmillan Co.

Mitchell, W. C. (1949). *Lecture Notes on Types of Economic Theory*. New York: Augustus M. Kelley. Vol. 1 and Vol. 2.

Mitchell, W. C. (1967). *Types of Economic Theory*, Joseph Dorfman (Ed.). New York: Augustus M. Kelley. Vol. I.

Peck, H. W. (1935). *Economic Thought and its Institutional Background*. New York: Farrar & Rinehart.

Schumpeter, J. A. (1949). Science and Ideology. *The American Economic Review 39* (March) 346–359.

Schumpeter, J. A. (l950). *Capitalism, Socialism, and Democracy*, 3rd ed. New York: Harper & Brothers.

Schumpeter, J. A. (1954). *History of Economic Analysis*. New York: Oxford University Press.

Stark, W. 1958. *The Sociology of Knowledge*. Glencoe, Ill.: The Free Press.

Stigler, G. J. (1965). *Essays in the History of Economics*. Chicago: The University of Chicago Press.

Zweig, F. (1950). *Economic Ideas: A Study in Historical Perspective*. New York: Prentice-Hall.

METAPHYSICS, SCIENCE AND VALUE THEORY (1926)

Edward Everett Hale

PREFACE

This chapter makes little claim to originality. It is scarcely more than a resumé of some of the reading in psychology, pragmatic philosophy, the method of science, and economic theory which I did during the second semester of the session of 1921–1922 at the University of Wisconsin and had done prior to that time. This reading, together with the round-table discussions of Professor Commons' seminar on Value, served to sharpen and define the more or less vague conviction I had had that value theory to date has progressed very little, if at all, beyond the metaphysical stage of speculation. I have attempted to correlate these readings and discussions and to sum up the conclusions toward which they seem to point. The conclusions embody suggestions as to what is needed in value theory to make it scientific and remove its metaphysics. In so far as I have been able to comprehend the argument, Professor Commons' volitional theory of value proceeds according to the scientific method, that is to say, it is a theory of the valuing process in economic society as it is actually constituted today, with all its institutions and forces and arrangements, and not a theory of that process in some supposed ideal economic society with institutions and forces and arrangements made to order for the convenience of the theorist. It deals with the economic behavior of individuals in society, not with underlying principles, norms, ultimate standards, and metaphysical concepts. The argument advanced in this study, then, may seem to be advanced

Edward Everett Hale: The Writings of an Economic Maverick, Volume 19-B, pages 27–55.
2001 by Elsevier Science B.V.
ISBN: 0-7623-0694-7

mainly as a defense of Professor Commons' theory and method. It was not, however, advanced with that purpose in view. My purpose, as has been stated, was to inquire how far current value theory is based on what seems to me to be metaphysical preconceptions and assumptions and what is needed to rid it of these and bring it in line with matter-of-fact inquiry and the scientific method as pursued in other fields of thought. It is an argument for the scientific as opposed to the metaphysical method and point of view. In so far, then, as Professor Commons' theory holds to the scientific point of view and follows the scientific method, its validity is recognized from the standpoint of the thesis here advanced. For my own part, and as far as my comprehension of the theory extends, I should consider it scientific in so far as it is 'behavioristic', but feel some doubt about it in so far as it is 'volitional'. I am quite uncertain regarding what part is or can be played by the Will. I am more uncertain, however, regarding what part has been assigned it by Professor Commons, and for that reason I, obviously, have nothing to say of it at present.

How much I am indebted for my criticisms and conclusions to others will be apparent from the multiplicity of quotations scattered through the pages of the manuscript.

INTRODUCTION

Among the systems of modern thought which have attained the dignity of a consistent and well-rounded development and which aspire to rank as a science, economics possibly falls shortest of the mark. Economists are wont to bewail the fact that their 'science' has such slight influence on the life and work of men and the 'practical' affairs of the world as compared with the enormous influence which has been and is exerted by such sciences as physics, chemistry, botany, geology, and even psychology. Policies of industry, business, and legislation are worked out today with little heed to the advice and instruction of the economists. Such, of course, was not true during the time of the Classical economists, when the new 'science' was hailed with delight as pointing the way out of the maze of baffling social and political problems with which men were then beset. And during the past few years professional economists have made efforts, many of them successful, to place their knowledge usefully at the disposal and service of the manufacturer, industrial leader, business man, and legislator. But the fact remains that economics generally is yet considered too abstract, too academic, too intellectual to be of any use to the busy man of affairs. The reason for this seems to me to, be not far to seek. It lies in the fact that of all the modern 'sciences', economics is possibly most tinged with metaphysical preconceptions and formulation. Physics and chemistry have long been past the stage of myth-making and alchemy. Astronomy, with the discoveries of Copernicus and Gallileo, ceased to be metaphysical astrology. Darwin's theory of evolution furnished the basic essentials for the scientific progress of biology. Philosophy, thanks to the work of such latter-day pragmatists as James, Dewey, Schiller and others, is getting away from empty speculations on absolute truth, absolute knowledge, and absolute standards of true and false in the direction of formulating its conclusions in terms of relativity and judging their worth by the practical significance of their results. And psychology, now definitely 'behavioristic', has cast loose from the metaphysical abstractions of hedonism and is treating the phenomena with which it deals in the approved scientific matter. But economics, still laboring under the metaphysical preconceptions of the founders of the 'science', continues its highly logical theorizing about the mythical economic activities of a mythical economic man in a mythical world, and states the conclusions arrived at by this process of reasoning in terms of self-evident propositions of universal validity, good for all times and all ages irrespective of any and all changes that might occur in the ethical, moral, and legal orders of the universe. From the time of the Physiocrats to that of John Bates Clark and Alfred Marshall, the explanation of the economic activities and life of man and the economic functioning of society has been stated, not in terms of what is actually happening in the world, but in terms of logical deductions from consciously chosen and preconceived assumptions. Most of the facts of actual life have been treated as 'disturbing circumstances' that must be ruled out in the interest of a consistent theory. Consistency of theory rather than adequacy of description seems to have been the aim of too many of the economists. Though they have proposed to describe and explain the economic order and functioning of society as it exists, they have always been careful to state certain and sundry disturbing circumstances which enter the equation and mar the unimpeded and perfect working of their systems. The economists have felt that their task was not to treat temporary aberrations and oscillations of the economic order, but to discover for the world the norm underlying these toward which things were constantly tending and by which they were constantly guided. Therefore, we have had, in turn, the 'Ordre Naturel' of the Physiocrats, the 'natural laws' and 'real value' of the Classicists, the hedonist principle of the Austrians, the 'static state' of Professor Clark, and that minor device, the 'representative firms' of Professor Marshall. The Physiocrats made no claim that their 'Ordre Naturel' was the actual order, but claimed that it would be the actual order if men would only discover and obey the natural laws that God had given the Universe. The Classical economists were always careful to distinguish 'real' value from 'market' value, 'real' wages from 'market' wages, etc. Their 'real' was that which would be realized could all the troublesome disturbing circumstances of actual life be removed. That is to say, their 'real' was not the real at all, but the ideal, a figment of the imagination. And Professor Clark admits that we do not now live in a static state, that no one has ever lived in a static state, and that the probabilities are no one will ever live in a static state. This, however, is of small moment. What really matters according to Professor Clark, is that, should such a state ever exist and should all the other assumptions postulated along with it hold true, the conclusions would be borne out as predicted. This might be true, but the innocent bystander feels constrained to ask, Of what concern is this in the everyday life of the common man? Surely, it would seem that speculation regarding the economic life of man on one of the distant stars would be equally as significant, equally as important, and equally as fruitful as speculation concerning what might be the economic realities in an ideal static state. All things 'natural' and 'real' and 'static'' and 'representative' I consider illustrative of the metaphysics of economics.

What then, is the distinction between metaphysics and science? Why is economics even today more metaphysical than scientific?

METAPHYSICS VS. SCIENCE

In a series of papers entitled Illustrations of the Logic of Science, appearing in the *Popular Science Monthly of November,* 1877, and subsequent issues, Mr. C. S. Peirce contrasts forcibly four methods of attaining belief which he calls, respectively, the 'method of tenacity', the 'method of authority', the *a priori* method, and the 'method of science'. Holding that 'the irritation of doubt causes a struggle to attain a state of belief', and terming this struggle 'inquiry', Peirce states that "the sole object of inquiry is the settlement of opinion." Men seek to reach a firm belief. Since belief is of the nature of a habit, why, ask those who follow the 'method of tenacity', may it not be attained by taking any answer to a question one may fancy, constantly holding that answer before one's self, and refusing to consider anything which might disturb it? By this method truth is arrived at by simply forming a habit of thought. Habits are very tenacious, and when once formed are not easily disturbed. But, Peirce points out, the social impulse is against this method. "The man who adopts it will find that other men think differently from him, and it will occur to him, in some saner moment, that their opinions are quite as good as his own, and this will shake his confidence in his belief." Then belief gives way to doubt, and opinion is again unsettled.

By the second method, that of authority, belief becomes a matter of commanded and dictated precepts, of rules laid down by some institution which are not to be questioned but are to be implicitly accepted. "Let an institution be created," says Peirce, "which shall have for its object to keep correct doctrines before the attention of the people, to reiterate them perpetually, and to teach them to the young, having at the same time power to prevent contrary doctrines from being taught, advocated, or expressed. Let all possible causes of a change of mind be removed from men's apprehensions. Let them be kept ignorant, lest they should learn of some reason to think otherwise than they do. Let all men who reject the established belief be terrified into silence." Peirce states that this method has, "from the earliest times, been one of the chief means of upholding correct theological and political doctrines, and of preserving their universal and catholic character. All religions have made more or less use of this method." This was the method used by the Church during the Middle Ages. During the Middle Ages nothing had been as firmly rooted in the minds of men as the need and goodness of authority. All questions of human thought, feeling and behavior were submitted to the authority of the Church as the ultimate test of truth and validity. Faith and submission were the two things demanded of the people both by the temporal and the spiritual leaders of the time. Questioning of the rules and precepts propagated by the Church through the Papacy was not admitted, indeed, was sternly repressed wherever it showed itself. Authority must be accepted even where the evidence of the senses contradicted it. Knowledge was of no moment, for the guarantee of salvation was not knowledge but faith. It is needless to point out that under such a regime not only the advance, but even the existence of science was impossible. For that reason, we find the beginnings of none of the modern sciences until after the close of the Middle Ages and the end of the rule of prescription and authority in the realm of the intellectual, moral, and physical domains.

But the method of authority is also an unsatisfactory method, for "no institution can undertake to regulate opinions upon every subject. Only the most important ones can be attended to, and on the rest men's minds must be left to the action of natural causes. This imperfection will be no source of weakness so long as men are in such a state of culture that one opinion does not influence another – that is, so long as they cannot put two and two together. But in most priest-ridden states some individuals will be found who are raised above that condition. These men see that men in other countries and other ages have held to very different doctrines from those which they themselves have been brought up to believe. They cannot help seeing that it is the mere accident of their having been taught as they have, and of their having been surrounded with the manners and associations they have, that has caused them to believe as they do, and not far differently. And their candor cannot resist the reflection that there is no reason to rate their own views at a higher value than those of other nations and other countries; and this gives rise to doubts in their minds. Hence, they cannot but doubt every belief which seems to be determined by the caprice either of themselves or of those who originated the popular opinions."[1]

A third method of arriving at belief is the *a priori method*. Peirce formulates this method as follows: "Let the action of natural preferences be unhindered and unimpeded, then, and under their influence let men, conversing together and regarding matters in different lights, gradually develop beliefs in harmony with natural causes." The a priori method is the metaphysical method, and Peirce notes that the most perfect example of this method is to be found in the history of metaphysical philosophy. "Systems of this sort have not usually rested upon any observed facts. They have been chiefly adopted because their fundamental propositions seemed 'agreeable to reason', – not that which agrees with experience, but that which we find ourselves inclined to believe . . . This method makes of inquiry something similar to the development of taste, but taste, unfortunately, is always more or less a matter of fashion, and accordingly metaphysicians have never come to any fixed agreement. The a priori method does not deliver our opinions from their accidental and capricious element. Sentiments in their development are very greatly determined by accidental causes. Some people, if they see that any belief of theirs is determined by any circumstance extraneous to the facts, will from that moment not merely admit in words that that belief is doubtful, but will experience a real doubt of it, so that it ceases to be a belief".[2] That is to say, the method of metaphysics has nothing to do with observed facts, actual experiences and phenomena. It concerns itself only with subtleties of the mind, with concepts gathered from the void, with reason. Its adepts postulate the all-sufficiency of the reasoning faculty of man to discover by logical accepted deduction from preconceived and implicitly accepted assumptions the guiding principles and underlying laws of the processes within any field on which the curiosity of man leads him to speculate. Its assumptions are susceptible of no proof because they do not lie in the realm of the perceptible. They are considered in need of no proof but are held to be self-evident propositions of universal validity. The validity of the conclusions arrived at by a process of logic and reasoning from these assumptions is vouched for on the ground that they are 'agreeable to reason'. 'Agreeableness to reason' is the ultimate test and the final ground of legitimacy of the conclusions of metaphysical inquiry. If the assumptions be granted, the conclusions are generally 'agreeable to reason', for the metaphysicians are usually masters of logical deduction. But only in so far as the assumptions are acceptable can adherence be gained for the conclusions. Since these assumptions are in large part matters of individual taste and preference, tinged by individual feelings and emotions, it is obvious that universal acceptance of them can never be attained.

It is seen that the personal element inevitably connected with any of the three methods of attaining belief outlined above vitiates their efficacy for attaining belief. "To satisfy our doubts therefore", Peirce states, "it is necessary that a method should be found by which our beliefs may be caused by nothing human, but by some external permanency – by something upon which our thinking had no effect, but which affects, or might affect, the thinking of every man." This method he finds in the 'method of science'. The fundamental hypothesis of the method of science is this: "There are real things, whose characters are entirely independent of our opinions about them; those realities affect our senses according to regular laws, and though our sensations are as different as our relations to the objects, yet, by taking advantage of the laws of perception, we can ascertain by reasoning how things really are, and any man, if he have sufficient experience and reason enough about it, will be led to the one true conclusion."[3] Professor Pearson also holds that if judgment on questions and problems is to gain universal adherence and acceptance, it must be formed apart from individual feelings and emotions. "Such a judgment," he states, "can only be based on a clear knowledge of facts, an appreciation of their sequence and relative significance. The facts once classified, once understood, the judgment based upon them ought to be independent of the individual mind which examines them . . . The classification of facts and the formation of absolute judgments upon the basis of this classification – judgments independent of the idiosyncrasies of the individual mind – essentially sum up the *aim and method of modern science*. The scientific man has above all things to strive at self-elimination in his judgments, and to provide and argument which is as true for each individual mind as for his own . . . *The classification of facts, the recognition of their sequence and relative significance is the function of science*, and the habit of forming a judgment upon these facts unbiased by personal feeling is characteristic of what may be termed the scientific frame of mind."[4] (The *italics* are Pearson's). Science aims at an exact and impartial analysis of facts, not at logical deductions from preconceived assumptions. Science holds that truth can be arrived at only by classifying facts and reasoning upon them. It cannot be arrived at by metaphysical speculation on super-sensual mental and spiritual phenomena.

There is thus introduced the conceptions of *fact* and *reality*. What are the realities and the facts with which science deals? Metaphysics also has its facts and its realities, as, witness, the 'verities' and 'realities' of classical political economy. Why have the 'realities' of science any greater or more valid claim to be the real than those of metaphysics?'. The 'realities' of metaphysics are not anything that any individual has ever seen or felt or experienced. The originators of metaphysical 'realities' always claim that the 'real' of which they speak is not the actual. The actual is temporary and more or less accidental, capricious and unstable. The 'real' is that which lies beneath the surface of things and events; it is the ultimate essence, the substance, the final truth. That is to say, the 'real' of metaphysics is not that which one actually experiences, but is that which one thinks ought to be and which he is inclined to believe. The 'real' is the 'ideal'. The 'realities' of science, on the other hand, are not the 'ideal', are not what one would like there to be or prefer to believe. They are the actual, the experienced. They are not what one thinks but what one sees and feels. They belong to the realm of the senses, not to the realm of the super-sensual. "The *real*," states Peirce "is that whose characters are independent of what anybody may think them to be. . . Reality, like every other quality, consists in the peculiar sensible effects which things partaking of it produce."[5] "*A sine qua non* of the existence of an actual object," Pearson maintains, "is some immediate sense-impression to start with, The sense-impressions which deter-mine the reality of the external object may be very few indeed, the object may be largely constructed by inferences and associations, but some sense-impres-sion there must be if I am to term the object real, and not the product merely of my imagination."[6] Thus, we see, it is the property of being the source of some immediate sense-impression that distinguishes fact from fiction, the product of reality from that of imagination. Sense-impressions are the *realities* with which science deals, and the source of these sense-impressions are facts.[7] All the effects of an object constitute the object. We only know what it is from what it does. Further than this we cannot go. The metaphysician attempts to peer behind the sensuous to find the nature of 'things in themselves', but science knows nothing of nor speculates on the nature of 'things in themselves'. Knowledge begins and ends with sense-impressions; all else is inference and assumption susceptible neither of proof nor disproof.[8] We know nothing else of gravity or electricity or love or houses than our ideas of what these thing do. As Peirce has it, " . . . the whole function of thought is to produce habits of action. . . . What a thing means is simply what habits it involves. What a habit is depends on *when* and *how* it causes us to act. As for the *when*, every stimulus to action is derived from perception; as for the *how*, every purpose of action is to produce some sensible result. Our idea of anything is our idea of its sensible effects; and if we fancy that we have any other we deceive ourselves, and mistake a mere sensation accompanying the thought for a part of the thought itself. It is absurd to say that thought has any meaning unrelated to its only function."[9] Metaphysics deals with the essence and substance of things; science deals with what things do. Metaphysics, in other words, is explanatory; science is behavioristic. Metaphysics attempts to answer the question, *why*? Science attempts to answer the question, *how*? Science attempts only to describe how a thing acts; metaphysics attempts to explain why it acts that way.

The descriptions of science are summed up in what are called 'scientific laws'. A scientific law is 'a brief statement or formula which, in a few words, resumes a whole range of facts' or routine of sense-impressions. A scientific law is a summary of the sequences and relationships observed among a vast range of phenomena. Pearson insists that scientific laws do not account for or explain the sequences and relationships; they merely describe them. The law of gravitation, for instance, 'is a brief description of how every particle of matter in the universe is altering its motion with reference to every other particle'. It does not tell why the particles thus move; it only tells how they move. All that we know is that a certain sequence has occurred and recurred in the past. That it will continue to occur in the future is a matter only of belief.[10] To this belief the scientist gives expression in the concept *probability*. The conclusions of science are stated, not in terms of absolute, immutable, and unchanging principles and postulates, but in terms of relativity and probability. There is nothing in science of fundamental principles and underlying laws governing the universe, society, and human beings. Scientific laws, as has been stated, resume briefly a wide range of phenomena gathered from observation and past experience, and describe sequences of perceptions, but 'science in no case can demonstrate any inherent necessity in a sequence, nor prove with absolute certainty that it must be repeated. Science for the past is a description, for the future a belief; it is not, and never has been an explanation, if by that word is meant that science shows the necessity of any sequence of perceptions'.[11]

The theory of probabilities is a mathematical concept for treating reasoning quantitatively. "Given a certain hypothesis," states Peirce, "there are two conceivable certainties with regard to it, the certainty of its truth or the certainty of its falsity." Neither certainty admits of absolute, but only of probable determination. "The general problem of probabilities is, from a given state of facts, to determine the numerical probability of a possible fact. This is the same as to inquire how much the given facts are worth considered as evidence to prove the possible fact. Thus the problem of probabilities is simply the general problem of logic."[12] From the number of cases of any particular sequence observed, science deduces what the probability is of that particular sequence repeating itself in the future. Unless repetition or routine of some sort exist, thought is impossible and knowledge unattainable, ". . . The actual order of the sequence is immaterial, but whatever it may be, it must nearly repeat itself if knowledge is to be possible. That the future will be like our experience of the past is the sole condition under which we can predict what is about to happen and so guide our conduct."[13] To guide his conduct it is unnecessary that man know why phenomena occur as they do. To know *why* might be, and likely would be exceedingly interesting. It would satisfy idle curiosity at least, but it would serve no purpose essential for the existence of the human race. In order to construct buildings and build machines, we need to know how bodies fall but not why they fall. To go from one place to another we need to know *how* trains run, and if we know that, we can go even though we be ignorant as to *how* they run. This disposes of the question of cause. "For science," says Pearson, "cause, as originating or enforcing a particular sequence of perceptions is meaningless we have no experience of anything which originates or enforces something else. Cause, however, used to mark a stage in a routine, is a clear and valuable conception, which throws the idea of cause entirely into the field of sense-impressions, into the sphere where we can reason and can reach knowledge. Cause, in this sense, is a stage in a routine of experience, and not in a routine of inherent necessity. There is nothing in any scientific cause which compels us of inherent necessity to predict the effect. The effect is associated with the cause simply as a result of past direct or indirect experience . . . When we scientifically state causes we are really describing the successive stages of a routine of experience. Causation is uniform antecedence."[14]

The distinction between science and metaphysics should now be clear. It is not found in the phenomena with which the two deal, for the scientific and the metaphysical (a priori) are only two different methods of treating the same phenomena. Pearson claims the whole range of phenomena, mental as well as physical – the entire universe – as the field of science. We have only to note astrology and astronomy, alchemy and chemistry, phrenology and psychology, the philosophy of Plato and that of the modern school of pragmatists (though it may be disputed that the latter is 'scientific') to see that science does not differ from metaphysics in point of subject-matter. Again, the distinction does not lie in the use of the inductive and deductive methods of analysis and approach. It is true that metaphysics relies wholly on the deductive method – abstract reasoning from supposedly axiomatic postulates, but science uses both methods, and necessarily so. The inductive method of approach is used, consisting of observation of wide ranges of phenomena, classification of facts observed, and recognition of their sequences and relationships. But a mere enumeration of data would never make a science or any other body of knowledge more pretentious than, say, a census report. Neither would the classification of facts and a description of their sequences. Economics, for example, from the time of the Physiocrats, has classified the facts with which it deals and pointed out the relationships and sequences supposed to exist among them in the manner of the exact sciences. "Science," according to Pearson, "is in reality a classification and analysis of the contents of the mind," and "science considers the whole contents of the mind to be based on sense-impressions," but "when we state that all the contents of our mind are ultimately based on

sense-impressions, we must be careful to recognize that the mind has by classification and isolation proceeded to conceptions which are widely removed
from sense-impressions capable of immediate verification . . . We are perpetually
drawing inferences from our immediate and stored sense-impressions as to
things which lie beyond immediate verification by sense . . . Science is based
largely upon inferences of this kind; its hypotheses lie to a great extent beyond
the region of the immediately sensible, and it chiefly deals with conceptions
drawn from sense-impressions, and not with sense impressions themselves."[15]
And the conclusions of science are expressed in the form of scientific laws,
which are purely mental concepts, the product of deductive reasoning. "Neither
a sequence of perceptions in itself nor the description involve the existence of
any law. The sequence of perceptions has to be compared with other sequences,
classification and generalization have to follow; conceptions and ideas, pure
products of the mind, must be formed, before a description can be given of a
range of sequences which, by its conciseness and comprehensiveness, is worth
the name of scientific law . . . it is not only the process of reaching a scientific
law which is mental, but the law itself, when reached, involves an association
of natural facts or phenomena lying quite outside the particular field of those
phenomena. Without the mental conceptions the law could not be, and it only
comes into existence when these mental conceptions are first associated with
the phenomena."[16] It is to be remembered, however, that a scientific law is a
description, not an explanation of the phenomena with which it deals, and that
it is arrived at, not by a process of logical deduction from consciously chosen
assumptions, but by a process of reasoning from the results of observation of
a great number of facts that are in the realm of the knowable, that is, of the
perceptible. Newton's law of gravitation "is not so much the discovery by
Newton of a rule guiding the motion of the planets as his invention of a method
of briefly describing the sequences of sense-impressions which we term plan-
etary motion."[17] Nor is the distinction between science and metaphysics to be
found in the distinction between 'realistic' and 'idealistic, the assumption being
that science is 'realistic' while metaphysics is 'idealistic'. Science is also 'idealistic' in the sense that it forms conceptions of the super-sensuous, as, witness,
the conceptions of molecules and atoms and electrons. These lie beyond the
realm of sense-impressions.[18] But the concepts of the scientist are recognized
as being only concepts, or ideals, if one wishes, and are not formulated as the
'real' and 'ultimate'.

The distinction between the two is to be found, not in the phenomena with
which they deal, but in the basis on which the phenomena are evaluated for the
purpose in hand; not in the way in which the data are handled, but in the purpose
for 'which they are presented. The distinction lies in the ground of legitimacy to

which appeal is made for substantiation of the conclusions reached, in the terms in which the formulations of the two are postulated, and in the point of view from which problems are attacked. Metaphysics evaluates the phenomena with which it deals on the basis of the cause and effect relationship which is supposed to exist between them. It may be objected that science also sets forth causal relationships. That is true, but the 'cause' of science is something quite different from the 'cause' of metaphysics, as has been pointed out above. Science uses cause as merely denoting a stage in a sequence of perceptions. Metaphysics uses the term to denote the inherent necessity of the next subsequent stage in a sequence. The scientist refuses to go back of a sequence of phenomena to seek the causes of this sequence, for the latter lie in the realm of the conjectural, the unknowable. He rests content to describe the sequence. But not so the metaphysician. The latter seeks to account for the sequence. He tries to go back of it to discover the guiding hand that directs it. The metaphysician attempts to peer behind the sensuous and to find there the guiding principles of our world, principles unconditioned and unaffected by the perceptive or reflective faculties in *man*. In this connection Professor Veblen notes that, for the Classical economists, "this ground of cause and effect is not definitive. Their sense of truth and substantiality is not satisfied with a formulation of mechanical sequence. The ultimate term in their systematization of knowledge is a 'natural law'. This natural law is felt to exercise some sort of a coercive surveillance over the sequence of events, and to give a spiritual stability and consistence to the causal relation at any given juncture. To meet the high classical requirement, a sequence – and a developmental process especially must be apprehended in terms of a consistent propensity tending to some spiritually legitimate end. When the facts and events have been reduced to these terms of fundamental truth and have been made to square with the requirements of definitive normality, the investigator rests his case."[19] Thus, we have had the *ordre naturel* and *loi naturelle* of the Physiocrats, the 'unseen hand' of Adam Smith, and the 'normal' and 'real' of Ricardo and other classicists.

For the legitimacy of its conclusions, metaphysics appeals to the ground of 'sufficient reason'; science, to the ground of 'efficient cause'. Metaphysics states its conclusions in terms of absolutes; science states its formulations in terms of probabilities. Metaphysics sees its problem in the discovery of the 'controlling principles' of activity; science finds its problem in the activity itself. Metaphysics deals with the nature of 'things in themselves'; science deals with the effects of things.

The claim has been made that economics, of all modern systems of thought which aspire to rank as a science, is most tinged with metaphysical preconceptions. The reason for the failure of economics to have attained the dignity of a science, if it has failed, in the light of the distinction that has been drawn between metaphysics and science, is to be sought, not in the facts with which the subject deals, not in the details of its theoretical structure, nor even in the conclusions which it reaches, but rather in the premises from which it starts its inquiry, in the point of view from which it attacks its problems, in the purpose it has had in view, in the basis on which it evaluates phenomena for that purpose, and in the ground of legitimacy to which it has appealed for proof of its formulations.

THE METAPHYSICS OF VALUE THEORY

A science has never arisen in any field of human thought until the belief has become dominant that the processes within that field possess definite relationships and follow definite sequences that admit of measurement and deductive treatment. As long as natural, individual, or social phenomena were felt to be accidental, disconnected, or unrelated, a science dealing with those phenomena was impossible. As has been pointed out, it is the aim of science to discover order and scheme amid the manifold variety of phenomena in any field with which it deals and to resume in brief formulae or statements the whole range of facts. Obviously, until it is thought that order and scheme exists, no description of sequences and relationships could be contemplated.

Starting with the speculations of the Physiocrats economics has aspired to be a science. The achievements of science in the material world, reducing wide ranges of material phenomena to a few simple principles and relationships, had, by the end of the eighteenth century, led men to believe that law reigned everywhere, in the inner world of human nature and social processes as well as in the external world of brute matter. The opinion was conceived that social processes follow laws and admit of measurement and deductive treatment equally with the processes of the physical world. It seemed scarcely consistent to assume one set of laws for the outside world and another for the inner. The whole realm of reality and knowledge, men thought, must be bounded by a single law. The astonishing growth of natural science would no longer permit all questions of thought, feeling, and behavior to be submitted for solution to authority as the ultimate test of truth and goodness. During the Middle Ages, as has been noted, authority – the Church – dictated all knowledge and belief for the masses of the people. But authority could not always govern the thoughts and minds of men.

A science, however, does not necessarily arise from the conception of order and scheme, of sequence and relationships, though generally speculation produces what purports to be a scientific description and explanation of the processes within the field which is felt to be adapted to each treatment. The

Physiocrats, in the middle of the eighteenth century, studied social processes from the standpoint of law and causation, and sought a unifying code for the loose bundle of economic facts with which the speculations of the Mercantilists and Kameralists had dealt. They found this unifying code in the 'ordre naturel' and 'loi naturalle'. Veblen states that "the economics of the Physiocrats is a theory of the working out of the Law of Nature in its economic bearing." Their philosophy was taken from the English individualistic and utilitarian philosophy and the French Revolutionary philosophy of the eighteenth century. The roots of the French philosophy can be traced back to the doctrine of the Stoics of welfare through obedience to natural law. The Stoical viewpoint was developed into theories of a State of Nature, natural laws, and natural rights. Such a philosophy was the inevitable development of rebellion against the intolerable monarchical regime in France. But it is obvious that the 'natural laws' and 'natural rights' and 'natural order' of the Physiocrats are all metaphysical concepts, products of the imagination looking for some guiding and controlling principle back of individual and social processes directing these toward the highest welfare of the human race. The 'ordre naturel' was the physical constitution 'which God himself has given to the Universe'. Such an assumption may be 'agreeable to reason', and therefore meet the test of metaphysical validity, but it is unprovable and undemonstrable dogma pertaining to the realm beyond the senses, and fails to meet the test of scientific validity. The Physiocrats, in their effort to reduce economics to a body of principles comparable with those to which the physical sciences were being reduced, made the mistake of treating social processes like physical processes, that is, they attacked economic processes from the point of view of physics and not from that of psychics. Their economics was an engineering 'science', not a social 'science'. Their concepts of wealth, production, and value clearly demonstrate the truth of this assertion. With them wealth consisted of concrete things destined for human sustenance, and only that activity was productive which resulted in adding to the wealth, that is, to the store of material commodities in existence. Since they considered that land alone had the power of producing commodities over and above the suit of commodities that had been in existence before, therefore, only labor on land was productive labor. Just as wealth consisted of concrete commodities, so value was the substance, the matter of which commodities were composed. The Physiocrats considered value a detail of production, measured by the productivity of the forces of nature. Theirs were technological concepts. Though they conceived order and scheme in social processes and relationships, and sequences existing among them, and though they developed a more or less consistent theory, yet they were metaphysical and not scientific because they sought to go behind the processes to find out why they worked as they did. That is to say, they were not content with a description but sought an explanation lying behind the economic activity of men in society.

Adam Smith is the successor of the Physiocrats, but his psychology and philosophy were drawn only in part from the same sources. He acquired his individualism from Hobbes through Hume, Locke, and Berkeley. Smith was particularly influenced by Hume. Hume had the scientific or matter-of-fact habit of mind which demanded a solution of every problem in terms of cause and effect, even though in his own solutions he failed to adhere consistently to this method. He was a skeptic touching almost everything that was generally accepted in his day. Unlike most of his contemporaries, and predecessors, too, for that matter, he was not content to formulate knowledge in terms of what ought to be or in terms of the goal toward which phenomena were thought to be tending. He had regard only for reasoning that proceeded step by step from cause to effect. He insisted on matter-of-fact explanations. So we find Adam Smith's generalizations to be substantially matter-of-fact. He was not given to talking in the abstract. Yet, in the final analysis, he proved to be no more content than the Physiocrats had been to describe merely mechanical sequences and relationships. He wished to get behind the obvious and find the hidden springs of action and control. Therefore, he, too, had recourse to the concept of natural law that exercises direction over the sequence of events in the interest of the highest welfare of man Leave the individual alone in his economic activities and an 'unseen hand' will so guide him that in following his own self-interest and aiming only to enhance his own well-being he will at the same time, and unconsciously, best serve the interests of his fellow man. Smith was not content to rest his case until he had stated the argument and the process in terms of a 'consistent propensity tending toward a legitimate end'. But the 'unseen hand' lies not in the realm of the perceptible; it lies in the realm of the mythical.

Economic theory after Adam Smith is value theory. The economists before Ricardo, – the Mercantilists, the Physiocrats, and Adam Smith, – were concerned with questions lying in the fields of production and exchange, with ways and means of promoting national prosperity and acquiring wealth. Little attention was paid by them to questions of distribution and valuation. The Physiocrats and Adam Smith discussed value from the point of view of production; later economists have discussed production from the point of view of value. "The former," as Veblen states, "make value an outcome of the process of production; the latter make production the outcome of a valuation process."[20] By far the greater number of the questions and problems with which economics has concerned itself since the days of Ricardo have been questions and problems of value. It is scarcely too much to say that in so far as economics has

aspired to be a science, it has looked to its value theory as the universal principle upon which to base the sequences and relationships of all social and
economic processes, and in terms of which to state its theoretical formulations.
It has been felt that if the value problem could be solved, the fundamental law
ruling the economic relationships of men would then have been discovered.
Under this single formula all the varied phenomena could be subsumed and the
sequences of economic life described and accounted for. And many have been
the economists who have thought themselves to have discovered the ultimate
principle and to have attained the final truth in value theory. Indeed, John Stuart
Mill, in 1848, was so content with his solution of the problem as to say,
"Happily, there is nothing in the laws of Value which remains for the present
or for any future write to clear-up: the theory of the subject is complete." But
unhappily, for Mill at least, later economists have not been content to take him
at his word, and many and diverse have been the speculations on the problem
of value since his time. Instead of considering that nothing on that question
remained to be cleared up, it seems rather that each succeeding writer has
considered that all that has been said before his time did little more than further
to obscure the problem and make more difficult the attainment of universal
acceptance of his own final and authoritative word.

The fact that economists have formulated such varied solutions of the problem
of value and have reached such diverse conclusions in their speculations on that
question serves as some measure of proof at least that they have not successfully
achieved the habit of mind characteristic of the scientific point of view and have
not always adhered to the scientific method of investigation. Peirce, asking how
true belief is to be distinguished from false belief, holds that "the ideas of truth and
falsehood, in their full development, appertain exclusively to the scientific method
of settling opinion. All followers of science are persuaded that the process of
investigation, if only pushed far enough, will give one certain conclusion to every
question to which it can be applied. Different minds may set out with the most
antagonistic views, but the progress of investigation carries them by a force outside of themselves to one and the same conclusion."[21] And Pearson insists that
"the scientific man has above all things to strive at self-elimination in his judgments, and to provide an argument which is as true for each individual mind as for
his own," and states that "the word science is used as applying to all reasoning
about facts which proceeds from their accurate classification to the application of
their relationship and sequence. The touchstone of science is the universal validity of its results for all normally constituted and duly instructed minds."[22] It may
be denied that universal acceptance and adherence is essential as proof of the
validity of the conclusions of any body of knowledge, but it will certainly be
admitted that almost universal difference of opinion is proof of the fact that the

method followed in reaching those conclusions is not such as recommends itself as valid to thinking men.

Today there is a growing discontent with and questioning of the value speculations of that school whose tenets and formulations were for many years generally accepted as final and authoritative, namely, the Austrian school. This questioning does not take the form of a denial of the logical consistency of the theory postulated by the Austrians and the validity of the conclusions, as such, drawn by them. It takes the form, rather, of a questioning of the premises from which the conclusions were drawn, of the point of view from which the facts were apprehended and the basis upon which they were evaluated. What is called into question particularly is the psychological premises on which the Austrians have based their psychological analysis of the value problem. In its broadest aspect, the struggle is between the scientific as opposed to the metaphysical point of view, the matter-of-fact as opposed to the animistic preconception, the cumulative causation as opposed to the teleological concept of evolution.

The value theory of the Austrians is based on the hedonistic psychology and English utilitarian philosophy of the eighteenth century. The shifting of the point of view after Adam Smith from problems of production and exchange to those of valuation is accounted for by Veblen as due to the developments of contemporary psychology, and especially as due to the formulation of that theory with which Bentham is commonly associated. It is Bentham's theory that furnished the psychology of the Austrians, though Boucke, in a recently published work, holds that "as a matter of fact, Bentham added very little of his own."[23] He states that Tucker and Paley had anticipated Bentham in the clear formulation at a universalistic hedonism, and that it is in Hartley, and not in Locke, Hume, or Bentham, that hedonism is given its final and most convincing form. Hartley in 1748, had this to say: "Our passions or affections can be no more than aggregates of simple ideas united by association. They must be aggregates of ideas, or traces of the sensible pleasures and pains which ideas make up by their number and mutual influence upon one another . . . Since the things which we pursue do, when obtained, generally afford pleasure, and those which we fly from affect us with pain if they overtake us, it follows that the gratification of the will is generally attended with, or associated with, pleasure, the disappointment of it with pain . . . The associated circumstances of the pleasures are many more than the pleasures themselves. But these circumstances, after a sufficient association, will be able to excite the motions subservient to the pleasures, as well as these themselves; and this will greatly augment the methods of obtaining pleasure."[24] And Hume, following Hartley, declared frankly that "the chief springs or actuating principles of the human mind are pleasure and pain; and when these sensations are removed, we are in a great measure incapable of passion or action, of desire or volition."[25]

The sensationalistic psychology and inductive logic of Hobbes, Berkeley, Hume, and Locke was developed into individualistic hedonism and utilitarianism, and gave rise to that monster of the imagination, the economic man. Hobbes may justly be considered the first of the materialists and the sensationalistic psychologists. Sensationalism, or empiricism, claimed that there is no reality beyond the senses and that all human wisdom is a product of sensation alone. Since sensations are purely mechanical and physiological phenomena which can be studied, analyzed, objectively treated and measured like other objective facts of the material world, the sensationalists reasoned that human nature, which manifests itself through reactions to sensations, is as accessible for analysis and measurement as are physical phenomena. Thus, Hobbes reduced consciousness to sensations, nerve responses to contacts with the outer world. He considered sensations to be the origin of all our thoughts, "for," he reasoned, "there is no conception in man's mind which hath not at first, totally or in parts, been begotten upon the organs of sense. The rest are derived from that original."[26] Hobbes recognized only four mental states, viz., sensation, imagination, memory, and desire. From these four are derived trains of thought and what men call 'reason'. "When a man reasoneth he does nothing but conceive a sum total, from additions of parcels; or conceive a remainder, from subtractions of one sum from another; which (if it be done by words) is conceiving of the names of all the parts to the name of the whole; or from the names of the whole and one part, to the name of another part."[27] Desire is conceived by Hobbes as simply a kind of motion "within the body of man which is commonly called endeavour; and this endeavour, when it is toward something which causes it, is called appetite or desire, and when the endeavour is from outward something, it is generally called aversion."[28] In his insistence on sensations as the origin of thought and knowledge and his contention that human nature may be analyzed from observation of the behavior of individuals, Hobbes would seem to hold the scientific point of view. But he neglected the effects of past sensations, 'stored sense-impresses', association, and the mechanism of thinking. Boucke states that "Hobbes was emphatic in his avowal of a materialistic thesis. He reduced psychics to physics, and put up the equation: Notion is motion; that is, matter and motion suffice to explain all experiences. He begins in his exposition with nerve vibration, which is held to move the minutest particles of neural and cerebral stuff. Contact with the outer world is made responsible for this agitation within. Responses result. Sensations become consciousness, or are it. And regardless of what the complexities of consciousness, they are derivable each and all from the first principle announced."[29]

But sensations, immediate 'sense-impressions', are not the sole origin of thought and thinking. Pearson, stating that "the immediate sense-impression is to be looked upon as the spark which kindles thought, which brings into play the still remaining impresses of past sense-impressions," cautions one to remember that "when we state that all the contents of our mind are ultimately based on sense-impressions, we must be careful to recognize that the mind has by classification and isolation proceeded to conceptions which are widely removed from sense-impressions capable of immediate verification. The contents of the mind at any instant are very far from being identical with the range of actual or possible sense-impressions at that instant. We are perpetually drawing inferences from our immediate and stored sense-impressions as to things which lie beyond immediate verification by sense, – that is, we infer the existence of things which do not belong to the objective world, or which at any rate cannot be directly verified by immediate sense-impression, as belonging to it at the present moment. Science is based largely upon inferences of this kind; its hypotheses lie to a great extent beyond the region of the immediately sensible, and it chiefly deals with conceptions drawn from sense-impressions, and not with sense-impressions themselves . . . Science is in reality a classification and analysis of the contents of the mind; the scientific method consists in drawing just comparisons and inferences from the stored sense-impression of past sense-impressions, and from the conceptions based upon them."[30]

Locke greatly improved the psychology of his predecessor and he is generally considered the central figure in the whole history of empirical psychology. He aimed at nothing less than revealing the limits of knowledge. In general he adheres to sensationalism, but adds the concept of reflections. Reflections, he says, "are the perception of the operations of our mind within us as it is employed about the ideas it has got, which operations, . . . do furnish the understanding with another set of ideas not to be had from things without."[31] Reflections are to be sharply distinguished from sensations directly traceable to outside stimuli, and all ideas, according to Locke, are derived from sensation or reflection. Simple ideas become compounded "by combining several simple ideas into one compound," or through like processes. Through association ideas are built into more or less regularly recurring and compact groups of thought. Idealogical concepts "are as capable of real certainly as mathematical" for "truth properly belongs only to propositions," that is, to ideas. Truth consists in the agreement of ideas. Thus did Locke develop the famous law of association as the key to chains of reasoning.

Hume follows Locke quite closely in his conception of the laws of thinking and feeling. He distinguishes between impressions and ideas, defining impressions as being "all sensations, passions, and emotions" and ideas as "the faint images of these in thinking and reasoning." Every simple idea springs from an impression, while complex ideas, developed from them after the manner described by Locke, may originate also from other ideas instead of from impressions. Impressions are of two sorts, 'those of sensation and those of reflexion', the latter being derived in great measure from our ideas.

James Mill took over the Hartley-Humian view of consciousness and rounded it out into a comprehensive *Analysis of the Human Mind.* "All sensations," he states, "are capable of being revived . . . An idea is a revival of a former state of feelings . . . Ideas are feelings which exist after the object of the sense has ceased to be present."[32] Ideas of the causes of pleasurable and painful sensations are never "ideas of the causes separately, but ideas both of the causes and their effects, inseparably joined in association. They are therefore always either pleasurable or painful, being complex ideas, to a great degree composed of the ideas of pleasurable and painful sensations . . . The anticipation of a future sensation is merely the association of a certain number of antecedents and consequents . . . A motive is an idea of a pleasure."[33]

Thus did hedonism become scientific and give birth to the 'economic man'. The association law was used to explain the rise of desire for pleasure even when the thing aimed at did not itself gratify the senses. The happiness of men was held to flow from their acting on remembrances no less than on stimuli at work. "The object of all mania intuitions," wrote Baron d'Holbach in 1771, "of all his reflections, of all his knowledge is only to procure that happiness toward which he is incessantly impelled by the peculiarity of his nature."[34]

Bentham, however, it is who reflects most faithfully the temper of Utilitarian economics. In the first paragraph of his Introduction to the *Principles of Morals and Legislation,* 1789, we are told that "nature has placed mankind under the governance of two sovereign meters, pleasure and pain . . . They govern us in all we do, in all we say, in all we think; every effort we can make to throw off their subjection will serve but to demonstrate and confirm it." From this conception of the motivating forces of human activity is deduced the famous hedonic principle which furnished the premise for all the speculations of the Austrian school on value theory and the economic functioning of man and society. Bentham states it as a self-evident proposition in need of no proof that "to obtain the greatest portion of happiness for himself is the object of every rational being."[35] The pursuit of pleasure and the avoidance of pain is the only effective human motive. And man pursues his own pleasure, not that of other people – self-interest is the guiding principle. "Dream not," says Bentham, "that men will move their little finger to help you, unless their advantage in so doing is obvious to them."

Pleasures and pains with Bentham are quantitative, not qualitative. He holds that there are no good or bad pleasures or pains. Pleasures differ in degree but not in kind. They differ as regards quantity, that is, as regards duration, intensity, extension, etc., but not as regards quality. Happiness is treated as atoms, particles. One pleasure is equal to any other of equal duration, intensity, extension, etc. Therefore, simple addition is all that is required to find out what is the greatest happiness for the greatest number or for the individual. Add all the pleasures consequent to any action, and that which gives the greatest sum constitutes the greatest happiness. Professor Commons calls this point of view the mechanistic and atomistic notion of happiness, and justly objects that Bentham's method does not allow us to place values on happiness. Bentham has a calculus of pleasures and pains but not a valuation of them.

It is needless to point out the inadequacy of the metaphysical hedonistic psychology. It is, of course, entirely discredited by modern psychology, and its shortcomings have been noticed by many since the days of Bentham.[36] But as illustrating the metaphysics of value theory, its relation to that theory requires some notice.[37] The hedonistic psychology reduces the individual to a mechanism, an automaton. As Veblen brings out the idea, "The immediate point of Bentham's work, as affecting the habits of thought of the educated community, is the substitution of hedonism (utility) in place of achievement or purpose, as the ground of legitimacy and a guide in the normalization of knowledge . . . Human action is construed in terms of the causal forces of the environment, the human agent being, at the best, taken as a mechanism of commutation, through the workings of which the sensuous effects wrought by the impinging forces of the environment are, by an enforced process of valuation, transmitted without quantitative discrepancy into moral or economic conduct. In ethics and economics alike the subject-matter of the theory is this valuation process which expresses itself in conduct, resulting, in the case of economic conduct, in the pursuit of the greatest gain or least sacrifice."[38] The human agent, then, is not an active agent, but is merely the middle term of a causal sequence, "of which the initial and terminal members are sensuous impressions and the details of conduct." Therefore, human nature may be left out of account, and the "theory of valuation process may be formulated quantitatively, in terms of the material forces affecting the human sensory and of their equivalents in the resulting activity."[39]

In accordance with such a view of human nature and the human agent, it is obvious a theory of value based on it might find the measure of value either in the pleasure obtained from the consumption of a given commodity, or in the sacrifice or pain undergone in producing or acquiring it. Ricardo and the later Classical economists stated their theory in terms of sacrifice undergone, that is, in terms of cost of production, while the Austrian school stated its theory in terms of pleasure derived. The reason why the Classicists found the measure of value in the amount of sacrifice (cost of production) may possibly be that, realizing the limitation of resources and the implications of the Malthusian

theory of population they were of a pessimistic nature and thought, consequently, in terms of pain rather than in those of pleasure. A more plausible
explanation, however, would seem to be found, first, in the fact that, during the
first half of the nineteenth century, the attention of men was absorbed with the
wonderful progress and increase of production which followed the inventions
that brought on the Industrial Revolution and inaugurated the era of the machine
industry, and second, in the fact that the psychology of the time offered no
method or instrument for objectively measuring and analyzing the subjective
phenomena of pleasure and pain. For these reasons, the Classicists made cost
of some sort or other the foundation and measure of value. Their value concept,
therefore, was a technological, not a psychological concept. Exchange value
was looked upon as a quantity of purchasing power existing in commodities,
similar to other powers possessed by them, such as, for example, heating power
in coal. Professor Commons points out that the 'use-value', concept of the
Classicists was also a technological concept, contrary to the contention of
Böhm-Bawerk that it was a psychological one. With them 'use-values' were
nothing more nor less than the physical qualities of things, intrinsic or embodied
in them. The nutritive value of food, for instance, was its use-value, – a physical
quality availing to sustain life.

But the Austrians, being pre-eminently optimistic, stated their theory in terms
of the pleasure derived from the possession or consumption of goods. They did
not overlook pain, or the sacrifice incurred in production, but they relegated it
to a distinctly subordinate position, holding that the pleasure anticipated would
in every case determine how much sacrifice men would be willing to undergo
in order to procure a particular good. By the 'marginal' analysis the Austrians
thought they had an instrument for measuring pleasure and pain. They used
marginal fractions of pleasure as the measure of value and marginal fractions
of pain as the measure of cost. They compared wants and feelings, not things,
and considered exchange-values adequately expressed by states of feeling and
consciousness in general. The Austrians considered human nature as
unchanging, passive, and substantially inert, and the human agent as simply a
medium through which was transmitted intact the force of desire for pleasure
and aversion to pain.[40] In view of this, as has been stated in another connection, man could be left out of account, and along with him all the forces and
institutions of civilization. These latter were taken as given and constant, for
the marginal utility analysis offers a study of a situation only as it exists at a
given time.

Present-day psychology, however, does not conceive human nature to be
immutable and unchanging, nor man to be passive and inert. It considers it
characteristic of man to do something, not simply to suffer pains and enjoy

pleasures.[41] The Austrians interpreted economic conduct in terms of rational response to the stimulus of anticipated pleasure and pain, but modern psychology expresses grave doubts concerning the supposed rationality of man, and emphatically denies that pleasure and pain are the only effective motives of activity. It has much to say of instincts, 'impulses', 'propensities', 'habits', 'temperaments' and 'intelligence'. The modern behaviorists, indeed, will have nothing to do with motives of any sort, and psychologists are generally agreed that, though one act may be accompanied by pleasure and another by pain, the one is not performed because it is pleasurable and the other avoided *because* it is painful, Pleasure or pains are *accompaniments* of activity, not causes of it. The activity, and not its motives, is the substantial fact about which psychologists today busy themselves with. By a calculus of pleasure and pain the Austrians attempted to explain what men are doing and why they are doing it, with particular emphasis upon the *why*. But we cannot tell how much pleasure an individual has nor how much pain he feels. All that we can know is what he is doing. The economic activity of men must be described in terms of that activity, not explained in terms of what are supposed to be its controlling principles, if economics is to become a science. Likewise, value can only be described in terms of valuing; it cannot be explained by means of metaphysical assumptions concerning its essence and substance. Professor Commons holds that there is no such thing as *value* but that there is a lot of *valuing*. By this he means, I take it, that the concept *value* is a metaphysical concept, a something whose existence is the product only of assumption or imagination; while the concept *valuing* is a scientific concept (a 'behavioristic' notion, as he calls it), being an ever-present activity of individuals, visible on every hand. All that we know of what is called 'value' is comprised in what we know of its effects, and these effects are perceptible in the valuing process.[42] What economics stands most in need of is fewer theories of value and a working theory of *valuing*. Metaphysical speculation has produced theories of value in abundance; scientific investigation and method will produce a theory of valuing.

CONCLUSION

It may be granted that the psychology of Bentham is inadequate and that the 'economic man' is only a creature of the imagination, but, some will say, economic theory today bases its value speculations on the results of modern psychological research. It is true, of course, that the economists have not disregarded the advances which have been made in psychology since the days of Bentham, and that modern economists have made efforts to bring the psychology of the Austrian theory up to date. Long ago it was recognized that the 'economic man' was entirely too clever, too subtle in his thinking, too precise in his estimation of utilities to be considered representative of any real flesh-and-blood man. Furthermore, he was too mechanical, too selfish, too little subject to his environment, and too individualistic. Clark and Anderson, among others, have recognized that it is not man as an individual that needs to be considered in value theory, for man is not independent and isolated. He is part of an organism, society, and is enormously influenced by his relations with his fellow men. Therefore, Clark and Anderson developed 'social value' theories based on social psychology. Value theory today, it may be claimed (and justly), does not consider pleasure and pain to be the sole effective motives of human action. Account is taken of the higher and lower psychological forces, and human nature is interpreted in terms of these, not in terms of pleasure and pain only. All this and more is pointed to as evidence that the psychological premises of value theory have advanced in step with the results of psychological inquiry and development. Admitted that a misconception of human nature vitiated the results of earlier theories, yet, it may be claimed, a more modern and correct conception of the nature of man reveals the motives of human action and furnishes a firm and substantial basis for an adequate psychological theory of value.

All this, and more, may be granted, but, as I see it, it has no bearing on the question at issue, and that question is, What is the purpose and function of a theory of value? In what terms is it to be stated? With what is it to deal? Psychological premises of unquestionable validity might yet yield nothing more than a value theory of misty metaphysical speculation, and it would do exactly that so long as the inquiry was directed toward *explaining how* men will act under given circumstances, what are the ultimate motives and standards of economic conduct, what is the nature of value, and similar matters. The thesis maintained in this work is that to be scientific and not metaphysical, a theory of 'value' must deal, not with value, but with valuing; must aim, not at an explanation of mythical concepts, but at a description of the activity and behavior of human beings in so far as that activity and behavior is concerned with valuing things; must be stated, not in terms of logical deductions from illogical, because merely assumed, premises, but in terms of summaries and resumés of wide ranges of observed facts and phenomena. The purpose and function of a theory of 'value' is not to explain the essence and substance of value and why things have it or men give it to them, but to describe the valuing process in terms of itself and furnish suggestions and a guide to administrative bodies, the courts, businessmen and others who are confronted with specific problems of valuing, with determining 'reasonable, 'just', 'fair', or 'adequate' values, and the like.

It may seem that a theory of 'value' which concerns itself only with a description of the valuing activities of men would be a decidedly unwieldy and barren theory. It possibly would, but a mere description of activities, as the argument which has been advanced has attempted to prove, is not what is implied by the scientific method. If science meant nothing more than a collection of facts and an insistence on data, the Historical School certainly could lay just claim to having produced a scientific economics. The work of the Historical School, however, falls short of being a science because the data which it so painstakingly collected and the facts which it so carefully observed were not developed into theories nor formulated in a consistent body of knowledge. Value theory, to be scientific, must be descriptive and not explanatory, behavioristic and not metaphysical, it is true, but it certainly must be formulated into a close-knit body of theory. It is not enough merely to collect facts and insist on data.

A scientific theory of value will concern itself with the valuing process, not with speculation concerning the ultimate nature and standard of value; it will describe what men actually do in their economic activity, not with what they might be supposed to do under an assumed set of circumstances; and, as Professor Commons holds, it will find that the 'real' values with which men deal are money-values, and not labor-values or pleasure-values or social-values. Economic science will first begin to be exact when it is quantitatively treated. A unit for measuring the phenomena with which it deals is essential. Since the 'real' values are money values, the dollar is the unit of measurement. Money is not the measure of commodities or of pleasures and pains, but it is the measure of human economic behavior, and it is this latter, not commodities or pleasures and pains, that constitutes the subject-matter with which scientific economics is to deal. Economic activity, not the technology of production nor the psychology of consumption, must be the subject-matter of economics if it is to become a science. If this be true, bringing the psychology on which the premises are based up to date is not sufficient to remove the metaphysics from value theory. It is doubtful whether psychology will have anything to do with the scientific value theory of the future.

NOTES

1. Peirce, Illustrations of the Logic of Science, *Popular Science Monthly*, November, 1877.

2. Peirce, Illustrations of the Logic of Science, *Popular Science Monthly*. November, 1877. (First Paper, The Fixation of Belief)

3. *ibid.*

4. Peirce, *op. cit.*, Second Paper.

5. Peirce, *op.cit.*, Second Paper. He goes on to specify further the nature of reality: "The only effect which real things have is to cause belief, for all the sensations which

they excite emerge into consciousness in the forms of beliefs. . . . The question, there-fore, is, how is true belief (or belief in the real) to be distinguished from false belief (or belief in fiction). Now, the ideas of truth and falsehood, in their fall development, appertain exclusively to the scientific method of settling opinion. All followers of science are persuaded that the process of investigation, if only pushed far enough, will give one certain conclusion to every question to which they can be applied . . . The opinion which is fated, (is sure to come and cannot be avoided), to be ultimately agreed to by all who investigate, is what we mean by truth, and the object represented in this opinion is real. That is the way I would explain reality."

6. Pearson, *The Grammar of Science,* Chapter II.

7. 'An external object is a combination of immediate with past or stored sense-impres-sions. The reality of the thing depends upon the possibility of its occurring in whole or part as a group of immediate sense-impressions'. (Pearson, *Grammar of Science,* Chapter II)

8. See Pearson, op. cit., Chapter II, Sec. 4, *The Nature of Thought.*

9. 'What we are sure of is a certain routine of perceptions and a capacity in the mind to resume them in the mental shorthand of scientific law. What we have no right to infer is that order, mind, or reason exist on the other side of sense-impressions, in the unknown plus of sensations or in things-in-themselves. Natural theology and metaphysics do this, for they assert that reason can help us to some knowledge of the supersenuous. Nonsense. The mind is absolutely confined within its nerve-exchange; beyond the walls of sense-impression it can logically infer nothing. In the chaos of sensations on the other side of sense-impressions we have no ground whatever for asserting that any human conception will suffice to describe what may exist there, for it lies outside the barrier of sense-impressions from which all human conceptions are ultimately drawn'. (Pearson, *Grammar of Science*, Chapter III).

10. Pearson, *Grammar of Science*, Chapter III.

11. Pearson, *op. cit.*, Chapter IV.

12. Peirce, *op. cit.*, Third Paper, *The Doctrine of Chance*, March, 1878.

13. Pearson, *op. cit.* , Chapter IV, sec. 12.

14. Pearson, *op. cit.*, Chapter IV, sec. 8.

15. Pearson, *op. cit.*, Chapter II, sec. 4.

16. Pearson, *op. cit.*, Chapter III.

17. Pearson, *op. cit.*, Chapter II.

18. But, let us note, 'the metaphysician asserts an existence for the supersensuous which is unconditioned by the perceptive or reflective faculties in man. His supersen-suous is at once incapable of being a sense-impressions, and yet has a real existence apart from the imagination of men. Such an existence involves an unproven and undemonstrable dogma. The conceptions of the scientist, for instance, that of the elements, molecules and atoms are in a sense supersensuous, – they do not at present represent direct sense-impressions. But the physicist looks upon that atom in one of two different ways: either the atom is real, that is, capable of being a direct sense-impression, or else it is ideal, that is, a purely mental conception by the aid of which we are able to formulate natural laws. It is either the product of the perceptive faculty, or of the reflective or reasoning faculty in man'. (Pearson, *The Grammar of Science*, Chapter III). But, 'The progress of-science is reduced to a more and more complete analysis of the perceptive faculty – an analysis which unconsciously and not unnaturally we project into an analysis of something beyond sense-impression. Thus both the material and the laws of science are inherent in ourselves rather than in an outside world. Our groups

of perceptions form for us reality, and the results of our reasoning on these perceptions and the conclusions deduced from them form our only genuine knowledge'. (Pearson, ibid.)

19. Veblen, T., Why is Economics not an Evolutionary Science, *The Quarterly Journal of Economics*, Vol. xii, July 1898.

20. Veblen, T., The Preconceptions of Economic Science, II, *The Quarterly Journal of Economics*, vol. XIII, 1899.

21. Peirce, *op. cit.*, Second Paper, January, 1878.

22. Pearson, *op. cit.*, Chapter I.

23. Boucke, *Development of Economics* (1921). p. 121.

24. Hartley, *Observations on Man*, vol. I, pp. 368–370. (1748)

25. Hume, D.A., *A Treatise of Human Nature*, Bk. III, Chap. 5, see. 3.

26. Hobbes, *Leviathan*, Part I. ch. 1. (1651)

27. Hobbes, *Leviathan*, Chapter V.

28. Ibidem, Part I, Chapter VI.

29. Boucke, *Development of Economics*, pp. 31–32,

30. Pearson, *Grammar of Science*, Chapter II.

31. Locke, *Essay Concerning Human Understanding*, Book II, Chap. 1, see, 4. (1689)

32. Mill, J. *Analysis of the Phenomena of the Human Mind*, Chap. 19. (1689)

33. *ibid.*

34. Baron d'Holbach, *System of Nature,* vol. I, chap. 1.

35. "Economic science," states Pantaleoni in the opening words of the first chapter of his *Pure Economics*, "consists of the laws of wealth systematically deduced from the hypothesis that men are actuated exclusively by the desire to realise the fullest possible satisfaction of their wants with the least possible individual sacrifice." Probably no better example of metaphysical assumption can be found than that furnished by this hypothesis. It is decidedly 'agreeable to reason', it seems a self-evident proposition, it is what all men are inclined to believe, but it rests on no fact in the world. So far as I know, no one has ever attempted to prove its validity. Pantaleoni, indeed, states that "the proof of the existence of the force postulated by economics is supplied both by self-observation and by observation of the motives from which other men act ... Egoism or self-interest is one of the most frequent and general causes of human actions. It is evident, certainly, that commercial or industrial activity, or the activity (whatever its nature may be) displayed by men in the pursuit of what is commonly termed wealth, has no other motive than egoism. Of course other forces, – compulsion of governments, customs, morality, ignorance, etc. – may actuate man's conduct, but such conduct is actuated only by self-interest so long as they consider these to be in accordance with the dictates of egoism." (*Pure Economics*, Chap. II). One wonders just why all this is so evident Pantaleoni himself experiences some slight doubt of the evidence in favor of it, for he goes on to ask: "But is the sole motive of every action the hedonic impulse? Bentham held that with reference to every act, every human being inclined to that course which, in his estimate of the conditions of the moment, will contribute in the comparatively highest degree to promote his happiness. It would be most difficult to establish proof of this hypothesis. But, even if it is impossible to prove that the sole motive of every human action is the desire to procure some pleasure or shun some pain, at all events this motive is, not only universal and most powerful, but likewise so multiform, that motives apparently most diverse from, are really reducible to, it." (*Pure Economics*. Chap. II). In view of the difficulty or impossibility of proof, the hedonistic principle

would seem to furnish a very slender base indeed on which to rear the structure of a science, but that is exactly what Pantaleoni and the other Austrians attempted to do. Pantaleoni makes the amazing statement that even though the hedonistic principle should not be true, nevertheless economic principles and laws deduced from it would be perfectly valid provided only they be deduced by correct and consistent logical reasoning. This makes the validity of conclusions a matter of thinking and not of fact, in the best approved metaphysical manner. I am inclined to believe that so long as 'economic science' rests on mythical assumption and logical inference from such assumption, that long it will be metaphysics and not science.

36. See, in this connection, any modern text-book on psychology, such as William James, *The Principles of Psychology* (1899) and *Psychology*, (1905); McDougall, *Psychology, The Study of Behavior;* Titchener, *A Text-Book of Psychology*; Dewey, *Psychology*; and Chapter VII of Grahem Wells *The Great Society.*

37. In several very able articles Professor Veblen has made reference to and pointed out the faulty conception of human nature involved in the Austrian theory of value. See, particularly, *The Quarterly Journal of Economics,* Vol. XII,. July, 1898, Why is Economics not an Evolutionary Science? (in the article as reprinted in *The Place of Science in Modern Civilization,* see pp. 73, et seq.); *The Quarterly Journal of Economics,* Vol, XIV, Feb. 1900, The Preconceptions of Economic Science, III. (in *The Place of Science in Modern Civilization,* pp. 155, et seq.); and *The Journal of Political Economy,* Vol. XII, no. 9, Nov. 1909, The Limitations of Marginal Utility.

38. Veblen, T. The Preconceptions of Economic Science' II, *The Quarterly Journal of Economics*, Vol. XIII, July 1899. (Reprint, The Place of Science in Modern Civilization, pp. 133–134).

39. Veblen, T., *op. cit.*, The Preconceptions of Economic Science, II.

40. "The hedonistic conception of man," states Veblen in a keenly satirical passage, 'is that of a lightning calculator of pleasures and pains, who oscillates like a homogenous globule of desire of happiness under the impulse of stimuli that shift him about the area, but leave him intact. He is an isolated, definitive human datum, in stable equilibrium except for the buffets of the impinging forces that displace him in one direction or another. Self-imposed in elemental space, he spine symmetrically about his own spiritual axis until the parallelogram of forces beats down upon him, whereupon he follows the line of the resultant. When the force of the impact is spent, he comes to rest, a self-contained globule of desire as before. Spiritually, the hedonistic man is not a prime mover. He is not the seat of a process of living, except in the sense that he is subject to a series of permutations enforced upon him by circumstances external and alien to him." (Veblen, T. Why is Economics not an Evolutionary Science? *The Quarterly Journal of Economics* vol. XII, July, 1899, Reprinted in T*he Place of Science Modern Civilization,* pp. 73–74).

41. See Veblen, Why is Economics not an Evolutionary Science? *The Quarterly Journal of Economics,* Vol. XII, July, 1898. (Reprint, The Place of Science in Modern Civilization. pp. 74–75.)

42. Consider what effects, which might conceivably have practical bearings, we conceive the object of our conception to have. They, our conceptions of these effects, are the whole of our conception of the object. What we mean by the force of gravity, for instance, is completely involved in its effects. When we say that a body is heavy, we mean simply that, in the absence of opposing force, it will fall. When we say that a body is hard, we merely mean that it will not be scratched by many other substances.

Our whole conception of every quality lies in its conceived effects. Take, for instance, force. To say that we understand precisely the effect of force, but what force itself is, we do not understand, is simply a self-contradiction. The idea which the word force excites in our minds has no other function than to affect our actions, and these actions can have no reference to force otherwise than through it effects. Consequently, if we know what the effects of force are, we are acquainted with every fact which is implied in saying that a force exists, and there is nothing more to known. (Peirce, Illustrations of the Logic of Science. Second Paper, How to Make Our Ideas Clear, *Popular Science Monthly*, January, 1878).

REFERENCES

Boucke, O. P. (1921). *The Development of Economics.* N.Y., Macmillan Co. (My quotations from Hartley, Hume, Hobbes, Locke, James Mill are as quoted by Boucke.)

Dewey, J. (1916). *Essays in Experimental Logic.* Chicago: The University of Chicago Press. Chapters XII and XIII.

Pantaleoni, M. (1957). *Pure Economics.* New York: Kelley and Millman.

Peirce, C. S. (1877). Illustrations of the Logic of Science. First Paper, – The Fixation of Belief. *Popular Science Monthly,* vol. XII (November), 1–15.

Peirce, C. S. (1878). 'Illustrations of the Logic of Science'. Second Paper, – How to Make Our Ideas Clear, *Popular Science Monthly*, vol. XII (January), 28–102.

Peirce, C. S. (1878). Illustrations of the Logic of Science. Third Paper, – The Doctrine of Chances, *Popular Science Monthly,* vol. XII (March), 604–615.

Pearson, K. (1908). *The Grammar of Science.* (3rd ed.) London: A. and C. Black.

Schiller, F. C. S. (1907). *Studies in Humanism.* London: Macmillan and Co.

Schiller, F .C. S. (1894). *Riddles of the Sphinx.* New York: Macmillan and Co.

Veblen, T. (1906). The Place of Science in Modern Civilization reprinted in *The Place of Science in Modern Civilization* (pp. 1–31). New York, B.W. Huebsch, 1919.

Veblen, T. (1908). The Evolution of the Scientific Point of View reprinted in *The Place of Science in Modern Civilization* (pp. 32–55). New York, B.W. Huebsch, 1919.

Veblen, T. (1898). Why is Economics not an Evolutionary Science? reprinted in *The Place of Science in Modern Civilization* (pp. 56–81). New York, B.W. Huebsch, 1919.

Veblen, T. (1900). The Preconceptions of Economic Science. reprinted in *The Place of Science in Modern Civilization* (pp. 82–179). New York, B.W. Huebsch, 1919.

Veblen, T. (1909). The Limitations of Marginal Utility reprinted in *The Place of Science in Modern Civilization* (pp. 231–251). New York, B.W. Huebsch, 1919.

Wallas, G. (1914). *The Great Society.* New York: Macmillan and Co. Chapter VII.

THE PROBLEM OF MONETARY STANDARDS (1933)

Edward Everett Hale

We were once told by former President Hoover that no greater disaster could befall this country than the abandonment of the gold standard. It has more recently been implied, if not openly expressed, that the action of our government in abrogating the Gold Standard Act of March, 1900, is morally indefensible if not wicked and sinful. Some regard this action as a shameful betrayal of trust – as a sanction from government for debtors to cheat their creditors by paying debts in paper dollars of depreciated value instead of dollars redeemable in gold at the price of $20.67 per ounce or 25.8 grains of gold 9/10 fine per dollar. It is curious how quickly a new way of doing things may become a tradition sanctioned by all the weight and authority that attaches to long established usage. It is very curious how that new invention, the gold standard, in the space of a few years, was erected into a moral principle, and how by this belief in and acceptance of this principle could be tested one's character as well as one's economic sanity.

For contrary to widespread opinion, the gold standard is not sanctioned by immemorial usage. It is in fact a recent phenomenon in human history, being

Edward Everett Hale: The Writings of an Economic Maverick, Volume 19-B, pages 57–66.
2001 by Elsevier Science B.V.
ISBN: 0-7623-0694-7

essentially a creation of the second half of the nineteenth century. Since the introduction of a money economy, men have experimented with an amazing variety of monetary standards, ranging all the way from oxen and tobacco to the precious metals and engraved pieces of gold. In the nineteenth century the nations of the world with few exceptions, were using either silver as the standard monetary metal or a mixed standard of silver and gold. It was only after the discovery of gold in enormous quantities in California and Australia in 1848 that a slow and gradual transition from these silver and mixed currency systems to the gold standard was begun. The transition was virtually completed in 1900 when the United States established gold as the standard money metal. During the world war all the belligerent countries were driven off gold, save the United States. From 1919 to 1925, a concerted and painful but finally successful effort was made to restore the gold standard. Yet the process of restoration had scarcely more than been completed before the extraordinary collapse in world price levels, initiated by the termination of the 'new economic era' in the United States in 1929, again subjected the standard to an unbearable strain. In 1930, a number of raw material producing countries, feeling first and most intensely the shock of declining prices due to the inelasticity of demand for their products, were driven off gold. In September, 1931, Great Britain suspended gold payments, and her suspension caused the immediate abandonment of the gold standard in the Scandinavian countries, in Finland, Ireland, and India, whose currencies were closely tied to sterling. Finally in March of this year (1933) we ceased redemption of our monies in gold, and by executive order on April 20 the President formally suspended the gold standard. Today France is the only major country remaining upon gold (even France has abandoned it now), so that the international gold standard has ceased to exist.

What caused the breakdown of the international gold standard? An answer to this question is best arrived at by considering the conditions essential to the successful operation of that standard. Due to the limited amount of monetary gold in existence, and to the necessity of each country to maintain adequate gold reserves back of its currency, gold can be used to settle international balances only under conditions such that not much gold actually passes from one country to another. These conditions exist when: (1) price levels in the various countries are sensitive to variations in gold reserves so that, e.g., a relatively small increase in the reserves will be accompanied by a rise in the commodity price level, and contrariwise; (2) the demand for international products is elastic, so that a rise in prices will produce an increase in the value of imports relative to exports, and contrariwise, (3) no restrictive or hampering barriers to international trade such as prohibitive tariffs or import and export quotas exist, and (4) payments between countries are the result primarily of trade and commerce and conservative international financing of commerce and industry.

Under these conditions no country could acquire or retain a disproportionate share of the world's gold supply. Let us assume that at some given time the balance of international payments was in favor of the United States, so that gold was flowing into this country. The accumulation of gold in our bank reserves would tend to lower discount rates. The reduction of discount rates would have two effects. First, it would cause the export of short-term and long-term funds seeking a higher rate of return elsewhere and thus lead at least to partial outflow of gold to other countries. Secondly, lower discount rates would stimulate expansion of domestic credit, an increase in the volume of business, and a rise in internal prices. As our price level rose, our imports would be stimulated and exports restricted, which would lead to a still further export of gold. As gold left this country, the rise in our price level would be checked while price levels in the countries receiving gold would rise until equilibrium has been achieved and the gold movement stopped.

But since the war these conditions essential to the successful operation of the gold standard have ceased to exist, and consequently the mechanism failed to work. Over the past fifteen years some 75% or 80% of the world's monetary gold has silted up in the United States and France. Whereas before the war, we were a debtor nation, we emerged from the war a great creditor country with some ten billions of war debts owed our government by our former allies. Then from 1922 to 1929, American private investors invested some ten billions more in foreign countries through the purchase of bonds and securities of their governments and business enterprises. Payment of interest and principal on these huge governmental and private debts amounts to hundreds of millions of dollars per year. In addition, after the war Europe continued to buy great quantities of goods from us to rehabilitate her war-wrecked industries as well as to supply the needs of her population. At the same time, our extremely high tariff made it difficult or impossible for foreign countries to penetrate our own markets. Prohibited or hindered thus from paying us in goods, they of necessity had to pay as far as possible in gold.

Yet from 1888 our bank credit failed to expand in proportion to our huge and growing gold reserves. It seems probable that the Federal Reserve authorities deliberately pursued a policy of sterilizing gold in order to prevent our own price level from rising above the level prevailing in the rest of the world and thereby encouraging imports even over our high tariff walls. There was, nevertheless some expansion of bank credit, but this increase went into security and real estate speculation instead of into commerce. Rising security and real estate prices together with high call money rates drew funds to this country instead of driving them out, as high commodity prices would have done. Thus the automatic regulation of the international gold standard ceased to function. It seemed that the more gold we accumulated, the more we tended to accumulate.

In France, likewise, there were special factors operating to increase the stock of gold and keep it there indefinitely. When France returned to the gold standard in 1926, French funds which had been deposited abroad were rapidly repatriated. Further the Bank of France and the French government adopted a deliberate policy of accumulating a huge gold reserve, primarily for military purposes. In addition the French people, remembering the war experiences, hoarded money in great quantities, so that gold imports failed to affect the price level as they might have done in the absence of hoarding. Too, due to the loss of a large part of their pre-war investments, the French were reluctant to invest further in foreign securities. And by means of successive increases in her tariff, France reduced her imports and hence the amount of her payments to foreign market countries. Hence she, like us, accumulated and still retains a huge stock of gold.

For other countries on the gold standard, this maldistribution of gold meant inadequate gold reserves, a constant threat to the integrity of their currencies, and a deflationary pressure on the their prices. As they lost gold, they of necessity adopted a restrictive policy in the issue of currency and credit, which caused falling prices and business depression for them. The threat to the integrity of their currencies caused a cessation of the flow of new capital from the creditor to these debtor countries and a withdrawal of previously made short-term investments. Loss of gold, falling prices, business depression, and banking crises caused flights from their currencies with the result that one after the other they were driven off the gold standard.

In Great Britain rigid wages, relative lack of progress in industrial technique, the progressive exhaustion of coal mines, the development of new foreign competition for her textile and steel industries, foreign tariffs, a crushing debt burden, an excessive export of capital, and low bank rates to encourage industrial reconstruction made the gold standard an increasingly difficult and finally intolerable burden.

As other countries abandoned gold, the United States was placed at a serious disadvantage in international trade, due to the appreciation of the dollar in the exchanges. Further, the disastrous fall in prices that followed the collapse of the new economic era, carried further and further downward by the competitive struggle of banks for liquidity and for the protection of their reserves at whatever cost to the rest of the economic structure, subjected our credit structure to an increasingly dangerous strain. As the purchasing power of the dollar increased, the burden of our enormous long-term debt became abnormally heavy.

The assets of financial institutions were undermined as debtors found themselves unable to meet their obligations. Fear spread as bank failures increased. Finally, a terrified flight from the dollar in the first months of this year closed all the banks in the United States and forced us off the gold standard.

If this analysis of the collapse of the gold standard is correct, the conditions requisite for its re-establishment should be clear. An essential condition is that the immense gold hoards of the United States and France be so redistributed among the nations of the world that each would have sufficient reserves to support its currency on gold. A second essential condition is that international trade and finance be so reorganized that settlement of balances would require relatively small shipments of gold. The realization of these two requisites would require: (1) the drastic reduction or cancellation of reparations and inter-allied war debts; (2) a substantial reduction of the principal or interest of American private foreign investments; (3) the reduction of tariffs, import quotas, and other barriers to international trade; (4) a more cautious and less irresponsible procedure in the flotation of international loans; (5) the economic and financial recovery of England and the United States, and (6) an abandonment of extreme nationalism. An international institution in a nationalist world, the gold standard is not adapted to withstand the centrifugal forces generated by nations indulging themselves in new extremes of self-determination.

It is reasonably safe to assume, in view of these various requisites, that there is little probability of the re-establishment of the international gold standard in the immediate future. We seem destined to witness the experiment of some hitherto untried monetary standard, in all probability some form of 'managed currency'. Indeed, Mr. Roosevelt has already stated with emphasis that he intends to reform the monetary system of the United States on the basis of the stabilized dollar.

Personally I am unable to view with alarm this departure from gold and prospective resort to a 'managed currency' system. The gold standard is by no means an ideal monetary standard. It suffers from the very grave defect that the value of gold is extremely variable. Variations in the value of gold bring accidental or fortuitous gains or losses to creditors and debtors when gold is used as a standard of deferred payments, and, as we have lately experienced, may undermine the entire credit structure of a country. This weakness of the gold standard has always been recognized, but its defenders have urged that gold possesses two marked advantages over any other monetary standard known to man – advantage so great as far to outweigh the disadvantage of its fluctuating value. Those two alleged advantages are: (1) that the gold standard stabilizes the foreign exchanges, and (2) that it provides a non-political and automatic regulation of currency and credit, and consequently prevents disastrous inflation or depreciation of money.

It is true that the gold standard stabilizes the foreign exchanges. If the national money of each country is exchangeable for a fixed amount of gold, the national monies of different countries must be exchangeable for one another at a ratio closely corresponding to the amount of gold which their monetary units contain. The rates of exchange of the monies of the two countries which are on the gold standard can vary only within limits set by the cost of shipping gold from one to the other. And there are obviously great advantages to this fixing within narrow limits of the rates of exchange between different national monies. It enables businessmen and financiers to make contracts and incur debts across national frontiers without worrying themselves about possible changes in the relative values of the national monies concerned. There is no fixed relation between the monies of two countries off the gold standard, and this introduces an element of great uncertainty into all contracts of an international kind, for no one knows when he contracts to receive or buy in foreign money how much of his own money he will actually get or have to pay out. This uncertainty hampers trade and the landing of capital abroad. This explains why exporters and importers and bankers are of all people most concerned with the maintenance of the gold standard. Thus it was the banking community that took the lead in forcing the world back on the gold standard after the war and it is the banking community that now most strongly urges the return to so-called sound money and most vividly pictures the dangers and perils of so-called inflation.

It is to be noted, however, that the gold standard, though it stabilizes the foreign exchanges and serves the needs of international trade and finance, produces an exceedingly unstable domestic price level which hampers domestic trade and finance. It protects importers and exporters and investors in foreign securities against loss from changes in the dollar value of sterling, say, but subjects those along with all domestic producers and traders and investors to risk of loss from changes in the goods or commodity value of the dollar, that is, in the purchasing power of gold. We have to choose between stability of the domestic exchanges and stability of the domestic price level. We can have one or the other, but not both. If domestic trade and investments are more important than foreign, it would seem that stability of the domestic price level is more important than stability of the exchanges. If so, the gold standard sacrifices a greater advantage for the sake of a lesser one.

Yet it may be thought that the second advantage claimed for the gold standard, viz, that it automatically regulates the volume of currency and credit and thus prevents disastrous inflation, is of sufficient value itself to outweigh all its disadvantages. By law we require that certain minimum gold reserves be maintained back of our currency and bank credit. This is thought to have the effect of restricting the total amount of currency and credit issue. But this is a pure fiction. It is not the gold reserve that sets the limit to expansion of credit but the law that prescribes the reserve. Congress passed that law and there is nothing in the constitution or elsewhere to keep Congress from changing the requirements at will.

Hence the only protection we ever had against undue inflation was simply the unwillingness of Congress to alter the requirements of the gold reserve. We have no more reason to assume that Congress will unduly inflate the currency when we are on an irredeemable paper money basis that we had when we were on the gold standard. In either case Congress controls the volume of currency and in neither case does gold regulate it. As far as our internal economy is concerned, the gold standard is a useless extravagance – it serves no purpose and is very costly. Hence this second alleged advantage is equally as fictitious as the first one.

Despite the horror with which 'hard money' economists and hard headed bankers and businessmen view any proposal for a 'managed money' system, the fact remains that the gold standard, as we operated it, was itself a managed currency system. This was true, not only because Congress managed the reserve requirements but also because out actual gold reserves always greatly exceeded the minimum required by law. We never permitted the volume of our currency and credit to be regulated by gold – expanding as the reserves increased and contracting as they decreased. The volume of our currency and credit then was necessarily managed by someone. It was, in fact, managed by the bankers with some, though generally ineffective, supervision by the Federal Reserve Board. The choice confronting us, therefore, is not whether we shall have a managed currency, for in practice and necessarily all currencies are managed, but whether management shall be by the banking fraternity or by some other agency or group. From recent experience some of us might reasonably question the benefits of the kind of management we have had from the bankers.

The essential problem, of course, relates to the aim or purpose on the basis of which currency and credit are to be managed. Whether a managed currency is desirable depends upon what it is managed for. On this point I would agree with Mr. Roosevelt, that the objective should be a dollar of stable purchasing power – that is, a dollar the value of which remains constant. Only such a dollar can secure justice between creditors and debtors, or provide against speculative and fortuitous gains or losses to all who contract to receive or pay money in the future. Only such a dollar constitutes real 'sound money', if that question – begging term has any meaning whatsoever. (Paul H. Douglas, *Controlling Depressions,* New York: W.W. Norton and Co., p. 195.)

Mr. Roosevelt proposed first to raise our internal price level or depreciate the dollar to the degree necessary to reduce debts to bearable proportions. Since the appreciation of the dollar from 1929 to 1933 increased the burden of debts two or threefold, justice seemed to require that the goods value or purchasing power of the dollar be reduced some fifty or sixty per cent so that debtors were required to pay back only as much as they borrowed. Irrespective of the requirements of justice, economic expediency makes the reduction of the debt burden imperative. It is impossible for debtors to repay with their 1933 dollar incomes debts contracted at the higher price and income levels of 1919 and to 1929, and attempts to force them to do so are in the nature of the case futile and ineffective. In every period of falling price levels since the beginnings of modern industrialism, it has been necessary to adjust the debts to lower prices and incomes. There are only three ways of reducing debts. One method, and the one pursued through the Hoover administration is by bankruptcy and reorganization. It is, of course, a most painful method, and would mean in our country, if pursued to its logical conclusion, the bankruptcy of most of our farmers, all our railroads, many of our industrial corporations, all our banks, and all our insurance companies. It is, in fact, a method so painful that it cannot be pursued beyond a certain point without generating open rebellion of debtors – as we have noted in the case of the mid-western farmers. The second, and by far the most equitable, method of adjusting the debt burden to lower price levels is by a legal reduction of the rate of interest on all evidences of indebtedness. This method, however, is politically impossible, for it would probably arouse open rebellion on the part of creditors. Investment bankers, insurance companies, mortgage holders, stock and bond owners would not submit without a violent struggle to a reduction of their income by such a direct, obvious, and rational device. The third, and politically most feasible method of reducing debts is by depreciation of the dollar, that is, by inflation of currency and credit. This method achieves exactly the same as would be achieved by a legal reduction of the interest rate – in fact, the two amount to one and the same thing – but it does so indirectly and more subtly, and consequently causes less determined opposition. It is the method that has been and will be used by the Roosevelt administration. We have had as yet very little inflation and may have a great deal more. [Parenthetical note by author: Keynes and inflation.] It is interesting to note that no major depression in the history of our country has ever come to an end without inflation of the currency or depreciation of the dollar. The long depression following 1837 was brought to an end in 1848 with gold discoveries in California and Australia, and the resulting inflation of currency through gold. The severe depression following 1873 ended simultaneously with inflation of our currency through silver dollars under the Bland-Allison Silver Purchase Act of 1878. The intense depression following 1893 ended with gold inflation after 1896 due to the cyanide process of gold extraction. This process greatly increased the production of gold by making possible the profitable working of low grade ores. (We have no reason to assume that the existing depression will prove the exception to the rule and end without inflation. Economic recovery is impossible unless the burden of debt is reduced, and its reduction is most feasibly affected by means of inflation.)

When and if the price level rises to the height desired by Mr. Roosevelt, we are promised stabilization at that level by the use of a stabilized or commodity dollar. The theory of the stabilized dollar is that the level of prices, in a country on the gold standard, can be controlled by varying the gold content of the monetary unit. If between any two given dates, the index number of prices should rise indicating a decrease in the value of gold, the amount of gold in the monetary unit, the dollar, let us say, would be increased so as to effect the decrease in the value of gold and give the dollar the same purchasing power as it had at the earlier date. In like manner the gold content of the dollar would be reduced in the event of a fall in the general level of prices. This, it is assumed, would have a dollar of varying weight and constant purchasing power, instead, as we used to have, a dollar of constant weight and varying purchasing power.

But a mere change in the gold content of the dollar could not itself affect the level of prices, because it would not place more dollars in circulation with which to buy goods. In our economy the dollars with which goods are purchased are almost altogether credit dollars created by the banks. Should the volume of bank credit be independent of variations in the gold content of the dollar, the price level would likewise be independent of such variations. As a fact, under our existing banking and credit system the volume of currency and credit has never been governed by the quantity of gold reserves. Past experience has amply demonstrated the lack of correlation between these two factors. The volume of bank credit has been regulated by variations in the price level, and not the price level by variations in currency and credit. This is inevitable in a system of free enterprise and private banking dominated by the profit motive and concerned for the security of the investments and loans. Neither the most persuasive exhortations, first of Mr. Hoover and later of Mr. Roosevelt, for the most extensive of open market purchases of governmental bonds by the Federal Reserve banks to increase the reserves and lending capacity of the member banks, availed to induce these banks to expand their loans, that is, to increase the volume of deposit currency, in the face of a falling price level. Bank credit of profit-seeking banks follows price changes. It does not and cannot be made to precede and cause changes in the level of prices.

Therefore, even if it be true that the price level can be controlled by manipulation of currency and credit, that control would be possible only if government should take over and operate our banking system. Government operation of the banking system will be the logical outcome of Mr. Roosevelt's plan to establish the stabilized dollar. In fact, through the Reconstruction Finance Corporation the Federal government has already assumed the function of financing trade and industry and through loans to banks and purchase of their doubtful assets is rapidly acquiring large ownership interest in them.

Further, the re-establishment of the gold standard on the basis of the stabilized dollar, or a gold dollar of varying weight, would seem to be superfluous to accomplish the end in view. Since, according to the theory, the variation of dollar gold reserves would work out its effect on the price level through proportional variation in the volume of currency and credit, it would seem simpler, and certainly would be less expensive, to vary the volume of currency and credit directly so as to maintain stability of the price level. The use of the variable gold dollar would be an unnecessary extravagance. It would be more logical and cheaper to continue the irredeemable paper money or fiat standard we now have and control it directly.

In my opinion control of currency and credit is one essential to stabilization of prices, but cannot by itself achieve that end. It requires to be supplemented by other measures and devices to eliminate or reduce the cyclical fluctuations of business and industry. The business cycle, together with instability of the price level, is, I think much more the result of gross inequality in the distribution of income than of defects in our money and credit system. If this is true, stabilization of price levels and of industry depends on reducing inequalities in the distribution of income rather than on control of currency and credit. Nevertheless, control of currency and credit is itself a necessary instrument in control of distribution of income. We should not, therefore, reject a managed currency system merely because it could not cure all the ills of our economy. It could at least cure some of them and should be welcomed on that account.

ECONOMIC PATTERN OF A DURABLE PEACE (1942)

Edward Everett Hale

It is a truism that the economic basis of a durable peace is to be defined in terms of the economic causes of war. The abolition of the economic causes of international violence would not alone guarantee the maintenance of peace, for war has other than economic causes, such as political, racial, religious, and even social frictions, but the economic factors are potent and their excision would greatly enhance the probability of a lasting peace.

There is widespread agreement that the economic causes of war since the rise of the modern nation states and the economy of free enterprise have been the competitive struggle among nations for markets and for control of sources of raw materials. Some analysts list the pressure of population among the major economic irritants, but I am inclined to believe that such pressure is rather a contributing factor to the competitive struggle for markets than an independent cause of international strife. Scarcity of markets creates unemployment, and unemployment seems an indication of a superabundant population. One does not hear of the pressure of population and the demand for *Lebensraum* in countries in which there is no chronic largescale unemployment, as in the United States prior

Edward Everett Hale: The Writings of an Economic Maverick, Volume 19-B, pages 67–76
2001 by Elsevier Science B.V.
ISBN: 0-7623-0694-7

to 1929, nor in countries in which the economy of free enterprise is not dominant. It is not China and India which seek Lebensraum at the expense of their
neighbors, but Germany and Italy and Japan. Solve the problem of unemployment and less will be heard of the pressure of population and the need for
living space.The nations have sought control of sources of raw materials both
for economic and political reasons. Economically such control has been deemed
advantageous as assuring domestic producers and uninterrupted supply of essential requisites of production, as placing foreign competitors at a disadvantage,
or as constituting a source of monopoly gain for domestic enterprises or for
government through restriction of output and the maintenance of high prices.
Politically such control has been deemed advantageous as contributing to
national self sufficiency in time of war.

The competitive struggle for markets is a struggle for export outlets for goods
and investment outlets for capital funds. Export outlets for consumer and capital
goods are sought because of the inadequacy of the domestic market to absorb
at profitable prices the output which the industrial system can produce, business
enterprise is obsessed with a fear of goods, a fear of scarcity of profitable
markets. Within a given country this fear inspires sabotage of industrial operation through monopoly and other schemes and devices to limit output and
maintain prices at profitable levels. In external relations this fear inspires restrictions on imports, encouragement of exports, limitation or prohibition of
immigration, and imperialist ventures for the control of colonial areas. All these
are fertile sources of international frictions and pressures. Lack of markets brings
depression, and depression closes down mills and mines and factories, abol-
ishes the job of laborers, restricts the farmers' market, and sharpens the
antagonisms among nations and races. The growth of unemployment in any
country during a general depression gives rise to a very dangerous psychological situation. People of every class find their livelihood disappearing, and each
class, failing to understand the causes of this general impoverishment, may irra-
tionally lay the blame on other classes or persons. They may choose the Jewish
financier, or the trade unionists, or the socialists, or the victor in the last war
as their scapegoat. And thus the psychological conditions for national and international conflict are dangerously promoted. In their efforts to find work for idle
hands and idle dollars, the citizens of one nation, if no domestic solution of
their difficulties is in sight, inevitably press outward for larger export markets
and fields for profitable investment, at the same time trying to keep foreigners
from underselling them in the home market and begrudging employment to
immigrants or any who can be construed as belonging to alien groups, national,
racial religious, or other. By way of a footnote and as bearing on the last point
mentioned, the *New York Times* of December 24, 1939, quoted Mr.Martin Dies

as stating that if Congress would make provision for the continuance of his committee, which otherwise would expire on January 3, 1940, "its investigations ultimately would result in the deportation of no less than 7,000,000 aliens employed in American industries while Americans go without employment." By means of tariffs, import quotas, and exchange restrictions a nation may secure a monopoly of the home market for home producers. By means of export subsidies, exchange depreciation, and the control of colonial areas, it may expand its export subsidies, export markets. By means of immigration barriers and the deportation of a part of its labor supply it may monopolize job opportunities for the native born. Whatever success it achieves in solving its economics problem by these means, however, is at the cost of increasing the unemployment of labor and capital in other countries. International frictions are intensified by a policy of dumping ones unemployment problem on the laps of ones international neighbors.

If modern wars in their economic aspect have resulted from competitive struggles among nations for markets, jobs, and investment outlets, the question may well be raised why war has not been almost continuous for the past two or three centuries. The answer is that it has. As concerns modern history at least, the assumption that peace is normal and war exceptional is highly unrealistic. Since the rise of the nation states, war has been a normal part of human and national life in the sense that only for relatively short and infrequent intervals has peace existed among all the nations of the world. That past wars have not been as all-inclusive and as vicious and destructive as the great wars of the twentieth century is due in part to the greater efficiency of modern engines of destruction (for in the weapons of war as in the tools of peace technological inventiveness never ceases), and in part to a conjunction of exceptional circumstances in the eighteenth and nineteenth centuries which lessened the intensity of the struggle for markets. In those two centuries markets and investment opportunities were constantly and rapidly expanding under the influence of certain unique forces – expanding on a scale sufficient to absorb an ever-increasing output of goods and an ever-enlarging labor supply, and to provide almost limitless investment opportunities for growing capital accumulations. The unique forces or exceptional circumstances referred to were, first, the pushing back of economic and geographical frontiers, including the opening up for exploitation of whole new continents and the building of new nations such as the United States; secondly, the provision of food, clothing, housing, transportation facilities, and all other necessities and amenities of life for a population that doubled during the nineteenth century; and thirdly, the exploitation of a vast number of capital – using inventions and of new industries resting on them. In that world of expanding markets and great investment opportunities, with a

limited number of financial and industrial nations to compete for them, a sufficient volume of employment of men and money generally could be maintained
without resort to expedients for monopolizing home markets or expanding
foreign markets at the expense of other nations.

But the twentieth century world is not blessed with an environment similarly
favorable to the functioning of the economy of free enterprise. It is a world of
rapidly declining birth rates, with virtually a stationary population now in its
western regions, a world of capital-saving inventions, of scarcity of new industries requiring large capital funds for their exploitation. It is a world with no
new continents or great unexploited areas to open up for construction and for
export of goods and money. The result has been a drastic decline in private
investment with consequent decline in income and employment derived from
capital goods construction. With reduced employment and incomes, consumption could not be maintained, and thus we have witnessed the tragic paradox
of poverty in the midst of plenty. Faced with growing unemployment of labor
and capital and the impoverishment and social unrest generated thereby, the
nations intensified their struggles with one another for the limited world markets
available, and two great wars and many lesser ones in the twentieth century
have been the result. War solves the problems of poverty and unemployment
of labor and capital, but does so only as long as the fighting continues. The
waging of war provides unlimited markets for goods, jobs for men, and employment for dollars. But when the fighting ceases the old scarcities reappear and
in an intensified form, for technological progress is speeded up by the demands
of the warring nations for more and better of everything.

While the inordinate productivity of modern technology throws into clearer
and clearer relief the scarcity of markets, at the same time its continued growth
and its spread to economically backward areas and industrially less developed
countries is making the common man throughout the world unwilling longer
to accept poverty and insecurity as his inevitable lot – poverty and insecurity
resulting not from the niggardliness of nature but from the folly of man, from
the prejudices and the economic mythology which prevent the utilization of the
productive resources at our command. Everywhere there is a conscious striving
for the higher living standards made possible by power production and the
application of science to industry, but thwarted by failure to adapt our customs
and conventions and habits of thought to the phenomena of this new world. It
is because of the growing gap between the forward-rushing world of economic
fact and the backward-looking world of economic thought that, while we are
conscious of the absurdities of man-made scarcity, we have been paralyzed in
action. The conflict in our minds between patent fact and cherished theory has
led to a sense of impotence and frustration. For two decades between the wars

we struggled desperately to make the facts conform with our theories. But facts are hard and stubborn things. We did not succeed in this effort. We may never succeed in this effort. We may have to revise our theories. But theories are hard and stubborn things too. Sometimes it has required a revolution to change them. It is doubtless in this sense that the present international struggle is frequently characterized as a revolution. Many do not agree with this characterization. British and American statesmen, for instance, do not regard themselves and their countries as engaged in a revolutionary struggle but as waging war for the preservation of the status quo, the restoration and maintenance of the imperial and national boundaries of the past two decades. Such war aims as they have thus far advertised to the world, as Professor Schuman has noted, call on the peoples of the world "to rally to a program of restoring Humpty Dumpty on the wall with the pious hope that he will stay on the wall a bit longer this time." Professor Schuman is disturbed by fear that the peoples of the world may not rally to this program with sufficient enthusiasm – sufficient, that is, to win the war. But this fear probably is groundless. He underestimates the rallying powers of modern propaganda. He may feel more hopeful now if by chance he has noted the ease with which the peoples of Texas and Oklahoma were rallied with great enthusiasm to an anti-New Deal crusade and an open shop and anti-labor drive in the midst of a war in which to date we have suffered one defeat after another and which surely cannot be won if our strength is dissipated by class war on the domestic front. If the existing international struggle is a revolution, it is so by intent of the common man, and the driving force behind it is the striving of the common man for the inheritance promised by technology.

Some peoples have despaired of a solution of the problem of production and employment within the confines of the economy of free enterprise and have turned to communism and fascism and nazism. They have traded legal liberty and freedom of enterprise for employment and economic security, and we cannot say with assurance that they feel the price is too high. But we feel that the price is too high and is unnecessary, and we seek to preserve the democratic way of life. The democratic way of life can be preserved and the economic basis of a durable peace can be laid if the democracies and those who seek to be democracies can find a solution of the economic problem of employment and production within the framework of the democratic organization of society. If no solution can be found there, democracy cannot be maintained, and the basis of a durable peace will be founded on some other form of social organization.

It is my thesis that the problem of production and employment can be solved in major part by domestic policies which do not beggar ones neighbors nor involve revolutionary changes in a way of life. Of course there is a price attached. The solution of the problem requires that some of our cherished theories and biases be laid on the shelf, and that is hard. It requires that we discard some of our economic virtues, such as thrift and saving and onerous work, and learn to practice some economic vices, such as increased consumption and easier living and that offends our moral sense. It requires, in a word, that our theories and practices be brought into line with the kind of world in which we live. The solution lies mainly in making the domestic market sufficiently broad and wide to absorb the output of goods which the industrial system can produce under conditions of full employment. If this is done, poverty will be largely abolished, security will be had, and the pressure for foreign outlets for goods and labor and money will be relieved.

Within the limits of full employment and capacity output, business enterprise utilizes productive resources to produce whatever amounts of consumer and capital goods it believes can be sold at profitable prices. The level of employment and output, or of income, is determined therefore by the extent of profitable markets, by the amounts of money spent for consumption and investment. If unemployment exists it can be reduced by an adequate increase of expenditures either for consumption or for investment or for both.

But how can expenditures be increased? The most simple and direct way is for the government to manufacture more money or have the banking system manufacture it through the purchase of new government bond issues, and to purchase goods with this new money, as government is doing today on an enormous scale, or to distribute it to people who will spend it for goods, as was done through the relief disbursements of our government during the great depression. But the relief disbursements did great violence to our theories, and government therefore could not make them on a scale sufficient to turn the trick. The waging of war is the only object deemed of adequate worth to warrant the manufacture and spending of money by government on an unlimited scale. This is unfortunate, for it makes war appear to some pessimistic and despairing folk as the only cure for chronic depression and unemployment. If Germany could have solved her unemployment problem in the '20s and early '30s, Hitler might never have risen to power to solve it by setting millions to work manufacturing munitions of war. Our prejudices and theories give way before the necessities of war; we must learn to bend them a bit before the necessities of peace. If hundreds of billions of dollars can be spent to wage war, surely tens of billions can be spent to fight depression and maintain employment, security and peace.

Fortunately, however, there are other expedients than the simple one of government spending of new money which will avail in some not inconsiderable degree towards the maintenance of markets, though truth to tell they too are unpalatable to many and they too require more or less government action. One way to increase expenditures on capital goods is to reduce the rate of interest. Business enterprise will find it profitable to borrow more money at 2%, say, for the purchase of additional machines and equipment than they would find profitable if they had to pay 5% or 6% on the funds borrowed. Further, a fall in the rate of interest will induce consumers to borrow and spend more for houses, automobiles, refrigerators, and all kinds of capital goods which provide direct services to consumers. Note the expansion of residential construction under the lower mortgage rates made available through the Federal Housing Administration, and the increase in purchases of electrical appliances with comparatively low interest on time payments effected through the Electric Farm and Home Authority. Lastly, lower interest reduce the objections to government borrowing money to finance the construction of public works, for the lower the rate of interest the lighter the tax burden to meet interest payments on the funds borrowed. Increased expenditures on capital goods expand employment in their production and increase the incomes of their increased incomes, and so on. In this way increased expenditures on capital goods induce a cumulative increase in the demand for consumer goods. This in turn increases the demand for capital goods with which to produce consumer goods. Thus, a reduction of the rate of interest expands investment and consumption, and employment and incomes.

But how can the rate of interest be reduced? This can be accomplished either by action of government or of the central banks. Government itself could enter the banking business, as it has done on a fairly large scale under the New Deal, and make loans at as low a rate as it chooses, including a zero rate. But for government to do this makes us very unhappy (at least it makes the bankers unhappy), so it probably is better or emotionally less disturbing to reduce the rate in a more orthodox way through action of the central banks. The central banks can push down the rate of interest by lowering their rediscount rates and by purchasing securities (usually government bonds) in the open market. The buying of securities by the central banks raises their prices, that is lowers their yield. The lower yields on such securities shift the purchases of the public to other securities, thus raising their prices.

But we have already noted that profitable private investment opportunities have become rather narrowly limited in the modern world. Even a zero rate of interest would not induce a sufficient volume of private investment to provide full employment. There is no escaping the necessity of government assuming the function of investment to the extent requisite to compensate for deficiency of private investment. Government investment in public works can go forward irrespective of the prospects of profits, for government is not a profit-making institution, and public investment widens markets and stimulates demand and employment in precisely the same manner as private investment. Unless by some miracle large new private investment opportunities appear which prove adequate to absorb the difference between the incomes derived from full employment and that portion of such incomes which people choose to spend for consumption, the maintenance of full employment will require a permanent public works program.

If we do not like this, our only alternative is to violate the puritan virtue of thrift and reduce the volume of saving. If employment is to be maintained there can be less investment only if there is less saving, this is, only if a larger proportion of income is spent for consumption. There are several ways in which consumption can be increased. One way, as we have noted, is for the government to distribute purchasing power directly to consumers. In the folklore the character of poor people who get something for nothing is said to be demoralized, and that is bad, but relief disbursements do prevent starvation, which demoralized the body if not the character, maintain employment, and keep the peace.

A second way to increase consumption out of a given national income is by a more equal distribution of that income. It is a fact that as one's income increases, his consumption increases, but not in proportion to the increase of his income. The more unequally income is distributed, therefore, the smaller the proportion of it is spent for consumption and the larger the proportion of it saved. On the assumption that that portion of income which is saved is not hoarded but is invested, i.e., spent in the purchase of capital goods, the older economics sanctions great inequality in the distribution of income as necessary to rapid increase in the capital equipment of the economy. If I were to speak frankly, I would characterize this as nonsense theory. It is not the volume of saving that determines the amount of investment, but the amount of investment that determines how much income can be saved. Employment and production, and hence income, are determined by the amounts spent for consumption and investment. A decision to save reduces the demand for consumer goods, and thus reduces the incentive to invest in capital goods with which to produce consumer goods. In the absence of some novel expedient to maintain investment despite restricted consumer markets, the greater the proportion of incomes which people try to save, the more their incomes will be reduced, until they have become so poor that investment does equal what little they can in fact save out of their small incomes. With great inequality in the distribution of income and with private investment opportunities narrowly limited, a huge volume of public investment would be required to maintain full employment and production, probably 15 or 20 billions of dollars per year. Since we were much disturbed by three or four billion dollars of government compensatory spending per year during the depression, it is doubtful if we would tolerate a program calling for 15 or 20 billions per year. We likely will have to increase consumption by effecting a more equal distribution of income. This can be effected by: (1) highly progressive income, inheritance, and profits taxes; (2) abolition of all regressive taxes, such as sales taxes, excises, poll taxes, and all indirect taxes which fall most heavily on the low income groups; (3) abolition of all special privileges granted by government, such as patents, holding company charters, exclusive franchises, protection of trade marks and trade names, and the like, which confer monopolistic and differential advantages on favored groups and persons; (4) a comprehensive system of social insurance financed from the ordinary revenues of government and covering all the contingencies life – death, old age, sickness, accidents, unemployment, etc. Reduction of inequality in the distribution of income does violence to our prejudices and even our morals, and we do not like it, but the alternative is either huge and continuous government expenditures, or restricted markets and unemployment and social unrest and international frictions, threatening war and revolution, which we might like even less.

To sum up: As concerns internal economic policies, what is required for a durable peace is the maintenance of full employment and maximum income through the stimulation of private investment by increased consumption and reduction of the interest rate towards zero, a permanent program of public works to compensate for any deficiency of private investment, and greater equality in the distribution on income.

In the international field the economic basis of a durable peace lies in the economic disarmament of nations – a limitation on the use of the economic weapons of tariffs, exchange depreciation, import and export quotas, monopolistic control of raw material sources, restrictions on immigration, etc. It is required that the nations relinquish their economic sovereignty to a greater or lesser extent, that an end be put to international economic anarchy. There must be agreements and guarantees among the nations that no one of them or group of them will pursue policies which will thwart the efforts of any given country to carry through its internal policies for the solution of the problems of unemployment and underproduction.

Thus there must be agreement that the central banks of the various countries will cooperate in the control of interest rates. One country cannot get its interest rates too far out of line with those of other countries without blocking its domestic efforts to enlarge employment and income or interfering with efforts other countries might be making to solve their internal problems. There must be unified action in the use of this device.

Again all countries must agree not to resort to currency depreciation as a means of stimulating their exports and reducing their unemployment at the expense of their international neighbors. With agreements to cooperate in the control of interest rates and not resort to currency depreciation except to the extent necessary to implement domestic policies, fluctuations in foreign exchange rates would be minimized and international trade facilitated thereby.

With internal policies effecting an increase of investment, employment, and production, tariffs and other trade controls would no longer be necessary for these purposes, and it would then be practical politics to discuss tariff reductions again. The demand for tariffs results in good part from the unemployment of the labor and capital funds. With the problem of employment of men and dollars solved, the pressure for tariff barriers would be greatly lessened.

Fourthly, immigration barriers should be lowered. The free immigration of peoples into a country in which standards of living are high is desirable from an international point of view provided that the growth of population in those countries to whose citizens are emigrating is not excessive. Countries of high living standards generally do not object to immigration as long as job opportunities are plentiful, as witness the example of the United States from the beginning of its history to the outbreak of World War I. A solution of the problem of employment would lessen the pressure for immigration barriers and thereby remove another source of international friction as well as cut the ground from under the demand for Lebensraum. I am well aware, of course, that there are other than economic objections to immigration, such as social, political, racial, religious, etc., but economic objections have proved most potent in practice, and such restrictions as are imposed on other grounds are generally not as all-inclusive nor as productive of international irritability.

Lastly, the 'open door' policy must be guaranteed in all colonial possessions. It would be better if there were no more empires or spheres of influence, but if this is too much to hope for, the political control of so-called backward peoples must not be allowed to generate international frictions by the country exercising that control being permitted to impose discriminatory restriction on trade and investment in those territories. The economic opportunities provided by the colonies must be open to all including the colonists, on equal terms.

These various measures should go far to establish an international basis for a lasting peace. In closing I cannot do better than quote the closing paragraph of J. E. Meade's thought-provoking little book, *An Introduction to Economic Analysis and Policy* (Oxford: Oxford University Press, p. 388): 'But above all it is necessary that countries should not meet the problem of unemployment by developing a favorable balance of trade at the expense of others, but by internal expansion, carried out if possible simultaneously in all countries; for the former method, if universally adopted, must lead to general impoverishment and eventually to war, whereas by the latter method the way is opened by prosperity and peace'.

Review of Harris, Seymour E. (Ed.):

THE NEW ECONOMICS: KEYNES' INFLUENCE ON THEORY AND PUBLIC POLICY

Edward Everett Hale

This is not a great book, but it is an important and useful one. It is in part a volume conceived, according to its editor, Professor Seymour E. Harris of Harvard, as a tribute to Lord Keynes, the man and the economist. In greater part and primarily, however, its purpose is 'to appraise Keynes' contributions to economics, to add up the gains and explore the weaknesses.' The occasion of the publication of this type of book at this time is, of course, the death of Lord Keynes on April 21, 1946, in his sixty-second year (he was born on June 5, 1883).

This book is a symposium containing contributions from twenty-six economists, including Keynes himself. Keynes is represented by one essay, four speeches, and a paper, which is largely his work, though formally prepared by the British Treasury. The essay is Keynes' reply in the *Quarterly Journal of Economics* of February, 1937, to criticisms of his *General Theory of Employment, Interest, and Money* voiced by Taussig, Robertson, Leontieff, and Viner in the November, 1936, issue of the *Quarterly*. Of the four speeches included, three were delivered by Keynes in the House of Lords of the British Parliament (one on the International Clearing Union, one on the International

Edward Everett Hale: The Writings of an Economic Maverick, Volume 19-B, pages 77–94.
2001 by Elsevier Science B.V.
ISBN: 0-7623-0694-7

Monetary Fund, and one on Anglo-American financial arrangements) and the fourth, on the Bank for Reconstruction and Development, was delivered on July 8, 1944, at the first meeting of the Second Commission of the Bank.

The major part of the book consists of forty-one essays discussing, amplifying, or criticizing various aspects of Keynes' system of thought. Eleven of these are reprinted from the journals in which they first appeared, and thirty are published here for the first time.

The remaining contents consist of a reprint of the obituary of Keynes, which appeared in the London *Times* on April 22, 1946, and a helpful bibliography of Keynes' writings, prepared by Editor Harris and Mrs. Margarita Willfort. With reference to this last item, Professor Harris expresses doubt that the bibliography is complete and asks that readers of the book please inform him of any omissions and errors they may discover. Even so, the bibliography covers twenty-two pages of fairly small print, no mean output for an individual to produce over a working span of thirty-five years. (The first item from Keynes' pen appeared in the March, 1909, issue of the *Economic Journal*.)

The larger part of the book is, as Professor Harris notes, "an interpretation by Keynesians of Keynes' economics and Keynesian economics." The majority of the twenty-five economists (omitting Keynes) represented in the book are definitely of the Keynesian school, including such well-known economists as Professors Alvin H. Hansen, Seymour Harris, R. F. Harrod, A.P. Lerner, J.E. Meade, Joan Robinson, and Paul Samuelson. Six economists who are definitely non-Keynesian are represented. They are Professors Gottfried Haberler, Wassily Leontieff, and Joseph A. Schumpeter, all of Harvard University; Professor Albert G. Hart of Columbia; Dr. Paul M. Sweezy, formerly of Harvard; and Professor J. Tinbergen of the Rotterdam School of Economics.

Editor Harris justifies giving most of the space to Keynesians on the ground that the best way to learn about any system of thought is from those who are sympathetic to that system, not from those who are hostile to it. He says that he is not a Marxist, but when he wants to learn about Marxian economics, he finds it more helpful to consult Marxists than anti-Marxists. In my opinion this is ample justification. Unfortunately, most of the critics of Marx and some of the critics of Keynes have never read the works which they criticize but have relied on what other critics, usually hostile, have said about those works.

Omitting the *Times* obituary and the bibliography, the book is divided into nine parts. Professor Harris introduces the volume with seven brief essays which variously: (1) define the issues in Keynesianism, (2) discuss Keynes' influence on public policy, (3) summarize earlier appraisals of the *General Theory* both by critics and by later Keynesians, (4) note three major criticisms that have been leveled against the *General Theory* (both that the theory is not general, that it is not dynamic, and that it fails to establish its thesis of equilibrium at under-employment levels), (5) raise the question of what remains of the *General Theory* ten years after its publication, and (6) asks whether the *General Theory* is merely an evolution from classical economics or is a revolution in economic theory.

Part Two contains three evaluations of Keynes, the economist: one by Mr. Harrod, a leading English Keynesian; one by Professor Schumpeter, a critic of Keynes to the right; and one by Dr. Paul Sweezy, a Marxian and hence a critic of the left. Mr. Harrod's judgment of Keynes, the economist, is that his great-ness cannot and will not be questioned. Keynes once described Ricardo as "the most distinguished mind that had found Economics worthy of it." "We must surely judge Keynes' mind," says Mr. Harrod, "to be more distinguished than that of Ricardo" (p. 72). Professor Schumpeter traces the relation of the *General Theory* to Keynes' earlier works, finds a more or less unbroken line of devel-opment, finds the *General Theory* – "Keynes' gift to scientific economics" – to be distinguished primarily because of its attractive wrapper, but withal impinging on economics and economists "with the salutary effects of a fresh breeze." "Whatever happens," he says, "to the doctrine, the memory of the man will live – outlive both Keynesianism and the reaction to it" (p. 100). Dr. Sweezy characterizes Keynes as "one of the most brilliant and versatile geniuses of our time . . . the most important and the most illustrious product of the neo-clas-sical school, . . . (whose) mission was to reform neo-classical economics, to bring it back into contact with the real world" from which it had wandered far since 1870 (pp. 102–104). Yet, he concludes, "Keynes could never transcend the neo-classical approach which conceives of economic life in abstraction from its historical setting and hence is inherently incapable of providing a reliable guide to social action" (p. 104). Keynes, like the neo-classicists, he says, assumed capitalism to be "the only possible form of civilized society," and hence, like the economists he criticized, "never viewed the system as a whole; never studied the economy in its historical setting" (pp. 106–107).

Part Three, in Editor Harris' words, subjects the *General Theory* "to micro-scopic examination." Three of the essays therein are written by three leading Keynesians – Professors Hansen, Lerner, and Samuelson – one by Professor Haberler, a non-Keynesian; and one by Keynes himself, being the *Quarterly Journal* article referred to earlier. Lerner's article is his brilliant summary of the *General Theory* which appeared, shortly after the publication of that book, in the October 1936, issue of the *International Labor Review*. This essays puts the sub-stance of the *General Theory* in language which makes it more comprehensible than the original. Professor Hansen's analysis and evaluation of the *General Theory* will be commented on below. Professor Samuelson differs from Schumpeter's view that the *General Theory* is the logical culmination of Keynes' preceding works. It is his opinion that "nothing in Keynes' previous works really quite prepares us for the *General Theory*" (p. 153). He finds the significance of the book to lie in "the fact that it provides a relatively realistic, complete system for analyzing the level of effective demand and its fluctuations" (p. 151). Professor Haberler seems to hold that insofar as Keynesian theory follows classical theory, it is valid and useful, but insofar as it departs therefrom it is in error and sin. He attributes most of Keynes' criticisms of the classicists to his alleged over-simplification of their theory in its older formulations.

Part Four deals with special aspects of the *General Theory*. This part includes two essays, one by Professor Hansen and the other by Mr. D. B. Copland, an Australian economist, which discuss the effects the *General Theory* has had on the concepts and tools of economic analysis and on public policy. Professor Tinbergen, the econometrician, contributes an article to this Part which comments on Keynes' important contributions to econometrics. The final essay in Part Four is by Professor Leontieff, who points out the respects in which he thinks Keynes has misrepresented and misinterpreted classical economics, misunderstood its postulates, and substituted more unrealistic and hence less tenable assumptions of his own. The tenor of Leontieff's criticism is indicated by a quotation he gives from Keynes' biographical sketch of Alfred Marshall, which was published in the *Economic Journal* in 1924. The quotation reads as follows:

> Yet after all there is no harm in being sometimes wrong – especially if one is promptly found out.

Leontieff thinks he has promptly found Keynes out.

Part Five consists of several essays which re-examine the theory of international trade and international economic policies in the light and in terms of Keynes' *General Theory*. Though Keynes' contributions to this important field are large and significant, time is lacking in which to discuss them here. This part also includes Keynes' four speeches previously referred to, and an essay by Joan Robinson which examines and appraises two different international currency proposals; one the proposal for an International Clearing Union put forth by the British Treasury (a proposal which, as we have noted, was largely the work of Keynes), and the proposal of the United States Treasury for a United and Associated Nations Stabilization Fund, Mrs. Robinson definitely regards Keynes' scheme as superior.

Part Six is concerned with policies appropriate on the basis of Keynesian theory for dealing with the problems of economic fluctuations and unemployment. For Keynes the waste of economic resources through unemployment seemed nonsensical and suicidal. He concentrated more of his energies on the solution of this problem than of any other. Professor A. G. Hart contributes an essay to Part Six on 'Keynes' Analysis of Expectations and Uncertainty' (Chapter 31). Keynes' theory of economic trends and stagnation is tied to his theory of the marginal efficiency of capital, which in turn depends largely on anticipations. Professor Alan Sweezy presents a survey of Keynes' views on economic maturity (Chapter 32), and includes a discussion of the criticisms that have been urged against the thesis of declining investment opportunity or secular stagnation. Professor Lloyd A. Metzler's article (Chapter 33) deals chiefly with Keynes' theory of business cycles. His main point is that Keynes' consumption function provides an easy answer to the problem of why both expansions and contractions of business activity are ultimately reversed. Classical theory never succeeded in answering this question satisfactorily, being forced because of its basic assumptions to rely for an explanation upon limiting factors, such as the inadequacy of monetary supplies. Mr. Gerhard Colm studies Keynes' views on fiscal policy (Chapter 34) and his influence on United States fiscal policy. He shows how difficult it is to measure the extent of this influence. Professor Higgins (in Chapter 35) lists the alternative approaches to full employment: rise in private investments and export balances, increase in the propensity to consume, and public loan expenditures; and shows why Keynes was inclined to rely primarily on the last two.

Professor Goodwin ends Part Six with a technical essay on the multiplier which greatly clarifies this concept if one can wade through the mathematical language.

Part Seven consists exclusively of a long article by Professor Lintner of the Harvard Graduate School of Business Administration on the Keynesian theory of money and prices. The analysis is acute, but cannot be easily summarized.

Part Eight includes three essays dealing with the relationship between money wages and the level of employment. Certainly one of the chief differences between the *General Theory* and the classical theory lies in their quite contradictory views on this extremely intricate problem. While these essays make clear the shortcomings of the classical theory that the volume of employment is an inverse function of the level of real wages, they also make quite clear that Keynes' thesis of the virtual independence of employment and money wage rates is established only by means of a large set of rather dubious assumptions.

Part Nine consists of reprints of what Professor Harris refers to as "some of the earlier contributions to Keynesiana." Two of the essays of this Part, one by Mr. R. F. Harrod and the other by Mr. J. E. Meade, give a systematic presentation of the run of the argument in the *General Theory*. The remainder of Part Nine consists of four short essays of Professor A. P. Lerner, which defend Keynes against his critics on two of the most controversial issues, the equality of savings and investment and the liquidity preference theory of interest. The defense is little less than a marvel of ingenuity.

What can be said of Keynes, the economist, and of the position of Keynesianism in the development of economic theory? Does the *General Theory* constitute a revolution in economic theory or merely a further evolution of the classical doctrine? Professor Harris, the editor of the volume under review, is unrestrained in his high appraisal of Keynes' work in general and of the *General Theory* in particular. He writes that during the last fifteen years of his life, Keynes was

> the outstanding figure in the world of economics. In the wide scope of his interests, in his eloquence and persuasiveness, in his virtually complete command over economic forums, both of subjects to be discussed and manner of discussing them, in the impression he made upon our quasi-capitalist system, in the influence upon economists and men of action of his day – in these jointly and probably in each separately, Keynes has not had an equal. (pp. 4–5)

Again to quote:

> The miracle of Keynes is that, despite the vested interests of scholars in the older theory, despite the preponderant influence of press, radio, finance, and subsidized research against Keynes, his influence in both scientific circles and in the arena of public policy has been extraordinary (p. 13).

With reference to the *General Theory*, Professor Harris writes:

> Its great contribution was to adapt economics to the changing institutional structure of modern society ... Up to 1936, when the *General Theory* was first published, accepted economics in general belonged more to the vanished age of competition, of capital deficiencies, of full employment or transitional unemployment and the like than to the twentieth century economy which tolerated and to some extent encouraged monopolies, rigidities, excessive savings, deficiency of demand, and unemployment. To make up for the growing lag, Keynes sailed boldly and vigorously into uncharted waters (p. 4).

Though Professor Harris admits that Keynes has not said the last word, that he has not solved all economic problems, that this theory will require supplementation, amplification, and revision, yet his final judgement is that

> ... Keynes was undoubtedly the great figure in economics of the twentieth century and may well prove to be the giant of modern economics ... Out of the straws of his predecessors, with some additions of his own, he built a structure which no economist or economic practitioner can afford not to inspect and use (pp. 6–7).

This appraisal is echoed, though with somewhat more restraint, by Professor Hansen, who ranks the *General Theory* as equaling the *Wealth of Nations* and the work of Jevons, the Austrians, and Walras in important significance in the development of economic thought. "No book in economics," says Hansen, "has made such a stir within the first ten years of its publication as has the *General Theory*." By virtue of it, "economic analysis has tackled new problems and is better equipped with tools of analysis" (p. 134). Nothing like the rapidity and scope of

the spread of the influence of the *General Theory* on economic thought and government policy has happened, in Hansen's opinion, in the whole history of economics. "Though it is too early to say," he concludes, "it does not now appear an
extravagant statement, that Keynes may in the end rival Adam Smith in his influence on the economics and government policy of his time and age" (p. 144).

Similar evaluations are ventured by other Keynesians, such as Mr. D. B.
Copland, Professor Lloyd Metzler of the University of Chicago, Dr. Gerhard
Colm of the Council of Economic Advisors to the President, and others. Even
rather severe critics of Keynes such as Professor Schumpeter and Dr. Paul
Sweezy agree that the *General Theory* has been most remarkable and has exer-
cised vast influence.

Thus Professor Schumpeter writes

> the success of the *General Theory* was instantaneous, and, as we know, sustained ... A
> Keynesian school formed itself, not a school in that loose sense in which some historians
> of economics speak of a French, German, Italian school, but a genuine one which is a soci-
> ological entity, namely, a group that professes allegiance to one master and one doctrine,
> and has its inner circle, its propagandists, its watchwords, its esoteric and its popular doctrine.
> Nor is this all. Beyond the pale of orthodox Keynesianism there is a broad fringe of sympa-
> thizers, and beyond this again are the many who have absorbed, in one form or another,
> readily or grudgingly, some of the spirit or some of the individual items of Keynesian
> analysis. There are but two analogous cases in the whole history of economics – the
> Physiocrats and the Marxists (p. 97).

And Dr. Paul Sweezy, the Marxian, writes

> I have no doubt that Keynes is the greatest British (or American) economist since Ricardo,
> and I think the work of this school sheds a flood of light on the functioning of the capi-
> talist economy (p. 108).

How account for this phenomenon? The Keynesians account for it on the ground
that the *General Theory* has made large and lasting contributions to economics
and at long last given us a kit of analytical tools by the use of which we can
solve the pressing economic problems of our time – the problems of appropriate
interest rates, central bank policy, inflation, deflation, wastage of economic
resources, and, above all depression unemployment. Keynesians such as
Professor Harris and Mr. Copland urge that the *General Theory* has at last
brought economic thinking into line with the changing institutional structure of
our society. Professor Hansen picks out the formulation of the consumption function as the greatest contribution of the *General Theory*. This formulation, he
holds, is "by far the most powerful instrument which has been added to the economist's kit of tools in our generation." Lack of this tool, he says, caused business cycle theorists from Malthus, Wicksell, Spiethoff, and Aftalion to "fumble
around in the dark, and never quite reach shore" (p. 135). The consumption

function has at long last, says Professor Hansen, elevated income analysis to a place equally important as price analysis.

Critics of Keynes such as Professor Schumpeter and Habeler, have, as might be expected, somewhat different ideas as to the cause of the victory of the *General Theory.* Professor Haberler attributes, as a partial cause,

> ... the brilliance of (Keynes') style, the versatility, flexibility, incredible quickness, and fecundity of his mind, the many-sidedness of his intellectual interests, the sharpness of his wit, in one word the fullness of his personality. (These, he says, were) found to fascinate scores of people in and outside the economic profession. Only a dullard or narrow-minded fanatic could fail to be moved to admiration by Keynes' genius (p. 161).

He further notes:

> The tremendous appeal of the *General Theory* to theoretically-minded economists has been attributed by many to the (alleged) fact that it uses for the first time in the history of economic thought a general equilibrium approach in easily manageable macroscopic (aggregative) terms (p. 162).

Yet in Professor Haberler's opinion neither the brilliance of Keynes' style and wit nor the attractiveness of macroscopic general equilibrium analysis is the major cause of the sweeping success of the *General Theory.* On the contrary, "we can safely assume," he says, "that the concrete content and the policy recommendations which Keynes and others deduced from his system had even more to do with its persuasiveness (even for his theoretically-minded followers) than its theoretical beauty and simpleness" (p. 162).

Professor Schumpeter in an even more straightforward manner accounts for the appeal of the *General Theory* to the fact that it once more reduces economics, which over the past decades "had been growing increasingly complex and increasingly incapable of giving straightforward answers to straightforward questions ... to simplicity" and enables "the economist once more to give simple advice that everybody can understand." Yet, Professor Schumpeter continues, "exactly as in the case of Ricardian economics there was enough to attract, to inspire even, the sophisticated. The same system that linked up so well with the notions of the untutored mind proved satisfactory to the best brains of the rising generation of theorists" (pp. 99–10).

This reminds one of Keynes' answer in the *General Theory* to a similar question relative to Ricardo's *Principles,* viz., what accounts for the victory of Ricardian economics over the Malthusian doctrine of inadequacy of general demand. Ricardo, says Keynes, "conquered England as completely as the Holy Inquisition conquered Spain." Keynes regards the completeness of the Ricardian victory as something of a curiosity and a mystery.

It must have been due," he says, "to a complex of suitabilities in the doctrine to the environment into which it was projected. That it reached conclusions quite different from what the ordinary uninstructed person would expect, added, I suppose, to its intellectual prestige. That its teaching, translated into practice, was often austere and unpalatable, lent it virtue. That it was adapted to carry a vast and consistent logical superstructure, gave it beauty. That it could explain much social injustice and apparent cruelty as an inevitable incident in the scheme of progress, and the attempt to change such things as likely on the whole to do more harm than good, commended it to authority. That it afforded a measure of justi-fication to the free activities of the individual capitalist, attracted to it the support of the dominant social force behind authority" (pp. 32–33).

Like Ricardo's *Principles*, the *General Theory* too was highly suited to the environment into which it was projected – the breakdown of capitalism in the great depression between the wars. Like Ricardian theory, the *General Theory* reached "conclusions quite different from what the ordinary uninstructed person might expect." We may note, among others, the conclusions that employment and real income are independent of the price level and money wage rates, that saving is a residual and is determined by the level of investment, that thrift is generally an economic vice and spending an economic virtue, that boondog-gling in a depression increases income and the wealth of the nation. *The General Theory*, like Ricardo's *Principles*, is "adapted to carry a vast and consistent logical superstructure." Here, though, the similarity ends.

Keynes' teaching translated into practice is not, like Ricardo's, austere and unpalatable. Quite the contrary. It calls for higher living, more consumption, and more leisure. Hence it is without virtue. It explains social injustice and apparent cruelty not as an inevitable incident in the scheme of progress, but as a result of stupidity and ignorance which prevent the formulation of policies and the use of controls already at hand to establish and maintain full employ-ment and maximum income. Since these policies, though, call for a rather severe redistribution of income and a vast deal of government interference in the activ-ities of businessmen, the *General Theory* is damned by authority and by the dominant social force that stands behind authority.

Undoubtedly all of the opinions noted as to the cause of the impact of the *General Theory* on economists and economic theory and public policy point to significant factors. I venture the thought, however, that possibly the most tren-chant reason is not mentioned in the list above. Schumpeter gives a hint of this reason, but he misses the essential point. He notes that in economics such enthu-siasm – and correspondingly strong aversions – as greeted the *General Theory* "never flare up unless the cold steel of analysis derives a temperature not natu-rally its own from the real or putative political implications of the analyst's message" (p. 98). The fact is that the *General Theory* seemed to be, and was taken to be, the answer to the maiden's prayer – not the most satisfactory answer possible, but a better one perhaps than the maiden could have dared hope for. For the orthodox, and indeed for the liberal-minded as well, the events of the interwar years were terrifying. The most direful predictions of Marx seemed to be coming true. Capitalism in most of the Western world, its habitat, appeared to be in its death throes. A socialist economy was established and stabilized in a nation covering one-sixth of the land area of the earth. In Germany, Italy, and some of the smaller European nations, capitalism was saved for a time only by resort to the desperate expedient of fascism. Even in the United States, the wealthiest and strongest of the capitalist countries, the system faltered, stumbled blindly, and collapsed completely in the spring of 1933. It was restored to partial vigor only by the most heroic endeavors of the pulmotor squad, and even their best efforts left the patient in a sickly condition, rather pale and anemic.

The most highly qualified and universally respected physicians of the accepted medical school of thought, that is, the classical or neo-classical school of economics, diagnosed the patient, assured him that his constitution was fundamentally sound, and that in consequence there was nothing wrong with him that a little time and patience would not cure. The physicians sought to cheer him by informing him that in their considered judgement his complete recovery to normal health was just around the corner. Since, however, the patient and all of his friends feared that he was dying, as indeed he was, neither the diagnosis nor the prognosis was very reassuring. The patient was so ill in body and low in spirits that he even came close sometimes to committing the ultimate heresy of questioning some of the medical doctrine (classical economics) in which the physicians were trained. What to do then to save himself and his soul! Where was the physician who could correctly diagnose the disease which had brought capitalism low (where it had not already proved fatal), discover its cause, and prescribe the proper remedy.

Just at this juncture, just, one might say, in the nick of time, the *General Theory* appeared. Its timing could not have been more propitious. No wonder it was greeted with such enthusiasm, with such acclaim, with such a heartfelt sign of relief. The relief was similar in intensity to that experienced by a thirst-crazed group of desert travelers on coming upon an oasis. This, I believe, is the real secret of the truly amazing success of the *General Theory*.

Keynes indeed seemed to tell us how we could save the essentials of our social and economic system at a cost which he assured us was not excessive. It would be necessary, he said, only to take a few pills and to remove a few excrescences and non-malignant tumors from the body economic. The really vital organs, he said, could be left intact and undisturbed.

Professor Harris, therefore, is absolutely correct when he insists, in the essay with which the volume opens, that Keynes was a defender of capitalism. "Only the stupidity," he says, "of those whom he supports can account for any other interpretation." And Professor Samuelson rightly insists that Keynes' philosophy "is profoundly capitalistic." Its policies are offered (and he quotes from page 380 of the *General Theory*) "as the only practical means of avoiding the destruction of existing economic forms and as the condition of the successful functioning of individual initiative" (p. 151). There can be no question that Keynes' motive was to save capitalism, not to destroy it. He tells us so in so many words in the final chapter of the *General Theory*.

Though the doctor assured the patient that the operations required would be minor ones, the patient, being extremely nervous and frightened, insisted that he would not permit them to be performed. We cannot blame him too much for his obduracy, for after all the doctor proposed to remove all bond and mortgage and other interest income by reducing the rate of interest to zero, and to socialize a great deal of investment. The patient screamed that these would be major, not minor, operations, and would cause him such pain as he could not possibly endure. Further, the patient complained loudly that the pills prescribed were too bitter to take. Again he was right. They would be bitter, for they consisted of a more equal distribution of income, less saving, more spending and higher living, and, for exercise, a little leaf raking now and then. The patient wanted none of this new-fangled dope. He would stick by the old Ricardian medicine even if it killed him. After all, he said, he would as soon be dead as to give up his interest income, to reduce his saving and capital accumulation, and to give a sizeable portion of his remaining income to the poor. This latter would be not only extremely painful to him but also, and far worse, destructive of the character and moral fiber of the poor. It would, indeed, undermine the very foundations of our way of life. It did little good for Keynes to insist to the patient that his really vital organs would not be touched, since he would be left with free choice, the quest for profits, and the allocating of resources in response to price incentive. After great urging and because of his dire extremity, however, the patient, though he resolutely resisted any of the operations proposed, finally agreed to try a little of the medicine. Whether it would have restored him in time to a relatively healthy state, we may never know because, before the course of treatment was completed, a more stimulating and powerful and possibly more agreeable medicine came along, the Second World War.

I think the doctor was trying to fool the patient. I think in fact that the doctor was fooling himself. The patient was well advised to reject the operations and to refuse to take most of the medicine, for they would have proved fatal. But we have carried this metaphor far enough, probably too far. Keynes refused to draw the logical conclusions of his system of thought. The reduction of the rate of interest to zero could not be effected short of complete socialization of the banking system, and the banking or credit system is the very heart of capitalism. Public investment to compensate for deficiency of private investment would inevitably in time result in government ownership of all industrial capital and all industries. The government would have to find something in which to invest after it had got all the farm-to-market roads constructed, all the school houses built, all the parks and playgrounds laid out, and all the leaves raked. And nothing else could be found except in those fields which previously had been posted and held for private investment only – the railways, the public utilities, steel, automobiles, and on through the whole list. Keynes failed or refused to recognize that he had laid bare the vital contradiction in the process of capital accumulation to which Marx had called attention three-quarters of a century earlier. He could maintain that his remedy would save capitalism only because he chose to ignore technological change and technological unemployment, and to treat depression unemployment merely as a symptom of a technical fault in the capitalist mechanism, not as a necessary device for the maintenance of a free labor market. We are now discovering that capitalism cannot function in a condition of full employment because of the irresistible inflationary pressure to which full employment gives rise. President Truman, recognizing this fact, has just called for a restoration of price and wage controls, that is, for the substitution of a regimented, governmentally controlled economy for the economy of free enterprise. The junior Senator from Texas dubs this proposal as an "un-American, communistic scheme," a climax to "fourteen years of New Deal delirium tremens." You can't fool the junior Senator from Texas. He knows that price controls and rationing are the opposite of the good old American system of free and unlimited private enterprise. He has no trouble detecting the devil lurking underneath the Keynesian rigmarole.

Keynes, further, could think that his program would save capitalism only because he completely ignored the problems of monopoly and the disturbing effect which monopoly has on the distribution of income and the utilization of resources. Keynes treats the state, as Paul Sweezy points out, "as a *deus ex machina* to be invoked whenever his human actors, behaving according to the rules of the capitalist game, get themselves into a dilemma from which there is apparently no escape. Naturally this Olympian interventionist resolves everything in a manner satisfactory to the author and presumably to the audience. The only trouble is ". . . that the state is not a god but one of the actors who has a part to play just like all the other actors" (p. 108).

Professor Schumpeter, then, is correct in his keen observation that the *General Theory* excludes from its formal analysis all phenomena that really dominate the capitalist processes. With the classical economists, capitalist evolution issues into a stationary state of full employment and maximum wealth and income.

With Marx capitalist evolution issues into breakdown. With Keynes it issues into a stationary state that constantly threatens to break down and is only prevented from doing so by his *deus ex machina*, the state.

Keynes and Marx, indeed, have much in common. *The General Theory*, like *Das Kapital*, teaches that unemployment and depression are the norms to which the capitalist economy tends. Both Keynes and Marx were aware of deficient demand and oversaving, of the declining profit rate resulting from limited investment opportunities, of the unwisdom of capital exportation. Both were highly critical of the excesses of the capitalist system. But Keynes was no socialist. For him the troubles of our society are due, not to the breakdown of a social system, but to a failure of intelligence. By the exercise of intelligence, he says, "capitalism could be made more efficient for attaining economic ends than any alternative system yet in sight." And he convinces himself that "in some respects the *General Theory* is moderately conservative in its implications." He could deceive himself, but he could not deceive the neo-classical economists, the un-American Activities Committee, the National Association of Manufacturers, or the East Texas Chamber of Commerce. The intelligence of the neo-classicists readily grasped the implications of the nefarious doctrine. The intuitions of the three latter served as well where intelligence might not have been equal to the task of piercing the rather abstract and abstruse argument to get at the subversive elements underneath the surface.

It never occurred nor could have occurred to Ricardo to draw the logical conclusions of his economic theory, but it did occur to the Ricardian socialists and to Marx, and they drew them. Keynes refuses to draw, or even to admit, the logical conclusions of the *General Theory*, but they are there nevertheless, and in plain sight for all to see.

This is indeed the Keynesian revolution. Those who look for it elsewhere necessarily fail to find anything very revolutionary. How could they? In methodology the *General Theory* is severely orthodox. Its technique, as several of the essays in this volume note, is that of static equilibrium analysis, just as was Ricardo's and Marshall's and that of other classical economists. For Keynes, as for the classicists, this technique involves a host of highly unrealistic assumptions. Keynes' assumptions, as noted by Mr. Arthur Smithies in his essay on 'Effective Demand and Employment' (Chapter 39), are the following:

1. That techniques of production and the amount of fixed capital are unchanged throughout the periods with which he deals.
2. That perfect competition exists throughout the economy. (There is not a single reference to monopoly or monopolistic competition in the whole of the *General Theory*.

3. That returns diminish and costs increase as output is increased. (This
   follows from the assumption of constant techniques.)
4. That the economy is a closed one.

Some part even of the classical marginal productivity theory of distribution is
incorporated in the *General Theory*. It is difficult, indeed impossible, to find
anything revolutionary in the technique of analysis or in the assumptions of the
Keynesian system.

Professor Haberler, in his essay on the 'The General Theory' (Chapter 14),
concludes that the same is true of its logical content. After an analysis of what
he regards as "the purely scientific content of *The General Theory of
Employment, Interest, and Money*," he concludes that "as far as the logical
content of Keynes' theory goes, i.e., apart from his judgment as to the typical
shape of the various functions and of concrete situations and apart from policy
recommendations, no revolution has taken place; the *General Theory* marks a
milestone but not a break in the development of economic theory" (p. 176).
Taking the logical content of the system, as Professor Haberler does, to be the
individual relationships ('functions' or 'propensities') of which it is composed,
the interactions of the various parts, and the working of the system as a whole,
I believe his judgment is essentially sound, though I think he minimizes certain
differences between the Keynesian and the classical systems and is in error in
holding generally that where they differ, as for example, in the theory of interest
or the relation between money wages and employment, the classical theory is
more realistic and useful. Surely, however, nothing revolutionary is readily
apparent in the consumption function, the marginal efficiency of capital function, the liquidity-preference function, the wage-unit and the labor-unit concepts,
and the assumption of a given quantity of money – and it is these that, according
to the *General Theory,* determine income and employment. Not revolutionary
indeed, but what a *tour de force*! "What a *cordon bleu*," exclaims Professor
Schumpeter, "to make such a sauce out of such scanty material."

Professor Hansen does not agree that the logical content of the *General
Theory* is not revolutionary, at least as concerns economic thought. On the
contrary, as we have noted, he regards Keynes' formulation of the consumption function as a revolutionary innovation in economic analysis. It is true that
Keynes is the first clearly and specifically to formulate this function and to use
it as an analytical tool, but surely the consumption function is implicit in the
whole analysis and argument of the underconsumptionists. It is virtually stated,
in fact, in Engel's Law of Consumption, which used to be included in the
elementary textbooks. This, though, is not to detract from Keynes' achievement. He is the inventor of the consumption function in the same sense that

Malthus is the inventor of the Malthusian doctrine of population or that Ricardo is the inventor of the differential rent theory. As Professor Hansen notes, "no man ever single handed invented anything." "In a sense," he continues in his essay on 'The General Theory' (Chapter 12), "there are no revolutionary discoveries. Nevertheless, in the progress of man's thinking new plateaus are from time to time cast up not unlike a geological upheaval. And these are revolutionary developments even though the constituent elements composing the structure can be found elsewhere and 'have long been well known' " (p. 133).

Schumpeter finds the revolutionary element in Keynesian economics to be its all-out attack on thriftiness and its espousal of spending. "Savings," says Professor Schumpeter, "had come to be regarded as the last pillar of the bourgeois argument" (p. 99). As we all know, in the orthodox theory, saving was held to be essential to capital formation and capital formation to be the very cornerstone of economic progress. Hence, though classical economists like Marshall and Pigou admitted the undesirability and inequity of the gross inequality which capitalism generates in the distribution of income, they nevertheless justify gross inequality as essential to rapid capital accumulation and increasing total income. Keynes attacked this pillar and smashed it into dust. Indeed his doctrine teaches, in effect, that an undue propensity to save reduces capital accumulation and impoverishes the nation, and that unequal distribution of income is one of the major causes of unemployment. "This," says Professor Schumpeter, "is what the Keynesian Revolution amounts to" (p. 99).

It may be. But the doctrine of saving has been subjected to repeated attacks over the past two centuries and more. Barnard de Mandeville delivered a telling blow against thrift in his *Fable of the Bees* which was first published in 1705 under another title. The underconsumptionists from Lord Lauderdale and Malthus to Hobson and Gordon Hayes have never tired in their spirited attacks on this doctrine. The thesis that saving is a vice and spending a virtue may be revolutionary but Keynes is not the subversive who began this revolution. He came on the scene some two hundred years too late for this role. His contribution consisted in lending his prestige and respectability to a doctrine that, in his words, had hitherto lived on only furtively, in the underworld of economics, espoused only by such unorthodox, and hence suspect, characters as Malthus and Hobson, or such disreputable characters as Karl Marx and Silvio Gesell. To lend the doctrine respectability is no mean contribution, but surely was no revolution.

No, the Keynesian revolution does not lie in the analytical tools which he forged. As Mr. Smithies notes, in the essay of his already referred to, the true greatness of the *General Theory* "could never have been achieved had its author been fully dependent on these analytical tools" (p. 559). It does not lie in the argument which, by the use of these tools, Keynes deduces from his unrealistic

assumptions. It does not lie in this or that specific element of his theoretical structure. It lies rather in the *obiter dicta* which are liberally sprinkled through the
book. It lies rather in the implications of the argument, in the logical import of the
system as a whole. It is revolutionary in the sense that Ricardo's *Principles* was
revolutionary. A host of what Marx refers to as "vulgar" economists busied themselves mightily to obscure or argue away the revolutionary implications of the
Ricardian system, but to little avail. It finally proved necessary to scrap that system and substitute what purported to be another for it – the marginal utility analysis, which sought to avoid the sins of its predecessor by concentrating attention on
the individual process of consumption in place of the social process of production
which had occupied the older classicists. By taking wants (and aversions) of the
individual as the basic data of economic inquiry and by assuming wants (and aversions) as given (that is, as determined by nature, not by the complex social environment of institutions, mores, folkways, and the like), the 'new economics' of the
eighteen seventies could treat economic society as merely an agglomeration of
atomistic individuals, and economic behavior as determined by universal traits of
human nature. Thus, they could deduce universal economic truths. In this way, not
only could economic classes and all the troublesome conflicts of class interest,
which were so clearly pictured in Ricardo's Principles, be got rid of, but the nature
and effects of the capitalist mode of production could be ruled out of the jurisdic-
tion of economics. We might say that the 'new economics' tried to save the day
by abstracting almost all, if not quite all, economic content from economic theory.

And now the *General Theory* and its 'new economics' have upset the apple cart
again. Once again the defenders of the status quo, both in theory and in practice,
have to try to repair the damage. Their efforts will doubtless be along the same
lines as the earlier attempt to obscure or to argue away the revolutionary implications of the *General Theory*. We find such efforts in some of the essays included
in the volume under review.

Professor Haberler tries to do this by finding nothing in the *General Theory* to
be worried about. After convincing himself, and possibly also the reader, that
there is not much that is new and nothing that is revolutionary in the logical or 'scientific' content of the book, he then denies what seem to me to be the obvious, viz.,
that the logical conclusions implicit in the system are revolutionary. "Differences
about policy," he says, "cannot logically be explained by basic theoretical dis-
agreement but must be explained by different judgments concerning concrete situations, administrative efficiency, the possibility of rational policy making, and,
perhaps most important, by different attitudes concerning the broad issues of government intervention and central planning versus *laissez faire*. It follows from our
analysis that specific policy recommendations derivable from the Keynesian system are not at all revolutionary. They are in fact very conservative" (pp. 176–177).

But the Professor is whistling to keep up his courage. He should take a look at some of the essays in this volume, such as Professor Harris' 'Keynes' Influence on Public Policy' (Chapter 2), or Professor Hansen's 'Keynes on Economic Policy' (Chapter 16), or Mr. Copland's 'Public Policy – The Doctrine of Full Employment' (Chapter 17), or Alan Sweezy's 'Declining Investment Opportunity' (Chapter 32), or Professor Higgins' 'Keynesian Economics and Public Investment Policy' (Chapter 35). Perhaps, however, Professor Haberler has read these and refuses to be perturbed because of his conviction that "radical schemes hitched to the Keynesian bandwagon have nothing to do, logically speaking, with the *General Theory* (he continues), what is needed to prevent mass unemployment is monetary policy and, at the most, a mild form of fiscal policy" (pp. 177–178). One can only conclude after this that Haberler has never read Chapter 24 of the *General Theory* itself.

Professor Schumpeter seeks to draw the poisonous fangs, by adopting a somewhat supercilious and patronizing attitude toward the *General Theory*. The model presented in the book is, he says, a simple one, and "the first condition of simplicity of a model is, of course, simplicity of the vision which it is to implement" (p. 92). Again, "Keynes refused to go beyond the factors that are the immediate determinants of income (and employment)" (p. 94). This enables him greatly to simplify his picture of the world and arrive at very simple propositions. Anyone can do this, says Schumpeter, if he is content "with arguments of the form: Given A, B, C . . . , then D will depend upon E." Since in the Keynesian system A, B, C, . . . "are part of the phenomena to be explained, the resulting propositions about what determines what, may easily be made undeniable and acquire the semblance of novelty without meaning very much" (p. 94). Still again, the *General Theory* abounds, he says, in overstatements – "overstatements moreover which cannot be reduced to the defensible level, because results depend precisely upon the excess" (p. 95).

Taking another tack, Professor Schumpeter finds the *General Theory* to be very narrowly circumscribed in its application and hence innocuous. We must note, he says of the book, "first, its specifically English quality; second, *ex visu of England's short-run interests and of the kind of Englishman the advisor was* (author's emphasis), its sober wisdom and conservation. It cannot be emphasized too strongly (he continues) that Keynes' advice was in the first instance always English advice, born of English problems . . . He was surprisingly insular, even in philosophy, but nowhere so much as in economics . . . Like the old freetraders, he always exalted what was at any moment truth and wisdom for England into truth and wisdom for all times and places" (p. 85).

The earlier attacks on the *General Theory* were less ingenious. Professor Seymour Harris, in a summary chapter (Chapter 3) on 'The Appraisal of the

General Theory, 1936–37', notes that not a single enthusiastic early review has come to his attention, though there were many critical ones. Pigou, in his review published in the May 1936, issue of *Economica*, sarcastically observed that "Einstein actually did for physics what Mr. Keynes believes himself to have done for Economics," viz., developed a real general theory (p. 29). "We have watched an artist," he continues, "firing arrows at the moon. Whatever we thought of his marksmanship, we can all admire his virtuosity" (p. 30). Professor Knight was equally bitter in 1937. Keynes' interpretations of classical economics are, he wrote, "the sort of caricatures which are typically set up as straw men for purposes of attack in controversial writing" (p. 31). And, he continues, "Chapter 24 of the *General Theory* is of special interest to the present writer as one inclined to take economics as a 'serious subject' rather than an intellectual puzzle for the diversion or even the improvement of the mind" (p. 31). Professor Knight found little in the book with which he could agree.

There were many other reviews of like tenor. They sound somewhat juvenile and somewhat archaic today, just ten years later. But one should not be too critical of them, for they represent the first startled and angry reactions and blind roundhouse swings at the renegade who was threatening to despoil the temple. Professors Haberler and Schumpeter do a much better job, as they should after a decade in which to marshall forces and decide tactics and strategy. Nevertheless, it is a losing battle – in fact, it is already lost. The damage has been done, and it is irreparable. What the bushy-bearded, heavy-handed German revolutionary did with malice aforethought and by frontal attack, the English aristocrat, a scholar of Eton and King's College, Cambridge, a director of the Bank of England, an advisor to the Chancellor of the Exchequer, a peer of the Realm, performed neatly, skillfully, and unconsciously, by flank attack.

REFERENCES

Keynes, J. M. (1936). *The General Theory of Employment, Interest, and Money*. New York: Harcourt, Brace and Company.

Pigou, A. C. (1936). Mr. J. M. Keynes' General Theory of Employment, Interest, and Money. *Economica*. (May), 115–132.

Knight, F. H. (1937). Uemployment and Mr. Keynes' Revolution in Economic Science. *Canadian Journal of Economics and Political Science*, 101.

KEYNES: GENERAL THEORY OF EMPLOYMENT, INTEREST AND MONEY

Edward Everett Hale

In 1852 John Stuart Mill, keenly aware of the inequalities and defects of the economic system of his day, and after a sympathetic study of Communism, stated that "if the choice were to be made between Communism with all its chances, and the present state of society with all its sufferings and injustices: if the institution of private property necessarily carried with it as a consequence, that the produce of labor should be apportioned as we now see it, almost in an inverse ratio to the labor – the largest portions to those who have never worked at all, the next largest to those whose work is almost nominal, and so in a descending scale, the remuneration dwindling as the work grows harder and more disagreeable, until the most fatiguing and exhausting bodily labor cannot count with certainty on being able to earn even the necessaries of life; if this or Communism were the alternative, all the difficulties, great and small, of Communism would be put as dust in the balance." (Mill, 1893, p. 159)

Eighty-four years later in 1936, John Maynard Keynes in his *General Theory of Employment, Interest and Money* asserts that "the outstanding faults of the economic society in which we live are its failure to provide for full employment

Edward Everett Hale: The Writings of an Economic Maverick, Volume 19-B, pages 95–104.
2001 by Elsevier Science B.V.
ISBN: 0-7623-0694-7

and its arbitrary and inequitable distribution of wealth and incomes," and in measured words states that "it is certain that the world will not much longer tolerate the unemployment, which, apart from brief intervals of excitement, is associated – and, in my opinion, inevitably associated – with present day capitalistic individualism" (Keynes 1936, p. 372).

Through the instruction and guidance of his father, J. S. Mill was steeped in the Ricardian economics and never reconciled or attempted to reconcile, his social sympathies and philosophy with the postulates of Ricardo. In any event, liberty for him was the supreme good, and the system of private property and free enterprise its best safeguard. Mill believed mankind not confronted with the harsh alternative of choosing between the system of property and free enterprise as it then existed and Communism with its sacrifice of liberty. There existed a middle ground. Liberty could be preserved by preserving capitalism with its defects removed. To this end Mill advocated universal education, a restriction of population growth among the workers by the development of prudential habits fostered by education and peasant proprietorship, the elimination of monopolies, limitations on the right of bequest and inheritance, and the promotion of systems of consumers' and producers' cooperation.

John Maynard Keynes is in the direct line of descent from Ricardo through J. S. Mill and Alfred Marshall. He is as steeped in Marshalian economics as was Mill in the system of Ricardo. Keynes, like Mill, is disturbed by the growth of radical theories and programs. He, too, regards liberty as the supreme good. Communism and Socialism, he states, would remedy inequality and solve the problem of unemployment at the expense of freedom and efficiency. Capitalism he believes, promotes efficiency and safeguards liberty, and for these virtues it is worth saving. By right analysis he is convinced its problems can be solved. His 'General Theory' is that analysis and his solution of the problems of unequal distribution and unemployment are progressive income and inheritance taxes, progressive reduction of the rate of interest towards the point of extinction of rate of pure interest within possibly a single generation, and socialization of investment.

Unlike Mill, Keynes reconciles his economic theory with his social philosophy. This reconciliation involves a shift from the Ricardian-Marshallian branch of theory to the heterodox branch represented by Bernard de Mandeville, Lord Lauderdale, Malthus, Thomas Chalmers, Si Mondi, Karl Marx, J. A. Hobson and Silvio Gesell. Keynes, no more than Malthus or Marx, ceases to be a classicist. He merely ceases to be orthodox. The classical theory is not incorrect. It is merely incomplete. More exactly, it fits one special case – the condition of full employment, and in real life this condition rarely, if ever, exists or has existed. It is therefor required to be supplemented by a general theory, applicable to all possible cases. Keynes undertakes to supply that general theory.

THE THEORY OF EMPLOYMENT

The classical theory of employment is that the demand for labor is determined by the marginal productivity of labor and the supply by the marginal disutility of workers. Thus wages will be established at the point of equilibrium where the value of the marginal product of labor is equal to the marginal disutility of the final unit of labor employed.

Keynes points out that this theory allows for frictional unemployment (time lags due to unforeseen changes), (change from job to job, etc.) and for voluntary unemployment but makes no allowance for involuntary unemployment. On its basis, there are only four ways of increasing employment:

1. Improvement in organization of foresight, which would diminish frictional unemployment.
2. Decrease in marginal disutility of labor.
3. Increase in marginal productivity of labor.
4. Relative decrease to the price of real wages.

Keynes agrees that the demand for labor is determined by its marginal product, but denies that the supply is determined by marginal disutility.

Further, Keynes denies that real wages depend on the wage bargains which labor makes with employers. It is other forces which determine the general level of real wages. There is no expedient by which labor as a whole can reduce its real wage to a given figure by making revised wage bargains with entrepreneurs.

Keynes' Theory of Employment

1. When employment increases, total real income is increased.
2. The psychology of the community is such that total consumption increases less than total income.
   a. Hence, employers would suffer loss if the whole of the increased employment were devoted to satisfying the increased demand for immediate consumption.
   b. Thus, to justify any given amount of employment, there must be an amount of current investment sufficient to absorb the excess of total output over what the community chooses to consume when employment is at the given level.
1. Given the community's propensity to consume, the equilibrium level of employment will depend on the amount of current investment.
   a. The amount of current investment will depend upon the inducement to invest.

The inducement to invest depends upon:

1.   The relation between the schedule of the marginal efficiency of capital, and
2.   The complex rates of interest on loans of various maturities and risks.

The volume of employment, therefore, is determined, not by the marginal disutility of labor, but by the propensity to consume and the rate of new investment.

THE PROPENSITY TO CONSUME

The amount that a community spends on consumption depends on:

1.   Its income
2.   Certain objective factors.
3.   The subjective needs and psychological propensities and habits of the individuals comprising it and the principles on which the income is divided between them.

The principal objective factors which influence the propensity to consume are changes in the money wage rates, changes in capital values, changes in the rate of interest, changes in fiscal policy, etc. But of these the effect is very small except that of changes in money wage rates. If any changes in money wage rates be eliminated, then propensity to consume is, in any given situation, a fairly stable function, and consumption depends on income. But if income increases, consumption does not increase in equal degree. The needs of the additional consumption do not require all the employment required to produce the increase in income. Hence, employment can only increase *pari passu* with an increase in investment.

The principal subjective factors which influence how much is spent or saved out of a given income are, in the case of individuals, the desire to provide for contingencies and old age, to provide for dependents, to secure independence, to secure funds to carry out speculative or business projects, to bequeath a fortune, and the bent of miserliness; and in the case of government or business enterprises, the motives of securing resources for increase of capital investment or to meet emergencies, of securing gradually increasing income, and of financial prudence. All these depend on the institutions and organization of economic society, on habits formed by race, education, convention, religion, morals; on present hopes and past experiences on the prevailing distribution of wealth and established standards of living. Those change slowly, and may be taken as given except over long periods.

Hence short period changes in consumption largely depend on changes in income, and not on changes in the propensity to consume out of a given income.

THE INDUCEMENT TO INVEST

Keynes states that the inducement to invest depends upon 1, the marginal efficiency of capital, and 2, the rate of interest.

He defines the marginal efficiency of capital as its prospective or anticipated marginal productivity. In his own words, "The marginal efficiency of capital is equal to that rate of discount which would make the present value of a series of annuities given by the return expected from the capital asset during its life just equal to its supply price", i.e. its replacement cost.

For any given rate of investment there is a corresponding marginal efficiency of capital. This investment demand schedule can be constructed and the rate of investment will be pushed to the point on the investment demand schedule where the marginal efficiency of capital is equal to the market rate of interest. Hence, the inducement to invest depends on the marginal efficiency of capital and the rate of interest.

The General Theory of the Rate of Interest

The classical theory makes the rate of interest depend on the demand for and supply of savings, with demand determined by the marginal productivity of capital and supply by the propensity to save. The rate of interest equalizes the amount of investment with the amount of savings. Increased savings reduces the rate of interest and stimulates output of capital. Increased investment raises the rate of interest.

Keynes criticizes this theory on several points. In the first place it neglects liquidity preference. In saving, an individual has to decide not only how much of this income he will reserve in some form of command over future consumption, but also in what form he will hold this command. The classical theory overlooks this second consideration – overlooks the fact that an individual might decide to hold his savings in the form of money or its equivalent. Whether one will so decide depends on his liquidity preference. In the second place, the rate of interest is not a payment for saving or waiting, for if one hoards his cash he receives no interest. It is a reward for running the risk of uncertainty of one kind or another. It is a measure of the unwillingness of those who possess money to part with their liquid control over it. It is the 'price' which equalizes the desire to hold wealth in the form of cash with the available quantity of cash.

Keynes, therefore, holds that the rate of interest is determined by: (1) liquidity-preference and, (2) the quantity of money. Savings and investments are not the causes, the classical theory teaches, but the results. They are the results of: (1) the propensity to consume, (2) the schedule of the marginal efficiency of capital, and (3) the rate of interest.

Thus, since employment depends on consumption and saving, since consumption and saving depend on income, since income depends on investment, and since investment depends on the marginal efficiency of capital and the rate of interest, there is a rate of interest consistent with a rate of investment which corresponds to full employment. The rate of interest on money limits the level of employment. As the rate of interest rises relative to the marginal efficiency of capital, employment decreases; as the rate falls, employment increases. Assuming liquidity-preference to be constant in any given situation, employment varies directly with the quantity of money up to the point of full employment.

Keynes is aware that the importance he ascribes to the rate of interest on money requires justification. Why does the rate of interest set the level of employment rather than the rate of return, measured in terms of itself, of non-monetary capital assets. The answer he gives is that the rate of interest on money is more reluctant to fall as output increases than is the rate of return on other assets measured in terms of themselves. This he accounts for by the following characteristics of money.

1. Money has a very small elasticity of production as far as the power of private enterprise is concerned. Thus, if the price rises, labor cannot be employed by entrepreneurs to produce more of it.
2. Money has an elasticity of substitution equal, or nearly equal, to zero. As its value rises, there is no tendency to substitute some other factor for it.
3. Money, because of its low or negligible carrying costs, satisfies liquidity more than other assets. This factor causes the rate of interest, below a certain figure, to be insensitive even to a substantial increase in the quantity of money in proportion to other forms of wealth.

On account of these characteristics, a rise in the money rate of interest holds back investment in the production of other commodities without being capable of stimulating investment in the production of money. In the absence of money, or any substitute for it, the ordinary forces of the market would tend to bring the rate of interest on other commodities, measured in terms of themselves, down until the emergence of full employment would bring about inelasticity of supply. Not so in the case of money. Thus 'unemployment develops because men want the moon; men cannot be employed when the object of their desire (i.e., money) is something which cannot be produced and the demand for which cannot be readily choked off. There is no remedy but to persuade the public that green cheese is practically the same thing and to have a green cheese factory (i.e., a central bank) under public control.

SUMMARY STATEMENT OF THE GENERAL HISTORY OF EMPLOYMENT

In summary, the independent variables or governing factors in the economic system are: (1) the propensity to consume, (2) the schedule of the marginal efficiency of capital, and (3) the rate of interest. The dependent variable of governed factors are (1) the volume of employment, and (2) the national income.

There is an inducement to push the rate of new investment to the point where the marginal efficiency of capital is equal to the rate of interest. A change in the rate of investment carries with it a change in the rate of consumption because it changes income. Consumption, however, changes less than the change in income. The change in investment and consumption determining the change in employment. But a change in employment changes the demand for money, i.e., changes the schedule of liquidity preferences, because it changes output, wages, and prices. The position of equilibrium will be influenced by these repercussions.

APPLICATION OF THE THEORY.

Notes on the Trade Cycle.

Keynes attributes the business cycle largely to cyclical fluctuations in the marginal efficiency of capital. The marginal efficiency of capital plays this important role in the cyclical fluctuations because it depends not only on the replacement cost of capital goods and their existing abundance or scarcity, but also on current expectations as to the future yield of capital goods. The advisability of new investment turns predominantly on expectation of the future. The basis of such expectations is very precarious and subject to sudden and violent changes. Keynes attributes the crisis stage of the cycle to a sudden collapse of the marginal efficiency of capital due to loss of confidence.

A fall in the marginal efficiency of capital tends to affect adversely the propensity to consume, and this aggravates still further the depressing effect of a decline in marginal efficiency. Under present conditions Keynes is of the opinion that the market estimation of the marginal efficiency of capital is offset by corresponding fluctuations in the rate of interest.

KEYNES: CRITICISM OF THE OVER INVESTMENT THEORY OF THE CYCLE

One school of thought attributes recurring booms and slumps to a tendency to over investment, and hence recommends the checking of over-investment by a high rate of interest. One fault of this theory is that the term over investment is ambiguous. Keynes states that it should mean a state of affairs in which every kind of capital goods is so abundant that even in conditions of full employment no new investment is expected to earn in the course of its life more than its replacement cost. In this situation the remedy would not be to raise the rate of interest but to redistribute incomes and otherwise stimulate the propensity to consume.

Generally, however, the term over investment refers to investments which are destined to disappoint the expectations which prompted them or for which there is no use in conditions of severe unemployment. In this situation the remedy for a boom is not a higher but a lower rate of interest. We do not wish to abolish booms and perpetuate a condition of semi-slump, but to abolish interest as a remedy for a state of affairs growing out of a prolonged period of abnormally heavy investment as a remedy would not be to raise the rate of interest but to redistribute incomes and otherwise stimulate the propensity to consume.

KEYNES' CRITICISM OF THE UNDER CONSUMPTION THEORY

Another school of thought attributes depression and unemployment to under consumption, or to social practices and a distribution of incomes which result in an unduly low propensity to consume.

Keynes believes that under existing conditions of unplanned and uncontrolled volume of investment and a long term interest rate which seldom or never falls below a conventional level, this theory is a correct guide to policy. If we do not or cannot increase investment, then employment can be increased only by increasing consumption.

Keynes, however, believes that there is still much social advantage to be obtained from increased investment and that this can be had by a proper control of investment and interest rates. He criticizes the under consumption theories for overlooking the possibility of expanding employment by increasing investment and for concentrating the attention exclusively on the increased consumption as the remedy. Keynes believes we should advance on both fronts at once by aiming at a socially controlled rate of investment, with the view to progressive decline in the marginal efficiency of capital and by pursuing all sorts of policies to increase the propensity to consume. He admits that it is doubtful if full employment could be maintained, whatever we do about investment, with the existing propensity to consume.

CONCLUDING NOTES ON SOCIAL PHILOSOPHY

As noted in our introductory paragraphs, Keynes points to its failure to provide full employment and its arbitrary and inequitable distribution of wealth and incomes as the outstanding faults of contemporary economic society.

Inequality in the distribution of wealth and incomes has been justified on the ground that the growth of capital depends on the strength of the motive towards individual saving, and the savings of the rich are necessary to this growth. His general theory proves this to be a fallacy, for up to the point of full employment the growth of capital requires high propensity to consume. An increase in the propensity to consume increases the inducement to invest by raising the marginal efficiency of capital. Under contemporary conditions of partial employment, therefore, the abstinence of the rich impedes or restricts the growth of wealth.

A high rate of interest has been justified on the ground that it is necessary to provide a sufficient inducement to save. But Keynes' theory holds that the extent of effective saving is determined by the scale of investment, and the scale of investment is, up to the point of full employment, promoted by a low rate of interest. The rate of interest, therefore, should be reduced to that point relatively to the schedule of the marginal efficiency of capital at which there is full employment.

Keynes believes that the demand for capital is strictly limited in the sense that it would not be difficult to increase the stock up to a point where its marginal efficiency had fallen to a very low degree. This would mean the death of the rentier, which Keynes regards as all to the good. He points out that the rentier class performs no necessary or useful economic function and that interest today regards no genuine sacrifice. Interest exists merely because of the scarcity of capital, and there are no intrinsic reasons why capital should be scarce.

Keynes regards his proposals of social and economic reform as conservative, and states that his scheme would leave wide fields to individual initiative and activity. To solve the problems of inequality and unemployment, it is not necessary that the state assume ownership of the means of production, as the socialists maintain. It is merely necessary that the state exercise a [telling] influence on the propensity to consume and control investment. The propensity to consume can be controlled through taxation, the fixing of the rate of interest, etc. The control of investment involves determination by the state of the amount of resources devoted to augmenting the means of production and of the basic rate of reward of those who own them. State control is needed, therefore, only to bring about an adjustment between the propensity to consume and the inducement to invest. All other matters may safely be left to private discretion, initiative and enterprise, and the free play of market forces. Thus the problem of unemployment can be solved and other defects of our economic system removed without impairing the efficiency of capitalism or abolishing the liberty it safeguards.

REFERENCES

Keynes, J. M. (1936). *The General Theory of Employment, Interest, and Money*. New York: Harcourt, Brace and Company.
Mill, J. S. (1893). *Principles of Political Economy*. New York: D. Appleton and Company.

LECTURE NOTES FROM ECONOMICS 327: COMPARATIVE ECONOMIC SYSTEMS

Professor Edward E. Hale, Spring Semester, 1948
(Notes taken by William C. Frederick)

INTRODUCTORY LECTURE

How Do Economic Systems Differ?

Certain elements which do not differentiate economies: (1) Mass production and machine technology. (2) Existence of a large amount of capital goods. Necessary to any advanced economic system. (3) Monetary income to people. (4) Goods and services sold in the market.

Any economic system is essentially an arrangement, organization, etc., with the function of producing goods and services to meet human wants and needs so that people may live adequately. Governing factors or requisites for producing goods and services required. (1) Means of production. Technological devices. Physical or mental energy needs to be expended. Natural resources – result of advance of technological and scientific knowledge. Not a product of nature but of science. Tools and implements. (Economic systems cannot necessarily be chosen and adopted arbitrarily. Example: Morgenthau's proposal to reduce Germany to an agricultural economy. German industry vital to whole European continent and related thusly to whole world. Proposals to change economies

Edward Everett Hale: The Writings of an Economic Maverick, Volume 19-B, pages 105–138.
2001 by Elsevier Science B.V.
ISBN: 0-7623-0694-7

limited by: population, real natural resources, state of industrial arts, culture, interlocking relations with other cultures.) (2) Institutions – rules and regulations to control actions of the people. Social customs, conventions, etc., which control actions of human beings. Difference in economies lies in institutional set-up.

Three Problems to Production of Goods

Allocating productive resources (labor, resources, etc.). What is the technology to be used to produce. Difference in manner of solving this problem differentiates economies. Socialism – central planning. Capitalism – free play of market and prices.

Motives to Production of Goods: Capitalism – profit motive. Sovietism – sometimes workers awarded by ribbons, honorary awards, etc. Army – ribbons, medals, honorary certificates, etc.

Distribution of Resulting Output Among People in Community. Distribution of income. Solution of these problems constitutes problem of securing economic order. Very difficult task in complex society. Large amount of cooperation required in a complex society such as ours in order to produce goods and services. Question of getting cooperation. The way in which that problem is solved differentiates economies. Solved through institutional set-up. Brings about economic order.

CAPITALISM

Institutions of Capitalism

Private Property: **Most** of productive equipment is owned by private persons. Private ownership of means of production. Carries right to exclusive use of or disposal of things owned. Owner determines at his own discretion how property will be disposed of. However, owner of private property is not entirely unlimited in his actions toward property. If this condition is not met, the system under consideration is not a capitalist system.

Free Contract: To set up relationship between individuals in order to secure economic order. (Crusoe and Friday) Relations determined by free contract. Determined by mutual and voluntary agreement between persons concerned. (Landlord and tenant, employer and employee).

Profit Motive: Gets productive resources into action to produce commodities of all kinds. Must realize or think he will realize pecuniary gain or reward. This must be present in a capitalist economy.

Inheritance: Right to control private property after death of owner. Not synonymous with private property. Relatively minor.

Price System: Capitalism relies on prices and free open market as device to direct or control allocation of productive resources.

Capitalism: A system by which people seek to make a living or accumulate wealth by buying and selling. Buying and selling on free market and based on contractual agreement between buyer and seller. Free market absolutely essential to capitalism.

Three markets essential to capitalism

Commodity market: Two necessities in order to establish the commodity market. (1) A development in technology. Before commodity market could be established it was necessary to invent and develop facilities for transporting goods over distances and for communication between buyers and sellers. Roads, canals, steam engine, railroads, auto, bus, and airplane. It was necessary to extend transportation facilities to get outside of a self-sustaining economy.

A Change in Institutions. What had to be changed? What was actually changed? Manors were self-sufficient. No buying and selling for a living. Produced food and commodities for consumption, not for the market. Towns – buying and selling was controlled by guilds. Guilds were corporations based on charters and franchises granted by the King or Parliament. They possessed both economic and political power. *Powers* – local self-government, election, majority vote, pass laws, own courts, enforce their laws, police force, taxation. *Privileges* – avoidance of tax collector by direct payment of taxes to the King, entitled to protection by the King on the King's highways (this gave access to the market). *Monopolistic privileges* – power to determine membership of guilds (closed shop), monopoly of one particular business (this gave guilds same powers as the lords and barons in the country). Guilds were a sort of capitalist system – made living by buying and selling. Different in structure from trade union organizations of master craftsmen. Members of guilds were owners and sellers of the product. Guilds provided social insurance, regulated prices, regulated competitive practices, and quality of product. Guilds were primarily monopolies. So it became necessary to destroy guilds in order to establish the free market. Destruction of guilds: *By revolution*. By the courts in England by taking away exclusive privileges: Merchant Tailors Case (1599). Merchant tailors guild was first to lose legalized monopoly. Tailors could sell outside 'legal' market if they sold an equal amount on legal market. Court decision ruled that the by-law was unlawful and that it violated common law and the liberty of the subject. The Case of Monopolies (1602). Queen Elizabeth granted a franchise to D'Arsey which gave monopoly on manufacture and importation of playing cards. When a competitor entered the market D'arsey brought legal action. Court decision declared patent was against common law and acts of Parliament. Monopoly restricted output and raised prices – therefore, they were against public welfare. Thus, common-law courts established the principle of allowing a man to get rich if the public welfare gained thereby. Dr. Bonham's Case (1608). In 1519 Henry VIII granted physicians the authority to pass upon qualifications of physicians in London and suburbs. Could prohibit unqualified from practicing. When Dr. Bonham set up a practice, he was arrested and jailed for failing to meet with the qualifications set up by physicians' organization. Court released Bonham and permitted him to practice even though not a member. Declared the privilege was against common right and reason. Thus the courts destroyed patents given to guilds and to court favorites. This led to a struggle between the courts and the kings and nobles. Glorious Revolution (1688) [See Strachey, *The Coming Struggle for Power*, p.12] Commonwealth Revolution: Parliament and judges against House of Stewart. These revolutions and the actions of the courts established free commodity market with unregulated and free competition. The courts are the foundation of capitalism. Enforce property rights, contracts, etc. Thus it became necessary for capitalism to control the courts. Feudalist courts: Manorial courts. Set up and maintained to govern tenants. Ruled by manor. Guild courts (see above). Common law courts. King sent out judges on circuits to try all cases. Took cases away from other courts, which slowly disappeared. Common law grew up here. Common law became customary law. Made laws out of customs. Business, agricultural customs became laws.

King set up: Star chamber. (Abolished in 1640); Court of exchequer. (Abolished in 1640); Courts of equity. Very powerful with power to issue injunctions. Served to give legal sanction to customs. Businessmen had no confidence in courts because King could remove judges at will. Settlement of 1700 took away this power. Judges appointed for life and were not removable. Government became a government of laws and not of men. Made contracts secure, gave confidence, and made possible the market. Thus the courts:

Established free competition.

Effected institutional change necessary to the establishment of a free market.

Destroyed guilds.

Established the capital market by taking over the functions of establishing contracts and rules of fair competition.

Capital Market: Two necessities to the establishment of money market. (1) The assumption by government of enforcing contracts in order to make them secure. Completed by latter part of the 16th century. Enforcement of contracts was legal beginning of capitalism. Came about during the reign of Queen Elizabeth. In capitalism the relations among persons are determined by contractual agreements (buy or sell, rent or lease, borrowing or lending, etc.). Contracts were formerly enforced by church or by guilds. In 16th century state took over this function. People began to live by buying and selling. Brought about by expansion of commerce. Legal enforcement of contracts became necessary. By beginning of the 17th century courts were enforcing verbal and implied contracts. This recognition of verbal or implied contracts was the beginning of capitalism. (Labor contracts). Brought into existence incorporeal property. Smith, Ricardo, common-law economists said there was no property other than physical. Incorporeal property: a positive, legal right to have someone else do something; a right against a second person. (Right to demand payment of a debt). A personal and physical relationship in dealing with corporeal property. (2) That the enforced contracts be made negotiable. Transference of property. Established in 17th century. Two circumstances prevented negotiability: Concept of property as only physical and tangible and concept of property as a purely personal relation. (Not binding on anyone else.) Legal enforcement of contracts brought about fact of reality of the new incorporeal property. With the invention of negotiability, contracts became a business relationship. Taken out of personal realm. Recognition of Bills of Exchange: In England there arose a controversy over foreign bills of exchange. Courts declared creditor could sell note and buyer had all rights which original creditor had. By 1699 negotiability was established. Negotiability of contracts made for confusion. Two different kinds of goods side by side. Opposing concepts of values. Development of negotiability created banking system, and made possible a rapid turnover of capital and low interest rate. Development of intangible property: Destruction of guilds left free and unregulated competition. Courts had to take over function of regulating competition. Courts, beginning in 16th and 17th century, took customs of guilds and put legal sanction upon them. Became the common law of business. Established rules for fair competition. First trademark case (1580). In London there was a manufacturer of woolen cloth named Hall. He conceived the idea of making it possible for buyer to recognize goods he's buying by a distinguishing mark and then advertising the mark. Another manufacturer put Hall's mark on his cloth. Hall brought suit and court ruled in his favor. Court extended concept of trespass to include infringement on any kind of business. Formerly applied only to physical property. Court said the other manufacturer was competing unfairly. First instance of court ruling that a competitor might lawfully be restricted from competing. Jollyfe v. Brode (1620). First decision that a person might lawfully sell a part of his liberty. Brode was a London merchant who sold his store and stock to Jollyfe. Brode sold at excess price of stock value, agreeing not to set up business in London again. However, Brode did open up again and Jollyfe brought suit. Court ruled in favor of Jollyfe and issued an injunction which required Brode to close shop. Thus, the court legalized a contract in restraint of trade. Started the modern law of goodwill by converting reputation into a piece of property. Right to the trademark and the concept of good will are the two cornerstones of fair competition. Copyrights (1688). Stationers Guild had monopoly on publication of books. In 1708 Parliament provided for the granting of copyright for 28 years. Made possible publishing business. Protects publisher, not author.

Development of patents: Intangible property then (consisting of goodwill, trademarks, patents, etc.) has a much greater value than physical property. Physical property can be duplicated relatively easy while intangible property cannot. Intangible property is a negative right against a third person; it can prohibit another person from doing something but has no right against customers. It is a right to buy and sell and to make contracts. Four types of intangible property above furnish an access to market. Incorporeal property is a positive right against a second person. Evidence of debt. May force a person to pay a debt, such as bonds, mortgages, etc.). Right to enforced contracts.

Labor market: Those who own means of production employ others to operate the means of production for them. Owners dependent upon hired workers. Two necessities for the establishment of labor market: (1) Workers had to be given the liberty to sell their labor power. Slavery and serfdom had to be abolished. Restraints were abolished by a series of revolutions which overthrew feudalism. (England, France, & America). (2) Means of production should be taken away from those workers. Established mostly by technological advance. Large industrial plants and machines made it impossible for each individual to control means of production. Enclosures in England drove small landowners off their land. Industrial Revolution brought textile industry to fore in England, making large tracts of land necessary for the raising of sheep for wool. The dispossessed agricultural workers were driven into the towns.

Laissez-faire Capitalism.

Development of Laissez-faire Capitalism: When all of the above rights were established, people began to think of these rights as natural and inalienable. Natural rights or individualistic stage of capitalism spanned a period from the late 18th century to about the first three quarters of the 19th century. Natural rights theory was based upon the idea that there exists a natural order with natural laws and natural rights. A system based upon the natural rights theory is conceived to be the best system, with more happiness, etc. Natural laws do not enforce themselves. Man is to discover, not make laws. In laissez-faire capitalism the natural laws (rights) were merely the laws (rights) of businessmen. Purpose of the Declaration of Independence: to serve notice to the world that the colonists were acting within their rights. A new theory of government was needed by American Revolutionists to replace the 'sovereign king' concept of Great Britain. The Declaration establishes the natural order theory which was above the English government. Natural laws were to be discovered by exercising 'right' reason and this would produce the best laws, rights, etc. George III had been violating these natural laws, and therefore the colonists were justified in overthrowing his rule. Natural rights theory holds that reason is the only just foundation of government. Government by the consent of the governed. These natural rights were incorporated into the basic law of the land in the Bill of Rights.

Individualistic capitalism based on laissez-faire. Motive was self-interest. Greatest happiness with least pain. Prize offered was property. The system was automatically regulated. Promotion of individual interests automatically promotes interests of whole system. Smith's theory valid only if equality of economic power and opportunity existed. Smith failed to see the importance of equality of economic opportunity. One must have equal power to enter into business. Liberty once meant absence of physical restraint to one's person. Today liberty means absence of legal restraint or duty. If not restrained by law, one has liberty; does not necessarily have a right but is not restrained by law from doing something. Liberty is not positive. Freedom is the ability to do as one wishes. Possession of rights. Therefore, a restraint upon liberty might increase one's freedom. (Minimum wage laws, etc.) Liberty is limited to the bargaining power of an individual. Main doctrines of laissez-faire capitalism also doctrines of anarchists (complete lack of restraint). Rights granted inversely to ability.

Restraint and Regulation of Laissez-faire Capitalism: Classical economists and the courts held that equality meant only legal equality. There are many other inequalities not necessarily within the law. Three types of government which exercise restraint: (1) State (political) government. State sets up rules and regulations to govern people and enforce laws. Enforces laws by fear or threat of physical violence to persons or property. (2) Economic government. Enforces rules by fear of poverty. Unemployment and bankruptcy. Power to withhold goods and/or jobs. (3) Moral or ethical government. Enforces rules by fear of public opinion. Persuasion. Largest segment of control exercised by economic and moral government.

Many labor cases were thrown out as a restraint of liberty. Coppage v. Kansas (1915). Hedges was a member of the Switchmen's Union. He had insurance with the union and his dismissal would forfeit the insurance. Coppage, the superintendent, would have an open shop. All union employees had to withdraw from the union and all employees had to sign a statement to the effect that they would not become affiliated with a union while working at that job. Hedges refused to sign and was fired. The state of Kansas prohibited yellow-dog contracts, so Hedges brought suit. The court ruled in favor of Hedges and the Railroad company appealed to the U.S. Supreme Court. Largely on the basis of the 14th amendment, the Court held the Kansas statute was unconstitutional. Employer and employee were free to contract and each can stipulate terms upon which he will contract. The decision was based upon the assumption that each party had equal rights and powers. Powers were not equal because employee had the alternative of working or starving. Economic coercion. States cannot force a person to deprive himself of those very rights which the state is supposed to defend. Courts took the view that the only restraint imposed was that of the political government. If not restrained by political government, then one had liberty. Economic coercion came from state legislatures. Unregulated industry system resulted in great inequality which meant that workers and consumers were greatly exploited. This led to government regulation to protect consumer and worker. Possible to control human behavior by exercising just one of the above three powers. Anarchists would control human behavior through economic and moral government, not through physical violence. Marxian communists would control human behavior only through moral government.

Three powers of sovereignty by which capitalism may be regulated: (1) Police power. Police power makes possible regulation concerning public utilities, public welfare, etc. Justifies abridgment of property without compensation. Removes opportunity to make profits. Reduces liberty of contract. Police power is 'due process of law'. In 1870 'due process' was procedure according to common law forms. In 1880s a new definition of 'due process' was developed. Hurtado v. California (1884). During the course of the trial the prosecution held that information against accused could be presented by district attorney instead of by grand jury. Hurtado said due process had not been observed. Supreme

Court overruled Hurtado and held that any legal procedure observing public welfare with no abridgment of liberties, etc., was due process. Form of procedure not important. Purpose is to get information before the court. (2) Taxing power. Takes away excess profits after they have been made. Taxing power recognizes private property. (3) Constitutional power. (Interstate commerce.) Instances of police power used in the U.S.: taxing state bank notes, oleomargarine. Not successful in trying to tax industries employing child labor. Regulation of laissez-faire capitalism has occurred from the last part of the 19th century. Barriers to regulation principally lay in provisions of the Constitution (5th and 14th amendments). Slaughterhouse Case (1860s). New Orleans municipal government said all cattle slaughtered in city must go through municipal slaughterhouse. Supreme Court upheld New Orleans city government and said that the regulation did not take away property from private owners. Railway rate case (1880). Court reversed decision made in Slaughterhouse Case and said property taken away was the right to charge for services to make profits. Government sets limits to use of economic power by an individual by establishing Restraints (police power). Regulatory laws were first passed to protect consumers. (Public utilities, etc.). In 1898 labor legislation first recognized by court. Safety and health of worker. Regulatory laws had to promote public welfare. Acts of legislature subject to review by courts to prevent private interest groups from controlling laws made. The whole long struggle for Liberty was a struggle for freedom of contract, which is the legal expression of the free market. 'There is nothing like a threat to property for rousing moral splendor in prosperous patriots'. Obstacles in the path of the establishment of the free market: Deep-rooted and formidable feudalistic institutions, fixed ideas, religious, political and social, all perforce founded on the impossibility of the market, stood flatly in the way.

Three violent engagements in the establishment of free market: (1) The Reformation. The religious field of thought. Improvement of navigation. Advance of agricultural methods. Improvement of transportation made exchange profitable for first time. Catholic Church held so much of the best land that the establishment of private profit-making agriculture was impossible, until the abbeys and convents had been dispossessed. Also, very important, that the men of the new middle class should have religious assurance that was necessary to them. In Spain, the power of the Church was not broken, and, consequently, capitalism did not exist there until 1931. (2) English Rebellion of 1640 and Revolution of 1688. The wealth of the new commercial class, whose very existence depended upon the maintenance and expansion of the free market, had grown out of proportion to their political power. Became suspicious of the King.

The prize of the revolution was the control of the State and the forging of a program to further their economic interests. The autocratic and prosperous Whig class in England triumphed in the struggle. (3) French Revolution (1789–1815). Revolution broke back of feudalism in Europe and brought bourgeoisie to full, recognized strength. French middle class differed from English middle class. Frenchmen were mostly small proprietors as opposed to English Whigs.

Labor Class Established by Two Means: (1) Tools, materials, and natural resources can be taken directly away from the workers. Example: English enclosures. 'Freed' agricultural workers from their land and brought into existence surplus wealth which should employ these 'free' hands at something else. (2) Workers can be dispossessed of means of production through specialization and concentration (which is essential to industry) of the means of production. The small independent producer will be forced into that class which has only its own labor to sell. Overthrow of feudalism did not result in a homogeneous society of free and equal producers for the market. Instead of destruction of monopolists, a new category of monopolists (of means of production) appeared. Instead of personal freedom for all men, there was created a new and far more extensive form of dependence.

MARXIAN SOCIALISM

Marxian Interpretation of History

Marx desired to exert an influence on future human behavior. He said that the philosophers have only *interpreted* the world in various ways, the point however is to *change* it. Marxian theory to be a tool for shaping history. One must have knowledge of the forces that have operated to produce social change in the past. What causes social change? The 18th century philosophers, classical economists, and early 19th century utopian socialists held that history consisted of merely a series of accidents. Utilizing this theory the utopian socialists reasoned then it would be possible at any time, and place to establish a new social system. Why not discover the best form of social organization and establish it? Acquaint people with new theory and people would immediately want to change to the new system. Adam Smith's laissez-faire capitalism came from this source of thought. In the social sciences, accidents may occur when causes of event cannot be explained within realm of the social sciences.

Idealistic theory and materialistic theory of history hold that history is altered change. *Idealistic theory*. Purpose, will, intelligence of some. Being determines course of history. Supernatural theorists. Explained history in terms of will of some supernatural God. Cannot be used to explain any future trend or event. Psychological theorists. Ideals, purposes, and aims of human beings and motives that control human behavior determine course of history. Great Man theory. Outside man unable to know what goes on in mind of the great man. *Materialistic theory.* Some aspect of physical or social environment that can be observed determines course of history. Chemical, biological interpretation of social evolution. *Social Darwinism.* Social life is result of struggle between groups with strongest race winning out. *Geographical interpretation.* Rise and fall of civilization is result of climatic conditions. Advanced cultures have always existed in temperate zone, according to theory. Assumption of the above three theories is that human behavior is determined by same forces that govern inanimate things. Tendency is to ignore social development and change. Man is an active force or agent in process of change.

Marx holds that history not determined by Providence, man's intelligence, or by Great Men. All history exhibits orderly sequence. Social organization follows a definite path. Social evolution controlled by objective forces and these forces determine the character of a culture, society, etc. "Its (the materialistic interpretation of history) premises are men not in any imaginary isolation and state of fixation, but in their actual empirically observable process of development in definite condition . . . There, where speculation ends, with real life, real positive science therefore begins, the representation of practical activity, of the practical process of the development of man." (Lindsay, Karl Marx's *Capital*, p. 28) Fundamental factor which controls social evolution is not to be found in ideas, but in the way in which men make a living. If man does not provide for physical and biological existence, he has not much interest in society. Procuring a livelihood is basic. Commands first attention. Material conditions of life are the prime mover. Limits are set by nature and by men. Manner of securing livelihood is conditioned by nature of productive forces available to them. Productive forces: (1) Raw materials (all things found in nature). (2) Tools, machines, etc. (3) Physical and mental powers of humans. (4) Scientific and technological knowledge.

In the process of making a living, relationships between men and men and between men and the productive forces are necessary. Relations between men (personal relations) necessary in order to gain needed cooperation. Relations between men and the productive forces are known as property relations. Both types of relationships put together are called the relations of production. In Marxian theory the productive forces correspond to technology and the relations of production correspond to economic institutions. Total of relations of production make up the economic structure of society. Productive forces and relations of production make up the economic system. Nature of relations of production is dependent upon the nature of the forces of production. Change of productive forces brings about change in relations of production. System of government is built upon the relations of production. (Code of ethics, philosophy, social institutions, political government, etc.). This (relations of production) is known as the social superstructure.

All parts of society are interlocking and each part affects all others. Why is general character of one social system distinct from another? Relations of production condition general character of entire society. In order to maintain any set of relations between men and men and between men and things it is necessary to set up political government to enforce laws, ethical codes, etc. Feudalism and capitalism had to devise some system of recognizing and enforcing customs and beliefs of the culture.

What brings about social change? (1) Forces of production change continuously. Change usually takes place in improvements in techniques of production. Process always going on. Dynamic and not static. (2) Relations of production are static. In any given society there will be one or more groups who enjoy positions of power and privilege or advantage and who desire to maintain those factors. Through possession of power, these groups are able to maintain relations of production intact. Therefore, a condition exists in which the continuously developing forces of production outdistance the relations of production. The relations of production then become obsolete and not in complete accord with the forces of production. Relations of production impede the development of the forces of production. (Example: guild system). Institutional relations mean that there are groups in society who enjoy positions of power and privilege. This brings about class struggle between those who hold positions of power and privilege and those who do not. Therefore, the class struggle is the basis of all history. When struggle reaches a point where economic system cannot function, then a new structure is set up to take the place of the old structure. Social changes brought about by class struggle.

Technological Interpretation of History by Veblen. Very sharp distinction between institutions and technology. Contradiction between institutions and technology. Fundamental factor making for social change is technological development. Only factor in social change is technological change. Marx: technological change itself does not result in social change. Conflict between institutions and technology makes social change necessary. Brought about solely through class struggle. Veblen: Social change brought about by effect of thinking about changes brought about by technological change. Technological change and development causes different way of making living which changes habits of thought (institutions). Habits of thought disappear through abandonment of outmoded ideas. No concept of class struggle. Change brought about automatically by technological change. Nothing anyone can do to hasten or retard social change. Marx: At a given time the relations of production might most effectively utilize the productive forces. Veblen: Institutional set-up always hinders development of productive forces. At most, ceremony allows productive forces to function.

Marxian Theory of Value

Commodity is unit of investigation of the capitalist system. Theory of value applicable only to capitalism. Characteristics of a commodity: (1) Must possess use value. Capacity or ability of a thing to satisfy human want. (2) Must have been produced by human labor. (3) Must be produced to be exchanged in the market. Other goods do not fall into the functioning of a capitalist economy. (4) Must be separable from the person of the laborer. Use value exists by virtue of relations of characteristics of commodity and human wants. Use value of one commodity differs from use value of another commodity qualitatively. Commodities bought in different ratios. Commodities have power of commanding other commodities in the market. Exchange value of one commodity differs from exchange value of another commodity only quantitatively. Exchange values all equal if taken in proper proportions. All commodities have in common: having been produced by human labor. If commodities are equal, each has in it the same amount of embodied human labor. Value, then, is embodied human labor. Use value = want-satisfying power. Exchange value (relative) = purchasing power or ratio of exchange. Ratio between amount of labor embodied in two commodities. Value (absolute) = embodied human labor.

Problems to Applying Labor Theory of Value: (1) Measuring quantity of labor power used in production of commodity (units of time, degree of skill, amount of time, etc.) Marx measures quantity of labor by units of time (hours). Marx used a concept of averages to arrive at the labor time socially necessary. Labor time socially necessary is the labor time required by worker of average degree of skill and ability working under conditions of production normal at the time. Marx probably meant modal average. Labor time required in those factories that are used in technique of production producing greatest amount of commodity. Problem of relation between different degrees of skill. Process by which wage rates are determined and established by custom. Classical economists described either 3 (or 4) classes and therefore 3 (or 4) different types of income: (1) Labor: Workers – wages, Capitalists – profits, (2) Land: Landowners – rent; (3) Capital: Investors – interest. Marx held that there are only two significant classes and two types of income: (1) Laborers – income from labor. (2) Capitalists – income from property. Property income called surplus value.

Why does surplus value exist and why does it accrue to property owners. Since all commodities are bought and sold at their values (according to definition of value) then surplus value could not be derived. Also in production of goods, each productive factor is paid according to its value. There would be, then, some commodity for sale in the market for more value than it has itself. Labor power, in action, creates value. Marx holds that the commodity for sale in the market for more value than it has itself is labor. Value of labor power determined just as is value of other commodities. Quantity of labor socially necessary for production of labor power. Worker must be kept in health and strength. Therefore worker and family must be sustained in order to supply labor power. Amount of goods and services necessary to maintain worker and family is then the amount which is necessary for production of labor power. Employer purchased labor power at full value. Employer, having purchased labor power, has control over his purchase. During the day, worker produces goods of more value than the value of the labor power which he expended in the production. Real value of his labor power is the amount of time required to produce labor's real wages. Length of working day = 12 hours. Necessary working time = 6 hours. At the end of 6 hours he has created goods equal to the value of one day's labor. But employer has contracted to have worker work for 12 hours. Therefore all goods produced after 6th hour are surplus value.

$$S = \text{surplus value.}$$

$$S^1 = \text{rate of surplus value} = \text{surplus working time/necessary working time}$$

Any capitalist seeking to engage in production of goods to realize surplus value has to invest in means of production. Two types of capital: (1) Variable capital. That part which is invested in or expended in purchase of labor power. Part upon which surplus value is realized. (2) Constant capital. Amount invested in all other means of production other than labor power.

$$V = \text{variable capital.}$$
$$C' = \text{constant capital.}$$
$$C = \text{total capital.}$$
$$C = V + c'$$
$$S' = S/V$$
$$p = \text{rate of profit} = S/(c' + V)$$
$$O = \text{organic composition of capital} = c'/(c' + V)$$

Organic composition of capital rises with amount of constant capital. With any given rate of surplus value (S'), the rate of profit (p) will be lower, the higher the organic composition of capital (O).

Given: $S' = 100\%$ $S' = S/V$ $c' = 50$ $V = 50$
$$O = c'/(c' + V) = 50/(50 + 50) = 50\%$$
$$p = S/(c' + V) = 50/(50 + 50) = 50\%$$

Given: $S' = 100\%$ $S' = S/V$ $c' = 75$ $V = 25$
$$O = 75/(75 + 25) = 75\%$$
$$p = 25/(75 + 25) = 25\%$$

Rate of profit depends upon two variables: S' and O.

The statements above together with the illustrative problems result in the 'great contradiction' of the Marxian theory: At any given time, it should seem to follow if rates of surplus value would be same in all industries, then highly mechanized industries would be less profitable than those which are not mechanized. In actuality, the rates of profit tend to be the same. Reason why contradiction appears is a misconception of function of the theory. Theory is not intended to be a description of the way specific prices are determined in the market.

The theory is intended to (1) describe the source of value, (2) what determines the total value of *all* things produced at a given time, (3) source from which property incomes are derived, and (4) the source of labor exploitation in a capitalist economy. Total value of all commodities produced in economy at a given time is determined by total amount of labor power expended in the production of those commodities.

Marxian Theory of Price Determination. In a capitalist economy investment of capital made to realize a profit. Greatest profit possible. Capitalist will invest in type of business which will yield greatest profit. As a result of efforts to seek greatest profit, rate of profits would tend to be same in each line of production. Brought about by competition.

Costs: (1) Wages to labor; (2) Interest on borrowed funds; (3) Prices paid for raw materials; (4) Taxes and other costs in producing output. Same as entrepreneur's cost theory. The total surplus value would tend to be divided among capitalists so that each would receive that percentage of total surplus value which his amount of invested capital bears to the total capital. Commodities would have to sell at price determined by cost of production. And if they did, in fact, sell at that price, the rates of profit would be the same in all lines of production.

Capitalism generates two basic contradictions: (1) Modern technology has made the productive process a cooperative or socialized process in which production requires close cooperation of many individuals. However, product produced by cooperation of many individuals is appropriated in its entirety by the few property owners. (2) Contradiction between meticulous and all-engaging process of production in individual enterprise and anarchy in production at large. (U.S. Steel very highly organized, while there is no coordination of economy as a whole). Frequent breakdowns are the result.

Marxian Theory of Economic Progress and Laws of Capitalist Development.

Law of Declining Rate of Profit. All economic interpretations have held that profits tend to decline. Differ in reason why this occurs. English classical economists attributed it not to anything which exists in capitalist economy but a result of the laws of nature. Outside of system. Non-economic. Rests on law of population increase (1798) and law of diminishing returns (1815). Malthus developed theory to disprove theory of socialism and anarchism. Diminishing returns – land is gift of nature and therefore fixed. Good land strongly restricted. Marx: direct result of way in which capitalist economy operates. Organic composition of capital tends to rise. Result of two forces: (1) Progress of technology itself (labor-saving machinery); therefore more constant capital per laborer. (2) Competition forces capitalist to accept new technological devices. This assumption based on given rate of surplus value.

Law of Concentration and Centralization. In development of capitalism, production becomes concentrated in fewer and fewer larger establishments and control of productive forces becomes centralized in the hands of fewer and fewer individuals. Concentration: Producer must enlarge the scale of the operations to maintain profits (absolute). *Rate* of profit falls, so an effort is made to increase absolute profits to offset loss with fall in rate of profits. Technological process makes large scale industry necessary. Smaller firms are slowly swallowed up with advance in technology. Centralization: With concentration comes centralization. Small capitalists forced down into the proletariat. Theory developed before corporations became dominant form of business. Until middle of 19th century, corporations were formed only by special legislative action. In 1847 New York state passed first incorporation law. Criticism: Development of corporations invalidates theory of centralization. Increase in number of owners instead of decrease. However, number of stockholders not as large as commonly supposed. (5,000,000 stockholders as compared to 45,000,000 family units.) Also, separation of control and ownership brought about. Change in kind of property. From corporeal to incorporeal and intangible. Separation of control from owners. Contradicts theory of private property. Stockholders are assumed to exercise control by voting for directors, etc. However, voting not on basis of person but on basis of shares. Also, inconvenience of exercising voting power.

Law of Increasing Misery. In progress of capitalism the economic status of workers will become progressively worse and worse. Absolutely worse or relatively worse? Marx was analyzing 18th and 19th century laissez-faire capitalism in England. Many developments have taken place which Marx did not foresee. Attitude of people toward well-being is largely relative to the condition of others about them. Labor and property incomes, historically speaking, have remained stable (65% to labor and 35% to property). Marx: Drops assumption of stable rate of surplus value. If surplus value could be increased this would offset declining rate of profits brought about by increasing organic composition of capital. Factors which might increase rate of profits and the misery of worker. If real wages of workers could be decreased. Might be done by reducing necessary working time. Reason for employer resistance to any increase in wages. If hours of labor could be lengthened, with no increase in wages. By speeding up workers. Improvements in technique of production. Laborer can turn out more goods per day (Per unit period of time). Contradiction: increase in rate of surplus value but decrease in rate of profits. Organic composition of capital increases with utilization of more machinery, thereby putting downward pressure on profit rate. In theory of surplus value, Marx assumes that labor is paid its full value. Law of increasing misery deals with actual operation of a capitalist economy. Also surplus value theory deals with aggregate producers while the Law of Increasing Misery applies to individual producers.

Law of Industrial Reserve Army. Technological unemployment. Not all production is for buying and selling. Some produce for use-value (farmer raising some food for his own use). In a simple commodity-producing economy (C–M–C), the end in sight is to obtain use-value as a result of exchange of commodities for money. In capitalism, producer begins with a sum of money with which he buys commodities (capital machinery) which he uses to increase sum of his capital wealth. Not interested in use-value. End is to increase money. M–C–M′ = (M + *M). Production only comes about as a result of increase in M. Classical economists assumed that the economy was a C–M–C type with use-value as an end to production. Purpose is to increase capital. Increase of investment means increase in constant and variable capital. M used for this purpose. Results in increased demand for labor which decreases profits by forcing up wages. Contradiction: Profit rate should decline. Classical economists explained contradiction by Malthusian theory. Marx: Upward pressure is offset through substitution of machinery for human labor. This builds up industrial reserve army which can be drawn upon when rage rates tend to rise. With full employment wage rates will rise. This stimulates mechanization of industry. Number of laborers necessary is thereby decreased. Classical economists: Mechanization cannot displace workers permanently. They soon will be shifted to some other job. When a machine is introduced into an industry which is competitive, it reduces cost of production. This results in lower prices for output. Quantity to be sold increases. With elastic demand, as much or more labor will be required to produce increased goods for increased sales as was originally required. With inelastic demand, any labor displaced will automatically be reabsorbed in other industries.(C–M–C). Argument based upon Says Law with these assumptions: Supply creates its own demand. Human wants are insatiable. Neither lack of will or ability to buy. Therefore, never a lack of jobs if demands are never satisfied. Marx: Malthusian theory is only relatively valid. Laborers are displaced by machinery, thus building up the industrial reserve army. When a machine is introduced into a monopolistic industry, price would not necessarily fall with reduction in cost. Any reduction of price would not equal reduction in costs. Results in unemployment. Consumers do not have as much to buy commodities with as before; profits of capitalists are increased. These increased profits are then invested in new fields, resulting in increased employment, thereby absorbing workers displaced in original industry. Assumptions of above argument: Total income (purchasing power) of buyers is independent of the volume of employment, or is not affected by admitted displacement of labor as result of mechanization of industry. Laborers as means of production and wages as cost of production. Classical economists overlooked fact that wages are income to workers. If machinery displaces labor, those laborers have income reduced to zero. There is, then, a decrease in total money income unless it can be proved that incomes of others are increased by a like amount. Thus reduction in income reduces effective demand in all industries, spiraling down, etc. Assumes (inelastic demand) that additional employment created in other industries will off set unemployment in mechanized industry. Assumes (elastic demand) that mechanization will create new jobs for those temporarily displaced. Assumes no one withholds money. All money is used for either consumption or investment. Based on assumption that economy is simple commodity-producing one (C–M–C). Factors which have tended to absorb displaced laborers: Expanding markets, wars, Other factors which absorbed displaced laborers and which are no longer existent: Population increase. Enlarges markets and stimulates investment. Process of producing the new machinery. Creation of industrial machinery required huge amount of labor. Territorial expansion. These factors have been more than sufficient to offset technological unemployment.

Law of Crises and Depressions. Withholding of money from system causes breakdown in productive process (M–C–M'). In C–M–C economy there would be no reason for withholding money inside the economy. Classical and neo-classical economists assumed C–M–C. Therefore they said no factor in the economy could cause periodic booms and depressions. All of money income realized from sale of output would be spent in buying output. All output was then taken off the market. Depressions were explained in terms of effects of some non-economic forces which impinge upon the economic system. Physical factors: Sunspot theory by English neo-classical economist William Stanley Jevons. Moore – weather conditions, Venus. Human nature: John Stuart Mill. Psychological make-up of humans. Phases of optimism and pessimism occur in humans. Affects economic activity of entrepreneurs. Marx: Assumes causes are to be found within the capitalist economy. Capitalism generates causes of crises. Crises did not exist before advent of capitalism. Assumes M–C–M' (= M + *M). Anything which affects level of profits (*M), affects the economy. Any decline in level of profits below a certain point would cause decreased investment, less production, etc. And vice versa with rise in *M.

Law of falling rate of profits does not apply to cyclical fluctuations, but is rather a long trend.

Factors on which law of crises and depressions is based: (1) Based largely on theory of industrial reserve army. New inventions, technological progress do not occur at continuous rate. Very irregular development. Reduction of costs results in much-increased investment to avail themselves of new profits available by new process or invention. Rapid accumulation of capital results in increased demand for labor. During unemployment this labor is drawn from industrial reserve army. During full employment, wage rates are forced up until they become so high as to reduce entrepreneur's profits so that production is cut down, laborers laid off, depression, industrial reserve army again built up, and process starts over again with invention of new machine or process. If labor-saving machinery was available at desirable periods, it would be helpful in averting crises. Line of cause and effect runs from rate of accumulation of capital to volume of employment to level of wages to rate of profits to level of economic activity. (2) Unsatisfactory distribution of income between laborers and property owners. Marx never developed an under consumption theory as such, but one may be formulated from his writings.

Productive process should be ultimate consumption of goods turned out. In capitalist economy, consumption is not primary motive, but profits. Thus, contradiction between technological process of production and capitalist idea of realization of profits. Ultimate buyer furnishes motive to production of goods. Social relations force restriction of consumption and force increased production of goods. Workers receive wages and spend it largely for consumptive purposes. Can never furnish adequate market for output of industry at profitable prices. If they could and if carried to a logical conclusion, all output would then have to accrue to workers, thereby meaning no profits. Capitalists save much of their income to increase capital accumulation. Used to buy productive goods. Results in ability to produce more consumption goods, but social relations lead to inability to buy consumption goods.

EVOLUTIONARY SOCIALISM

Introduction

Marxian theory of history held that a socialist society would succeed capitalist economy. Would be brought about by forces within capitalist economy. Determined but not pre-determined. Veblen's criticism of Marx was directed primarily at the theory of history. Darwinian evolution – change but not toward any objective. Only this type of change is scientific. Marxism, then, was not scientific. Darwin generalized Malthusian theory of population increase to apply it to all animals. Survival of fittest in struggle for scarce food supply. Struggle between institutions and survival of institutions best fitted to social environment. In Darwinianism there is no objective, but in Marxism there is an objective. This is primary criticism of Veblen. (Social evolution is like *in kind* to biological evolution.)

Contradictions in Society. Marx applied theory of history to prediction of future conditions.

Downfall of capitalism did not come about when Marx predicted it would. He made errors in estimation in his predictions. Capitalist economies had greatest period of expansion from 1850 to 1900 and there very strong at beginning of 20th century. These factors brought about a split in socialist thinking. Germany, France, and Great Britain. This brought about evolutionary socialism. Marxism needed to be revised to bring theory into accord with the facts. Revisionists: Edward Bernstein. Fabians – Sidney and Beatrice Webb and George B. Shaw founded English movement.

Fabians: Aim at reorganization of society by the emancipation of land and industrial capital from individual and class ownership, and the vesting of them in the community for the general benefit. Only way the advantages of the country can be shared equitably by whole people. Work for extinction of private property in land and of consequent individual appropriation in form of rent for use of earth and resources therein. Work for transfer to community of the administration of such industrial capital as can conveniently be managed socially.

Held that evolution toward socialism was an evolution of a democratic, gradual, ethical, and peaceful character. Emphasis on *natural* evolution.

Revisionists: Collapse of capitalist system not imminent. Theory of social evolution was correct in general tendencies, but wrong in estimate of time evolution would take. Social conditions have not developed to so acute an opposition in classes as was depicted by Marx. Middle class. Development of corporations. Invalidated centralization of ownership. Middle class increasing in number and growing in strength. Concentration not borne out by facts. Many small-scale industries survived and even increased in number (agriculture, textile factories, retail merchandising, handicraft, co-op movement, etc.). Tendency was in opposite direction from large to small. Forces leading to centralization were not universal. Development of trade unionism with consequent bettering of working man's position. Invalidated law of increasing misery. Not one proletariat but many divided groups represented by unions of skilled workers. These groups were not interested in welfare of unskilled workers: AFL. Greater security for lasting success lies in a steady advance rather than by a catastrophic crash. Governments began assuming responsibility for welfare of laborers through passage of labor legislation. Also pointed to legislation which regulated certain aspects of capitalist economy which Marx had criticized.

Revisionists: If process of social evolution takes longer period of time, that process wily assume forms and lead to development of forms which could not be foreseen. Contradiction had not developed into acute stages which Marx had predicted but had been relieved by legislation, etc. Marxism should therefore be revised to fit the facts.

Objective of socialists: to organize workers into political parties and that these parties should take normal action to gain control of political government and thereby bring about principles of socialism. Pointed out that suffrage is now present to a much greater extent than in Marx's time and that weapon could be used to bring about social change instead of revolution. Suffrage in U.S. spread by competition between Western and Eastern states for population. Suffrage in G. Britain spread by political rivalry between Tories (land openers) and Liberalists (merchants and capitalists). Suffrage on the Continent brought about by various means. Immediate and particular social problems were objectives of socialists. Gradualism was favored by evolutionary socialists. Most pressing problem was to extend suffrage to workers in order to make desired changes by peaceful methods. Marx: Development of modern technology until conflicting relations become so acute that capitalism would break down. Definite degree of capitalist development. Class struggle as active agent to absolve contradiction set up by technology. Revisionists said these factors were not producing conditions which would lead to socialism. Better way to change than through class struggle. Interests of working class widely varied and sometime contradictory. Only a weak feeling of solidarity. Peaceful transition from capitalism to socialism was ultimate objective of the Revisionists. Appealed to middle-class intellectuals who desired social reform.

Significance of Evolutionary Socialism: Very radical break with Marx. Forces of production will be hampered by relations of production. This will be the beginning of a revolutionary period, during which an organized working class will overthrow capitalists and establish a new economic superstructure. Marx emphasized that capitalism is a temporary system and contains seeds of own destruction. Evolutionary socialists deny capitalism contains seeds of destruction. Persuasion and education are tools used to realize socialist goal, instead of revolutionary methods. Based on 'accidental' interpretation of history; man can establish type of economy desired. Result would be to eliminate Marxism from establishment of socialism. Gradual elimination of all evils of capitalism. Capitalism would exist indefinitely Effect would be not to establish socialism but to bolster up and perpetuate capitalism.

During latter half of 15th century, capitalism had its greatest growth. General outlook of people was optimistic; world looked secure, safe, etc. Since 1910, outlook has been radically changed by two World Wars and the depression of the 30's. Many capitalist countries have fallen or have been radically weakened. Also, there was the rise of two new economic systems – Soviet Russia and Fascist Germany. The events following 1910 seemed to bear Marx out; but in events preceding 1910 Marx seemed wrong. As a result, many evolutionary socialist movements became weaker while revolutionary socialists became stronger (Soviet Russia). Economic, social, and political events since 1910 have not been conducive to development of evolutionary socialism but have encouraged the spread of revolutionary socialism.

COMMUNISM

Introduction.

Twentieth century will be as much influenced by Russian revolution as much as the nineteenth century was influenced by French revolution (1789). Basic obstacles in way of study of Russian communism: Lack of historical perspectives, lack of reliable information, difficulty in maintaining a scientific objective. Communism strikes at heart of many of capitalism's basic institutions.

Physical Similarities between U.S. and U.S.S.R. Both are very large: U.S. – 3,000,000 square miles. U.S.S.R. – 8,250,000 square miles, nearly the size of the North American continent. This factor produces certain similar problems: (1) transportation, and (2) physical unification of people into one nation. For a long time the existence of geographical frontier influenced people and institutions of the U.S.. Same thing in U.S.S.R. today. Some degree of similarity in consequent developments. Both rather thinly populated. Dispersed. U.S. – 45 people per square mile. U.S.S.R. – 22 people per square mile. Both have had much room to expand without encroaching upon neighbors. Both are countries of polyglot people. Diverse social customs, nationalities, etc. Melting pots. U.S.S.R. on a much larger scale: 189 separate nationalities; 150 languages and dialects; 40 different religions. Social level fluctuated sharply between these groups. Both are very richly endowed with natural resources – forests coal, iron, copper, oil, manganese, etc. Most resources necessary to operation of modern industrial system with machine process.

Economic and political similarities: (1) Each born of a revolution. Pre-existing institutions destroyed and new civilization erected on ashes of old. (2) Revolutions There revolts of the common man against rights of the few. U.S. – middle class against aristocracy. U.S.S.R.-proletariat against small group of nobility and aristocrats. (3) Both are federal unions. Union of states with government based on written constitution.

U.S.S.R. composed of 16 union republics (states) with power divided between central government and state governments. Supreme Council is the highest legislative body. Two houses of equal powers. Members chosen directly by electors. Council of the Union. 600 deputies chosen on the basis of population. One deputy to each electoral district of 300,000 people. Council of the Nationalities. Deputies elected by political subdivisions (each Union Republic elects 25 members, etc.). To secure representation of all nationalities (resembles structurally the U.S. Senate). Constitution of U.S.S.R. provides for legislative, judicial, and executive branches of government. Balance of power not similar. Legislative branch has supreme power. (Similar to Britain). Representative government in U.S.S.R. with voters qualifications of 18 years, irrespective of race, social status, past activity, property relations, etc.

Determination of Soviet policy.

Economic policies of U.S.S.R. between the two World Wars: Sharp changes in economic policies. Abolition of capitalist money market, capitalist rewards to labor, etc., and establishment of communism. 1921 – slight reversion to capitalist theories and institutions. 1928 – First of 5-year Plans. Went back to socialistic trend. Policies based on opportunism or on determined policy and theory of Marx? Seems to be based upon policy and theory of Marx for a development of a socialist state. Stalin and Lenin – each economy is a link in a chain; therefore, they interact upon one another. Explanation of revolution in backward, underdeveloped Russia. Class struggle. Revolution brought about through instrument of a small, class-conscious group. Russian revolution occurred in manner in which Marx predicted, led by Lenin, Trotsky, etc.

Marxian theory of the state: as an instrument of class domination, tactic of revolution, dictatorship of the proletariat, and disappearance and withering away of the proletarian state.

The State as an Instrument of Class Domination. The state is a product of class divisions, conflicts, and antagonisms in society. Conflicting economic interests. Lenin – society divided against itself; contradictions. Purpose of the state is to keep down contradictions and maintain order. The state will exist only as long as classes exist. Is by its very nature a class organization. Controlled by dominant economic class and used as an instrument of exploitation of the economically weaker class. Instrument of power used by capitalist class to oppress the working class.

Tactic of Revolution. The state, therefore, cannot be used as a means of bettering the conditions of the oppressed class. Socialism cannot be realized by the use of parliamentary methods. State designed for protection and promotion of capitalist class. Cannot be used to realize the opposite purpose of protection and promotion of the proletariat. First necessary step toward the establishment of socialist state is the destruction of the state by direct, revolutionary action by the proletariat.

Dictatorship of the Proletariat. Communism can be realized not through capitalist state but through new apparatus created by proletariat. Workers' soviets set up by proletariat. To consolidate revolution and carry it to a conclusion is purpose of dictatorship of proletariat. New state apparatus needed. Set up by 1917 revolution. Tendency is to say that dictatorship of proletariat is merely a dictatorship of Communist Party. There is no one in Soviet Union who has absolute *legal* power to exercise powers of a dictator. Use dictatorship to mean control and use of state power by a class in the interests of the people. Structured form not important in definition of dictatorship, but important point is exercise of state powers by a class. Strong and resolute administration by the proletariat dictatorship of proletariat. Stalin-dictatorship is a dictatorship of the Communist party. Party not endowed by law to govern. The party has no legal authority to modify laws of Soviet Union. Acts on basis of persuasion rather than by legal means. Tremendous influence on policies of U.S.S.R. Stalin holds position similar to Prime Minister in England, President of U.S., etc. Communist party actions not based on legal actions but the party controls policies by controlling public opinion sources. Any state is regarded as a dictatorship of one class over another. Dictatorship lies in domination and not in structure. Communist party controls U.S.S.R. not through legal action. Is not a political party in U.S. sense. U.S. – Competition for political power. Relatively free to act. Parties do not stand for fixed, immutable policies. Policy varies with political tides. The larger the membership, the better; easy to join or resign.

U.S.S.R. – Membership severely restricted and function is totally different from U.S. political parties. A leadership organization. Function the formulation of policies and administration of policies through propaganda, etc. Lenin – Advantage of small, highly disciplined organization over large, unwieldy group which might develop factions and dissenting views. Class conscious, revolutionary-minded group. Will of members subjected to will of the party. Any sacrifice toward advancing policies of the party. Membership around 4 million (2%). Maintenance of power by Communist party by variety of means: (1) Persuasion and inducement rather than by force and threats. Effort to instill in workers devotions to ideals of communism. (2) Always acts as a unit. Active, highly-trained, rigid discipline. Unity of action and purpose is result. Individuals expected to criticize proposed policies but must accept policies after they are adopted by the party. (3) Elaborate, reliable system of reporting. Informed of opinions of whole country. Stands ready to modify policies (not aims) in response to public opinion. (4) Has definite, planned program. Complete set of principles, a theory, and a program based upon the theory. Party members must be in agreement on principles, theory, and program. Party members are trained to take political positions of power. (5) Leaders keep ears to ground. Policies may be changed to meet changed conditions. How does party safeguard itself against those who are not sympathetic toward party policy? Membership requirement extremely rigid. Ineligibles: Priests, private employers of labor, Czarist regime members. Must be recommended by 2 party members. Put on probation for 6 months. Peasants and white collar workers. Exercise of rigorous party code. 'Poverty, obedience, and chastity'. Income limited (however, royalties to authors, government officials' expenses, etc.). Obedience most strongly enforced. Moral conduct – judged from *effects* of action upon the party. Conduct of periodical purges: 2% expelled each year. For drunkenness, embezzlement, contrary political opinions, too close association with bourgeois influences. Wholesale purges. All party members must appear before boards to prove loyalty to party. U.S.S.R. seems to be operating economy on basis of Marxian theory. Opinion made on basis of Marxian theory of state.

Functions of Dictatorship of Proletariat. (1) Consolidating conquest of revolution. (2) Effect the transition from capitalism to communism through stage of socialism. Essential instrument to prepare way for and guide development of a socialist society to a communist society. Economic condition of U.S.S.R. would affect in no way the seizure of political power as concerns Marxian theory. Would eventually have an effect on economic institutions. First problem was to destroy capitalist regime of power and overthrow of the capitalist state. Dictatorship of proletariat must be maintained during transitional period. Economic policies then were designed to maintain the dictatorship. Post- war (war communism) policies determined by necessity and were not dictated by Marxian theory. NEP was not a retreat from Marxian theory. Lenin had no hard and fast far-ranging plan for future but held that changing conditions might bring necessity for changes in policy. (Objective never lost sight of.) It became necessary to meet demands of peasants in order to maintain dictatorship of proletariat (85% of population). They were given main desire, which was land and free market and therefore they acquiesced. First 5-year Plan socialized agriculture even against wishes of some of the peasants. During World War II, U.S.S.R. policies dictated by necessity. Postwar U.S.S.R.: Internal policies are determined by Marxian theory. External policies are affected by fact that it is a nation-state concerned with national interests such as national safety, foreign affairs, etc., much like any state power.

Goals of Communism in the Soviet Union

Goal of communism is not a dictatorship but a classless society. Dictatorship of proletariat merely a means to the end of a classless society. U.S.S.R. is a defective communist society. Capitalist principles carried over to the present communist society. Those who do not produce shall not eat. Distribution on basis of amount of work done. True communism: No state, no classes; distribution from each according to ability, to each according to need. Conditions of communism: No classes, no distinction between manual and intellectual labor, work no longer irksome, Increase in production, making distribution according to need possible.

In communist society all individuals will have the same access to the means of production. Abolishing capitalist institutions and development of a 'social conscience' will do away with need for a political state and will lead to a pure communist society. Lenin did not state how long it would take to establish the above Conditions or that they would ever be actually realized. Communist society (if established). There would be no political government. No use of physical force or coercion. All work voluntarily performed. No pecuniary reward. Absence of classes. (Class – relationship of people to means of production.

Purely economic.) Means of production collectively owned. Disappearance of division of labor. No group confined to one line of work or task. Abundance of wealth. Economy of plenty. Final goal is a classless society. Revolutionary Soviet leaders have succeeded in establishing a socialist society in U.S.S.R.

Some planning in *any* economy is necessary (technology, war, etc.). New Deal was partly socialist in function. Russia has developed into industrial nation with no disastrous business cycles.

Foreign policy of U.S.S.R.

Two considerations to be made in understanding actions of U.S.S.R.: (1) U.S.S.R. based on Marxism theory of socialism. Determines internal policies and actions. (2) U.S.S.R. is a great nation-state. Has vital national interests which they desire to protect. These interests are largely independent of type of government in power. Actions taken to protect these national interests are not based on Marxian socialist philosophy. Russian point of view influenced largely by long period of Czarist absolutism. Average Russian view on causes of World War II and things that should be established with the consequent peace differs greatly from Western viewpoint. U.S. – Wished to restore pre-war world conditions. U.S.S.R. – World War II caused by conflicts within societies of the great nation-states. European capitalist countries tried to isolate these conflicts by destroying U.S.S.R. Buffer states set up by capitalist countries to isolate U.S.S.R. These states became fascist. U.S.S.R. dose not want these conditions restored but wants these buffer states to be friendly to U.S.S.R. In the enemy states, the remnants of systems which had served fascism and Nazism would be swept away. Hoped for recognition by world that socialism had succeeded as evidenced by victories of Red Army. They never forget tremendous sacrifices and costs of defeating Germany. During World War II U.S.S.R. lost 7 million soldiers and 5–6 million civilians. Russian casualties at Stalingrad equaled all American casualties in both Europe and the Pacific.

At Kharkhov alone the Russians suffered as many casualties as the American forces suffered in the whole course of the Pacific War. Germany and her allies occupied large portion of U.S.S.R. Containing most industry of the nation. Russian viewpoint: Democratic elections in Spain, Argentina, etc., as well as in countries dominated by U.S.S.R. Trusteeship of Pacific Islands vs. Russian seizure of Karelia. Chaupultepec conference on 'solidifying' Western hemispheres. U.S.S.R. pacts with Eastern countries Middle Eastern oil not equally distributed when held by U.S. and Great Britain. Faction of U.S. & G.B. in UN vs. U.S.S.R. and Eastern nations. Russian mobilization vs. U.S. intention to have large air force and possession of atom bomb.

Thus the very origin of the State is bound up with class antagonism. It is evident that 'society thus far, based upon class antagonism, had need of the State'. But the forms of the State rest upon conditions of production, which as we have seen, determine classes of society. 'The will of the State as a whole, is declared ... through the domination of this or that Class, and in the last instance through the development of the forces of production and the conditions of exchange'. The State is therefore 'the summarized, reflected form of the economic desires of the class which controls production', and this is true of both the modern epic and 'the earlier epochs of history'.

An organ of class domination; the official form of the antagonism of classes in civil society; an organization for the oppression of one class by another. The four distinct features of the States: (1) The organization of inhabitants by territories. Overthrow of blood kinship groups. (2) The creation of the public power of coercion. It is an instrument of the ruling class, for it is divorced from the mass of the people. It constitutes the essence of the State. It is a concentrated and organized force with a historical tendency to grow stronger and stronger. (3) The right of levying taxes and contracting public debts. In order to maintain this power of coercion, contributions of citizens become necessary. Taxes are inadequate. The privileged position of state officials, raised above society. Purpose of the State: the protection of private property. Function of the State: the oppression of the non-possessing by the possessing classes.

Overthrow of bourgeois state by revolution. Brought about primarily by contradictions between forces and relations of production. Tactics: Organization of the proletariat: into a Class. into a political party. Practically synonymous. Proletariat must be united internationally. On its actual fight for emancipation, the proletariat should act differently according to the stage of the political development of its own country. Last decisive struggle to be fought out in the democratic republic. All legal and reformist measures are viewed not as a substitute for revolution by force, but as the auxiliary means to the overthrow of the bourgeois State. These measures are utilized simply for destructive purposes. All abstract conceptions and milder measures are rejected in Marxian tactics. Important: Marxian tactic is dynamic, not static. The general outline was laid down, its details are not fixed. It must make due allowance for the relationships existing in various phases of the development of various societies.

Notes from Lenin's State and Revolution, p. 745, 748, 750;
Engels Handbook of Marxism, p. 328.

... as long as the proletariat still needs the State, it needs it not in the interests of freedom, but for the purpose of crushing its antagonists; and as soon as it becomes possible to speak of freedom, then the State, as such, ceases to exist.

Democracy for the vast majority of the people, and suppression by force, i.e., exclusion from democracy, of the exploiters and oppressors of the people -this is the modification of democracy during the *transition* from capitalism to Communism. p. 745.

What we are dealing with here is not a Communist society which has *developed* on its own foundations, but, on the contrary, one which is Just *emerging* from capitalist society, and which therefore in all respects – economic, moral and intellectual still bears the birthmarks of the old society from whose womb it sprung. p. 748.

And so, in the first phase of Communist society (generally called Socialism) 'bourgeois right' is not abolished in its entirety, but only in part, only in proportion to the economic transformation so far attained, i.e., only in respect of the means of production. 'Bourgeois right' recognizes them as the private property of separate individuals. Socialism converts them into common property. To *that extent*, and to that extent alone, does bourgeois rights disappear. p. 750.

Notes from the Origin of the Family by Freidrich Engels. (From the Handbook of Marxism, p. 328.)

The State is therefore by no means a power imposed on society from the outside; just as little is it 'the reality of the moral ideas,' 'the image and reality of reason' as Hegel asserted. Rather, it is a product of society at a certain stage of development; it is the admission that this society has become entangled in an insoluble contradiction with itself, that it is cleft into irreconcilable antagonisms which it is powerless to dispel. But in order that those antagonisms, classes with conflicting economic interests, may not consume themselves and society in sterile struggle, a power apparently standing above society becomes necessary, Whose purpose is to moderate the conflict and keep it within the bounds of 'order'; and this power arising out of society, but placing itself above it, and increasingly separating itself from it, is the State.

The three great forms of exploitation: (1) Slavery in the world of antiquity, (2) Serfdom in the middle ages, (3) Wage labor in the more recent period. p. 335.

The Party: (1) The party is the vanguard and General Staff of the proletariat. It must be bound very closely with the class. (2) In order to lead the working class, the Party must be an organized detachment, composed of members of unwavering loyalty and discipline. (3) The Party is the highest form of class organization of the proletariat. For the purpose of guiding and directing all proletarian organizations in the same channel the Party must exercise paramount influence. (4) The Party is the weapon and machinery for the purpose of achieving and maintaining the dictatorship of the proletariat. (5) The Party is the expression of the unity of will, and is incompatible with the existence of factions. (6) The Party is strengthened by purging itself of opportunist elements.

FASCISM

Characteristics of 'Official' Fascist Philosophy

Vague in nature as compared to capitalism and socialism. Intellectual background also rather vague. Fascists consider themselves men of action rather than theorists.

Actions are taken and then theories worked out to fit the actions and rationalize them. Machiavelli; Pareto; Trieachie, German philosopher. Sorel – French syndicalism. Advocated leadership of the elite who possessed the genius of the people. Hegel – German philosopher. (I) State as the ultimate and absolute social organism; (2) mystical nationalism.

Fascist theory – anti-rational and anti-intellectual. Revolt against rationalism of 18th and 19th century. (Science, laissez-faire capitalism, Marxian socialism.) Seeks to arouse feelings and emotions rather than reason. Appeals to folklore, prejudices, biases, rather than to facts. Answers questions by force and authority rather than by facts. History determined by strength and will-power of Great Men. Theory of State. Unlimited and irresponsible sovereignty of the State over individuals. Regulates every aspect of human existence. All things subordinate to the state. The state is an end in itself as opposed to Marxian socialist theory that state is merely a means to an end. The state is regarded as an actual existing entity. Main function – to safeguard the spirit of the race. Individual exists for the State. Many duties, no rights. Individuals should subject himself to whatever State may demand. Supremacy of the State must be maintained at all costs, irregardless of scarifies required of individuals. Denies representative government based on universal suffrage. Individuals lack intelligence to govern themselves. Final decisions to be made by one man. The elite – those who have intelligence and capacity to govern. Chain of authority runs from the highest officials down through the lesser officials to the people. Chain of responsibility runs from the bottom up. Fascist theory is reactionary in that it looks back instead of forward.

Observations on Fascism by Rauschning, Laski, Neumann, and Sweezy.

In general, they say that fascism has no basic philosophy; that the 'official' philosophy is merely a means of propagandizing the people. Only symbolic value. Aims of Fascism: Rauschning. A ruthless and calculating pursuit of power by leaders for destruction of everything that is. Laski. Power built upon terror and hopes which conquests give rise to. Organizing principle, if any, is that power is the sole good. How to account for seizure of power by fascists? Possible only when people are confused as to objectives of society. Expression of society in process of dissolution. Fear overwhelms hope. Procedures of society are thrown aside because common agreement cannot be reached. All sense of security is gone. Various groups are set off against one another. Power of state to enforce laws is weakened drastically. Outlaw is in position to challenge the State power itself. If State is incapable of bringing about order, then the outlaw is given free rein to remedy conditions. Large industrialists (profits), small merchants (free competition), workers (wages and interest), and ex-soldiers supported Hitler. All of these groups thought their interests would best be represented by Hitler. All rules of society must be swept aside. First, he must pacify his fellow-outlaws; second, he must sweep aside all opposition to his own rules. Fascism a result of the decay of capitalism. Expediency of property owners in reacting against social legislation seeking to modify relations of production. A destruction of capitalism. Use nationalism to justify foreign conquest which will relieve decay of capitalism. Dictator must then solve problems which allowed him to gain power. Constitution is swept away and dictator becomes supreme law of the land. Rule of terror and propaganda then take over. Exploit to the limit national patriotism. Large army necessary for this. Therefore, whole economy of nation must be geared for war. To have no fixed principles or policy. Actions determined on basis of expediency. Neumann. (Marxian). Fascists have no basic policy or aims. Device for manipulating the masses. Domination of the people. Disagrees as to character and objectives of fascism. Aim: Maintenance, preservation, and promotion of monopoly capitalism. Profits cannot be made without totalitarian political power. Monopoly capitalism cannot exist with: Democracy (government by people), liberty of contract, freedom of trade and investment, freedom of labor. Monopoly capitalism extremely sensitive to cyclical and structural changes which leads to control of credit structure. Fascism would appear as a totally monopolistic capitalist economy. Paul Sweezy. (Also a Marxian). Agrees largely with Neumann. Emphasizes international aspects of fascism. Fascism is one of the forms which imperialism assumes in age of wars of re-division of world among big powers. Several advanced capitalist nations about equal economically. Monopoly capitalism dominant. Contradictions have reached such a stage of maturity that capital export becomes outstanding feature of world economic relations. Severe rivalry between countries, with rise of cartels. Territorial divisions of unoccupied parts of the world between large nations. In advanced countries, nationalism and militarism necessary to imperialism. Incentive to people and growth of State power. Fascism develops as a result of rise of imperialism. Contradictions of capitalist economies. Effects of international wars upon the economies of the nations of the world. Internal structures of nations involved are weakened. The conditions give rise to revolution which may result in: (1) counter-revolution, (2) Socialist revolution, or (3) a stalemate in which classes are in a state of equilibrium. Working class shares in power, has unions, bargaining power, etc. Capitalists still have control of means of production. This condition is very unstable since great pressure is put on profit rate by virtue of working man's strength. Industrialists then maintain monopoly by prices. Middle class impoverished and middle class becomes unemployed as a result of technology. Resulting disorder leads to development of fascism.

Marxian Viewpoint of Fascism

Fascism does not affect basically the class struggle. Theory held that rich must remain rich and the poor, poor. Lower class interests subordinated to those of the State. Fascism – replacement of capitalist democracy by totalitarian capitalism of capitalist monopolies. German and Italian fascism had support of big business. Fascism repaid this debt by destroying labor unions, laws, etc. Facts underemphasized by the Marxists. Fascists could build great mass movements which appealed to all discontented groups in the community. Techniques of building mass movements: Skillful exploitation of nationalistic spirit. Offered expansion through action. (Economic uncertainty, Treaty of Versailles, anti-Semitism.) Economic depression: Capitalists feared laborers' mood and welcomed anyone who assured them that working movement sentiment would be destroyed. Labor movement torn by conflict between left and right. Bitter struggle.

Fascists were more skillful in propaganda than left groups and stole thunder of revolutionary socialists. Left had never developed method of bringing about revolution which they favored. Built on fear between groups and promises to those groups. Lower middle class was backbone of fascism in Germany. Lost heavily in chaotic inflation. Lower middle class sees itself squeezed between monopoly capitalism and demands of workers movements. Blames depression on monopoly capital and monopoly labor. Middle class interests favor: restoration of strong State power, war of revenge, destruction of labor unions, etc. The use of power was more than just a simple tool in hands of monopoly capital. Fascism was driven to destruction of liberal capitalism. Problems which Fascists had to solve in order to retain power: (1) Unemployment could not be solved by initiative of free private business enterprise. Reasons: inflation, economy depression, destruction brought by war. (2) Unemployment could not be solved by inflation because memory of the chaotic inflation was still in the German mind. Embarking upon a tremendous public works program was the answer to unemployment. Spirited foreign policy necessary to restoration of national tradition. Large rearmament program probably necessary to recovery of German economy. Served two-fold purpose of re-arming nation and restoring national tradition and glory. Therefore, jobs were providing for the unemployed, and made it possible to back up the new spirited foreign policy. Government had to control investment in order to maintain armament program. Also had to control exports and imports in order to dovetail everything with armament program. Profits had to be retained in industry in order to build up economy.

Rearmament brought rise in wages and, consequently, prices – bringing inflation. In order to combat this, the government had to fix prices and wages. Price fixing required rationing. By 1939, capitalism in German, and Italy had lost all traces of 'liberal' capitalism. State capitalism replaced 'liberals capitalism'. State carried right to intervene in the economy if political interests or over-all safety were endangered. Business enterprise was promised security from competition, socialism and communism, and labor disturbance. Restriction on wages (labor unions) brought about reduction in purchasing power which destroyed many small businesses. However, big business was limited to purpose of the state program. Since Nazi party is in control of political power, they determine the policies of the state program. These party leaders make decisions designed to keep themselves in power.

Most of productive forces were going to the armament program. Nazis had to combat discontent by doing two things: (1) Control profits to pacify wage earners. However, this did not create hope for better conditions. (2) Had to promise great future benefits for present sacrifices through imperialistic foreign conquest. Conquest was inevitable end of fascism. It was necessary in order to restore the economy and restore the national tradition. Program won approval of all groups through restoration of national prestige and of each individual group for its own interests.

Comparison of Fascism and Communism

Development of communism. Revolution of the working class. Immediate goal: socialist state. Ultimate goal: communist state. Development of fascism. Fascism rose in countries with a disappointed national ambition as a result of World War II. Came as a result of wanting to restore national wealth and prestige. No goal of bringing about a revolution of classes. Essentially a counter-revolution. By its very nature, fascism led to war, destruction of Western institutions, etc. Russians also had similar problems to those of the fascists, with exception of restoring national tradition: Employment and depression taken care of by: unlimited resources, increasing population. (Unlimited market.) No *economic* incentive to foreign conquest. No basis in socialist theory for international wars in order to bring about a socialist, and eventually, communist society. Brought about through class revolution transcending national borders. Search for raw materials and/or markets are factors which lead to international wars between large nations. Both U.S.S.R. and U.S. have abundant supplies of most raw materials. U.S.S.R. for years will have to import capital goods and export raw materials. U.S., as a mature industrial nation, exports primarily capital goods.

Similarities of fascism and communism: Both opposed to laissez-faire economics. Subject social life to regulation. Disparage parliamentary government. Permit only one political party. Antithetical to liberal capitalism. Almost nothing positive in common. Communism is working class movement. Fascism is financed by industrial capitalists. Fascism preserves private property, free enterprise, and profits. Fascism proclaims sovereignty of the State. Communism professes to destroy the State.

ECONOMICS 389: MARXIAN AND NEO-CLASSICAL ECONOMIC THEORY (DEVELOPMENT OF ECONOMIC THOUGHT FROM 1848–1900)

Edward Everett Hale

MARXIAN ECONOMIC THEORY

Marxian theory was first developed by Karl Marx (and Engels). Later contributions have been made by Lenin and Stalin. Stalin's major contribution was that he built an economic system on the Marxian theory, in one country. Mao Tse-tung built his system not on the industrial proletariat, but on the peasants. Lenin and Stalin were not much interested in the peasants; their major interest was to keep the peasants quiet in the period they built their Marxian economy based on the industrial worker.

Paul M. Sweezy says: "Marxian economics is essentially the economics of capitalism while 'capitalist' economics is in a very real sense the economics of socialism."[1] The reason is that the whole Marxian theory is an analysis of the capitalist economy. Marx's theory and analysis is strictly in the classical tradition, and he drew heavily on Ricardo and Smith; however, they came to different conclusions. Marx tried to find the 'laws' of capitalism. His economics is not economics of socialism. Marxian economics is the theory of capitalism.

Edward Everett Hale: The Writings of an Economic Maverick, Volume 19-B, pages 139–275.
2001 by Elsevier Science B.V.
ISBN: 0-7623-0694-7

MARX'S THEORY OF HISTORY

In his economic analysis, Marx applied his theory of history to a contemporary stage in economic development. Those of you who have had economics
388 (classical economic theory) will remember that my (Hale's) point of view
is that economic theory is never motivated by what Veblen called 'idle
curiosity'. It arises out of economic problems and issues of its time. It has a
very practical objective. The economists developed theories in order to solve
problems. All schools of thought have this objective; however, the marginal
utility school is hard to fit in here, but even in this case the objective was to
a limited extent to find a theory for policy. It is certainly true in the case of
Marx. He wanted to find a basis for his policy recommendations. Marx was a
very complex personality, more so than most other people. He was a philosopher and a revolutionary; and of the two aspects the revolutionary was the
primary aspect. It does not mean that Marx created theory in order to obtain
an 'apology' for the achievement of certain objectives. Marx was a scholar who
was seeking the truth. Like Adam Smith, the advocate of *laissez faire*, Marx
developed his theory on the basis of which he made certain policy recommendations (opposite to those of Smith). Both Smith, Marx, and Keynes developed
theories and recommended certain actions, but you cannot conclude on the basis
of this fact that they simply 'cooked' a theory to fit their objectives.

Of course, it is difficult to say with accuracy whether their theories influenced 100% of their policy recommendations or whether they had an idea of
the best policy and to a certain degree developed their theories as a rationale
for their policy recommendations. But it is surely wrong to assume that these
scholars simply 'cooked' up a theory in order to support a preconceived goal.
They were all seekers of the truth.

Philosophers have always tried to understand the world; have attempted to
ascertain causes of change in the world; and to discover the motivating forces
which bring about change and development. (If you, as in the case of Marx,
are interested in bringing about changes or promoting changes in the social
order, you have to know the forces which bring about this change.)

There have been thousands of theories with regard to the change creating
forces. One of many is the 'great man' theory, which is still widely held. Such
men as Alexander the Great, Caesar, Napoleon, even Hitler have been assumed
(and are still assumed) to be the factors which have caused social change, historical change. Marx inquired into the sources and causes of institutional change.
Why is society organized on the basis of feudalistic institutions at one stage in
history and on institutions of a commercial nature at another stage in history?
The first part of Marx's thesis is that: (1) the most significant fact in human

society is to make a living. This is done by acquiring those goods and services on which human life is dependent. If man does not succeed in acquiring the means of subsistence then he dies, passes away, and philosophy, art, religion, literature and other aspects of culture are not matters to worry about. Food, clothing, housing, and other necessities are basic in human life; only after these things have been acquired does man devote himself to philosophy, religion, art, literature, etc. (2) The second question is: what is necessary to make a living? Marx answered: in almost all societies known hitherto two things are necessary. According to Marx, these two 'things' are:

(1) *The forces of production.* In this concept are included: labor power (all the mental and manual and managerial skills of human beings) and the things which result from men's labor power: tools, machines, scientific knowledge and 'know-how'. These things are the factors which constitute the Marxian concept of the powers of production. Quite similar to the Veblenian and Ayresian concept of technology.

(2) The second force, or means·to making a living, which is essential in any class society (not essential in a classless society) constitutes what may be called 'the rules of the game'. (This is somewhat similar to the Veblenian and Ayresian concept of institutions, but not quite the same). That is to say, in order to carry on any process of production you have to have a functional division of labor along class lines (some work for others, some control those working for others). In any society you have to have such a division of labor. Some problems have to be solved in order to let production go on. Some mechanism must be set up to solve the problems. *The* problem is the problem of the economic order. How is the allocation of resources to be made?

The set of forces involved in the 'rules of the game' is what Marx called *the relations of production* (as mentioned above, this concept is somewhat similar to the Veblenian/Ayresian concept of institutions; but not quite the same). The forces include those that determine the allocation of resources, the incentive to get resources into action, and the distribution of the output. The relations of production have two aspects: (1) relations between men and things – property relations – and (2) relations between men and men – social relations. The property relations may range the whole way from private enterprise to state ownership. The personal (social) relations may range the whole way from slavery to men working according to contract.

Marx defined classes as determined by the type of relationship between men and the means of production and by the type of relationship between men and men. In a classless society, men have the same relation to property and to themselves (man to man). In such a society, no jobs would result from ownership. There would still be different types of jobs, but managerial functions would not be limited to a managerial class. In a classless society, Marx assumed that different types of jobs would be attractive to different persons. In a class society, people are not attracted to manual labor because of the class stigma attached to manual labor. The forces of production and the relations of production make up society. (As mentioned above, the first concept is equal to technology and the second concept is somewhat similar to institutions in Veblen's work).

Inasmuch as the making of a living is essential, all other things must depend, or rely on it. Consequently, the forces and relations of production are basic. Other aspects of society and culture are ultimately conditioned by this system. These other aspects are such things as government, ethics, literature, philosophy, art, etc., every aspect of society. All these things Marx called '*the social superstructure*'.

The sequence is this: the forces of production are basic and they determine ultimately the relations of production; next the entire social superstructure (art, philosophy, government, etc.) is ultimately determined by the relations of production; that is, you move from the forces of production to the relations of production, and from there to art, philosophy, government, etc.

The relations of production are property relations (relations of men to things) and personal relations (men to men; such as slave owners to slaves, etc.). These (economic) relations shape all other aspects of society such as government and culture, arts, religion, philosophy, etc. The reason for this is that all these social arrangements have only one purpose: to compel men to conform to the present relations of production, to protect the owners of the means of production, to compel workers to carry out their contracts. The fundamental purpose of the legal system, for example, is to protect private property and relations among men once they have entered into a contractual relationship. The same is true of our moral ideas. Theft is frowned upon because it does violence to property relations, etc.

According to Marx, the reason that the American constitution protects property is simply that this is its function as a part of the social superstructure.

The relations between religion and the economy were studied by Weber and by Tawney is his *Religion and the Rise of Capitalism*. Capitalism required a Protestant religion. It had to get rid of feudalism of which the Catholic Church was an inherent part and supporter. Hence in order to foster capitalism, it was necessary to get rid of the Catholic Church and establish a church which would be conducive to the rise of capitalism which is anti-feudalistic in spirit.

What causes social change?

The forces of production are highly dynamic (like 'technology'); they never stand still; man is ever extending his know-how, he invents new tools; each generation builds on and extends the achievements of past generations.

The relations of production, on the other hand, are static and change-resisting (like 'institutions'). The reason for this is that any set of relations of production means that *one* class stands in a position of having power, prestige and control. In a class society this controlling class is composed of the property owners. Any class that derives its power from its position in the relations of production will not give up its superior position. The dominant class prefers to maintain the existing relations of production; it will not give up its position. The dominant class prefers to maintain the existing relations of production and resists or prevents other classes from threatening its position. As the property owners constitute the ruling class, they are in a position to fend off any threat.

At any point in time, the relations of production may be adjusted to the forces of production and you have efficiency in production and distribution. As the forces of production are dynamic, however, they develop and expand cumulatively. The relations of production, on the other hand, are static. Therefore the 'spread' between these two factors increases and results in increasing conflict between the two factors, and it becomes more and more difficult to make efficient use of the forces of production. Sooner or later, it becomes impossible to utilize the increased efficiency of the factors of production. You have contradiction and conflict between the two factors. (It becomes impossible to make use of the advanced technology within the framework of the system; it becomes impossible to keep all workers employed; you have unemployment, crises, etc., because of the resistance of the relations of production).

The Stage is Set for Social Change

What is called for is a revision in the relations of production; a setting-up of a new set of relations of production, adapted to the dynamically changed forces of production. According to Marx, the only way to do this is through the class struggle. The class struggle is the result of: (1) the relations of production (the social structure), and (2) the contradiction between the forces of production and the relations of production.

The exploited class (the proletariat under capitalism, the serfs under feudalism) will gain from a change, whereas the exploiters gain from no change (in the relations of production).

[Marx on ideas: Marx believed that ideas do not develop in a vacuum and once they are there they become a fact just like any other fact. Thus ideas can be used like any other fact. Marx does not deny the value of ideas nor the place of ideas in the process of change. What he does deny is that ideas develop out of nothing. Our ideas, for example, are different from those of our predecessors. Ideas, such as the idea of the importance of 'great men', play a part in making history. Economic forces are the ultimate causes and sources of history, however. In other words, history has more to do with making men great than great men have to do with making history!]

This raises the question of whether or not Marxian theory is teleological.[2] I say yes and no. I must agree with Douglas Dacy (unpublished U.T. thesis) that the dialectics implies teleology. Dialectics is used as a final term by Hegel and Marx. The final term is the classless society, the ultimate result of the class struggle. In a classless society all individuals stand in the same relation to the forces of production; nobody has a special interest in maintaining existing situations. In this sense Marx is teleological.

For Veblen there is no final term, no end to the process of social development. In this sense the Veblenian scheme is *not* teleological.

Marx is not teleological in the sense that the course of process towards a final term is fixed in the beginning. Everything is brought about by causes. If causes are different, different results will materialize. Most people think that Marx's theory is a theory of inevitability, from capitalism to socialism and from socialism to communism. If you by inevitability mean that Marx thinks that everything is pre-determined then he does not have a theory of inevitability.

Another philosopher [blank] said that if he knew everything which had happened in the past in the universe he would be able to predict what would happen in the future. This statement involves the assumption that there are no causes for development; what will happen has already happened, and what has happened in the past has no importance in the future. So the whole past can be scratched out and so can the future. This is a theory of pre-determination. There is a no cause-and-effect relationship. It does not matter what people will do, the course of events goes on irrespective of people's actions.

Marx did not think that he inevitably could predict the classless society. If he believed that he would not have devoted his whole life to stir up revolution. He thinks that the class struggle has to be stirred up and that is the task of the revolutionist. If people are not told so, they have no concept of class-consciousness.

Maybe the Veblenian thesis has an element of inevitability to a larger degree than the Marxian scheme, because Veblen did not try to take part in the parade. 'Veblen was sitting in the grandstand looking at the parade'. Marx on the other hand, 'took part in the parade, marching ahead waving the banner'. Marx did all that he could to stir up the class struggle; he believed that you could stir up the class struggle and speed up the process of social change. Lenin said that never had he nor anyone else said that the communist society would be obtained. It depended on the circumstances. He probably assumed, however, that the probability of realizing the communist society was great.

In the Veblenian scheme we are, during the process of change, influenced by technology, which influence causes social change. In this scheme social change depends on change in ideas brought about under the impact of the dynamic force of technology.

Marx never denied that ideas and great men had influence on the cause of history, but he denied that ideas and great men were basic. Had Napoleon not lived in a period of war, he would not have become a 'great' general and dictator. Napoleon was the result of circumstances of history.

For Marx the ultimate result of the conflict between forces and relations of production, the classless society, would not be a stationary state, because technology will go on. Further stages are not, however, implemented by the class struggle. Perhaps this would be the Veblenian world. Marx had a stage theory of evolution whereas Veblen had a theory of continuous development.

It is a strange phenomenon that when the Bolshevik revolution took place in Russia, Veblen (who was at that time with the *Dial*) was sympathetic to the revolution. This in spite of the fact that the Bolshevik revolution was a Marxian revolution and Veblen had been highly critical of Marxian theory. In all his writings on the Russian revolution Veblen never mentioned Marx or Marxism.

There is no doubt that Veblen got certain elements of this theory – technology and institutions – from Marx, but Veblen never recognized the influence of Marx on his thinking. In general he never made a footnote in his publications except to refer to his own works.

Marxian Economic Theory

As we have seen, Marxian economics is simply a particular application of his theory of history to a certain point in economic development. As the factors which bring about change in the social order are the forces of production and relations of production and the conflict between these two forces, and as Marx wants to bring about change, he is naturally searching for these forces. His theory of capitalism is aimed at discussing the nature of the contractions between the forces and relations of production.

The amazing thing about Marx's economic theory is that it is derived from Adam Smith and David Ricardo. He takes the theories of these men and draws different conclusions. He does make some changes.

The Labor Theory of Value

The labor theory of value came from John Locke. He used it to justify the institutions of private property in a society with division of labor. How division of labor is brought about, and how the labor theory is applied is shown by Smith in *Wealth of Nations*. Locke assumed that everyone had a natural right to dispose of what he has produced by his own labor. But when you have an economy with division of labor, individuals produce only part of the goods they use themselves; they sell their own produce and buy that of other people. So what they produce they do not own, and what they own they do not produce. However, the individual still commands the value of his own labor, because he exchanges the produce of this own labor for the produce of an equal amount of labor. So the labor theory of value excuses the institution of property, an excuse biased on many assumptions. Even Locke treats inheritance differently from 'self-created' property. He admits that inheritance should be taxed, because an inheritance tax is basically a tax on the right of transfer, not a tax on the property itself.

Marx takes the labor theory of value and uses it in his own scheme of theoretical analysis. He seeks a unit. According to Marx, the significant factor about capitalism is that it is a commodity producing economy.

The Commodity

Looked at from the point of view of the basic device on which the capitalist economy relies in order to solve the problems of economic order – allocation of resources, incentive to utilize resources, distribution of income – capitalism is a market economy. It relies on the 'free' market. Marx follows the classical economists in that respect, i.e., he assumes free competition. This goes on to mean that he is unaware of the existence of monopoly, but the reference on which Marx relies is the British economy in the 19th century and it was not too unrealistic to assume competition.

In the capitalist economy each individual relies on production and sale for a living. Because of this fact Marx selects a commodity as his unit of investigation. A commodity has four characteristic which make it proper as a unit of investigation.

These four characteristics must be present in any good to make it a commodity.

It must possess use value. This idea in Marx is not quite the same as Smith's concept, but is very similar. It is identical to Ricardo's concept of use value, i.e., the ability to satisfy wants. It is an absolute term.

It must be produced for sale in the market. The purpose of producing a commodity is to offer it for sale. Only goods which enter the market are commodities. Certain processes will therefore be outside the capitalist economy, e.g., goods produced for their own use by farmers. Such phenomena occur in any system, that is, there are certain processes which are not part of the system within which they take place. No system is 100% pure.

It must be a product of human labor. Labor must have been expended on its production. Any good existing in nature which is in a form to satisfy human want without labor being expended on it is not a commodity. The classicists assumed land and natural resources to fall in this category. Virgin land may be such a good. [Virgin land is of course outside the economy, so in fact it is no good at all: however, the classicists assumed it to be so.]

It must be separable from labor, able to be sold apart from the person who has expensed his labor on it. This is not a necessary prerequisite to distinguish capitalism from slave economy. Under capitalism, the laborer sells his labor skill, not himself.

A student had the opinion that Marx required a good to have a physical appearance in order to be a commodity. If this were the case, labor power would be ruled out as a commodity and this fact would contradict the whole Marxian scheme. Hale finds the source of difficulty in a lapse in the part of the translator of the Modern Library edition (a translation from the 4th German edition, whereas the older American edition is a translation of the 3rd German edition of Das Kapital). The statement regarding the physical form of the commodity is not found in the older American edition, and must be based on a misunderstanding of the German text. Marx could not possibly have meant that a good must have a 'physical' appearance in order to be a commodity; such a statement would have rendered his entire theory invalid.

These definitions are important. You cannot criticize definitions as definitions; you can only say that a concept defined is useless for the purpose to which it is put. Definitions will always be more or less arbitrary. You cannot criticize definitions as such. Marx is interested in an investigation of the capitalist economy and tells us clearly that this is his purpose, so we must accept it. It is the same with Ricardo. He limited his investigation to reproducible goods and you cannot criticize Ricardo on this ground. It is his privilege to investigate, and to limit his investigation to, reproducible goods. All you could say is that you would not limit yourself to such an investigation. So with Marx, much of the criticism of Marx is beside the point, because it has been directed towards his selection of topics for inquiry.

Commodities are bought and sold in the market. Marx took a look at the conditions in the capitalist world and saw that the process in the market had strange elements. One was that all commodities exchange in the market at definite ratios to one another. This is the case whether you derive the ratio directly by exchanging commodity for commodity, or indirectly by the use of money.

1oz. gold = 1 ton coal = 10 yds. Cloth = 10 bushels wheat. This means that when you take commodities in certain given quantities they are equal to each other; any commodity is, in a certain proportion, equal to another. Marx says that this means: (1) all commodities have some one element in common and (2) this common element exists in certain *measurable* quantities in all commodities. So when two commodities are equal it means that this common element exists in the same quantity in both commodities. If they did not have this common element they could not be equal. What is this common element? Marx arrives at the answer in a somewhat dangerous way, i.e., by the process of exclusion, one by one of the elements they cannot have in common. This is dangerous because you cannot be sure that you have excluded all the elements which are not common in the two commodities.

Elements which are not common, and which therefore Marx excludes, are such things as shape, weight, chemical elements, physical elements, mass, geometrical properties, etc. All these can be ruled out because these components are not to be found equally in say gold and cloth, cloth and coal, coal and wheat, etc. And here Marx gets out of dangers resulting from the process of exclusion, because all these qualities give commodities use *value*, not *exchange value* (referring to ratio or exchange between different commodities). With respect to use value different commodities are *qualitatively* different; physical, chemical properties and so on give commodities different use value because they give different commodities different want-satisfying abilities. *Marx follows Adam Smith by saying that the use value of shoes and bread are different, because they serve to satisfy different, immeasurable and incommensurable wants.* Commodities are, however, equal in exchange value in a certain proportion; on the other hand, use value is different in different commodities. (2) *Marx therefore rules out use value.*

You have then: (1) the power of a good to command another commodity in the market has relation to its exchange value, whereas (2) use value is the want-satisfying ability of a commodity. Marxian analysis eliminates (2).

Exchange value is a ratio and therefore represents a *quantitative* and *measurable* relationship. When certain commodities have the same exchange value they exchange one to another in certain quantities. This relationship cannot be based on use value, because use value is a *qualitative* matter and differs from commodity to commodity.

Now the question is what determines exchange value. To solve this problem we have to locate or isolate the element common to all commodities. Marx has ruled out all want-satisfying qualities – use value, so that the only element left is human labor. All commodities are produced by human labor. All commodities may be considered embodying labor.

The element common in all commodities which makes them equal in exchange value is human labor – embodied human labor. This embodied labor is what Marx calls Value. The three Marxian concepts of value are: (1) *use value,*

(2) *exchange value,* and (3) *embodied labor or value. When commodities are equal, it means they have the same Value.* Exchange value is determined by the quantity of labor required to produce the commodities. Exchange value is a relative matter (one bushel of wheat for five pair of shoes), *but Value is an absolute matter.* [Ricardo's value was a relative term.] What makes exchange value relative is that the same quantity of labor produces either one bushel of wheat or five pair of shoes. The embodied labor, Value, is the same, whereas the quantity of the two commodities are different. The exchange ratio is therefore determined by the absolute matter, Value, which enters the two commodities in the same amount. That the different commodities' Value is determined by embodied labor is Marx's *first approximation.*

What is the critique which can be leveled? Is it possible to compare two commodities which are quantitatively different unless they can be reduced to a common denominator? Exchange value is a quantitative matter.

In the Marxian scheme each individual is legally free to sell and exchange goods in the market; no policeman forces people to sell or buy; they are legally free to do so – economically it is different. In a capitalist economy the only way to produce is for the market, it is the only way to earn a living. If a person earns his living in another way, he is not operating within the framework of capitalism. Marx is only concerned with the fact that if a man wants a ton of coal he has to give up ten yards of cloth or one oz. of gold or five pairs of shoes. Up to this point in this analysis, Marx is only interested in the fact that goods exchange in certain ratios, *which is a fact.* So far we have only got definitions (sic).

Marx's fundamental assumption is that all goods have a common element, a common denominator; use value is dropped. In exchange value only quantitative comparison is of importance to Marx. [Nassau W.] Senior could not reduce pain cost and abstinence to a common denominator; therefore comparison was rendered impossible.

What Marx does is abstract from all use value (labor power has of course use value in itself.) What he means is that in all commodities there is a common denominator. Commodities differ only in quantity – one oz. of gold sells for $35, one pair of shoes for $10—this is a quantitative difference. The common denominator is one of definition; i.e. all goods have embodied labor in the abstract (abstract from use value because use value is a qualitative matter – different want-satisfying abilities).

The marginal school questioned this concept of embodied labor in the abstract, and they created the concept of utility as the common denominator. Smith and Marx assumed that use value is qualitatively different. You can only heat a house with coal, not with gold; if you are hungry, you can only eat bread, not coal. *You cannot say that so much hunger satisfaction equals so much heat satisfaction;*

therefore you cannot compare use value, only exchange value. To determine exchange value, Marx developed his concept of Value. Next time we shall see how Marx measured value (embodied labor) by abstraction.

[Use Value and the Labor Theory of Value]

Use value is just ability – the want-satisfying ability of commodities; exchange value is purchasing power – the ability of one commodity to command others; *Value* is embodied labor. Value is absolute, exchange value, relative. Ricardo uses the concept of 'value' as a relative term; *he states explicitly that he does not consider value to be equal to cos*t, what Malthus assumed Ricardo to say. Cost and value are only the same when you include entrepreneurs' cost – then you have absolute value. *My thesis is that Marx is closer to Smith than to Ricardo.*

Most theories are developed to the end of solving particular problems so that the theory is shaped by the problems the writer is attacking. Ricardo had a specific problem. Marx also had a specific problem, but it was completely different from Ricardo's. For Ricardo it was the distribution of income, posed by problems centering about the question of the Corn Laws. He asked: *what is the effect on the distribution of income resulting from the abolition of the Corn Laws?* [What is the] [e]ffect on the wealth of the nation? Ricardo was convinced that free trade was the best policy. He was a free trader before he developed his theory, but he was aware that there were great obstacles to overcome in order to convince the public that free trade was the best policy. These obstacles were: (1) the abolition of the Corn Laws would harm the landed interests which controlled the policies of England; and (2) a general fear that a depression would result from cancellation of the Corn Laws. This fear was based on the prevailing theory of value; i.e. the entrepreneurs' cost theory. People feared that a decrease in corn prices (resulting from free importation) would lower wages and prices, since wages were an important element of entrepreneurs' cost which determines prices. Lower prices were associated with depression.

Ricardo, therefore, had to develop his own theory of value, according to which lower wages would not mean lower prices but only increases in profit. *Ricardo was not interested in explaining the price level at any one time, only in what causes relative value to change over time.* If, at one time, a pair of shoes exchange for ten yards of linen, why do the same pair of shoes exchange for only five yards of linen at another time? He was not interested in absolute value, only in relative value; not in exchange ratios at any one time, only in exchange rations over time.

Marx's problem is entirely different; he was a revolutionist.

Ricardo was not interested in the source of value; Smith was. Ricardo used the wage scale as a 'general scale' of reductions that a change in relative value could be measured over time. In Smith's primitive society, on the other hand, labor is the source of value. Smith and Marx had the same idea.

Marx wanted to investigate the capitalist economy in order to discover why and how the operation of the economy creates conflict between the forces of production and the relations o production. His theory of value has as its purpose the provision of a basis on which to discover this contradiction. He is interested in: (1) the source from which value is derived. (2) He wants to make use of value to explain the source of property income, to explain how it is possible that certain people derive their income by virtue of ownership, not by labor. This to enable him (3) to discover the consequences that flow from the existence of these property incomes. These are the functions and purposes of his value theory.

It is an attempt to explain capitalism, identical with Smith's purpose and problem, namely, to inquire into the causes and nature of the Wealth of Nations. Later is was Keynes' problem for which he sought a solution and explanation. Hence the similarities between Smith, Marx and Keynes. Ricardo, on the other hand, *was interested in the causes of a change in the* distribution of income. Ricardo set the path for investigation which orthodox economists followed and devoted their whole time. The people in the 'underground' – Malthus, Marx, the underconsumptionists, and Keynes – devoted themselves, as Smith had, to the problems of production, the Wealth of Nations. In fact, after the interlude of orthodox theory since Ricardo, Keynes came back to the labor theory of value!

Keynes said that in a couple of generations the interest rate would drop to zero; this means the elimination of the whole renter class. When this happens, the value of any commodity will be determined by labor costs – labor theory of value. Keynes' intention, according to his own statement, was to save capitalism. He would do this by partial planning. Marx, on the other hand, would have total planning; he would 'drop the axe on the neck of *laissez faire* in one blow', by changing the whole society, turning over the institutions of capitalism. Keynes would make it a gradual process, although he saw it inevitable that investments would be socialized in order to compensate for the savings gap inherent in a mature capitalist economy. Keynes, a true Britisher, was a graduationist. The British are 'graduationists', not from inborn qualities, but because of the structure of their society. Abolition of capitalism is the logical consequence of Keynesian theory, whether he realized it himself or not. Marxian process is revolution; institutional change is necessary, and must occur within a very short period of time.

The function of Marx's labor theory of value is to create a foundation on which the contradiction between the forces and relations of production can be disclosed. It is not a petty problem of price determination. However, it does appear that Marx was concerned with the determination of prices. His statements are misleading; it looks as if he were concerned with specific prices. Non-Marxian writers have attacked him on this ground. Böhm-Bawerk for instance said that the labor theory was completely unable to explain prices and price changes; therefore maintaining that he had completely demolished Marx's labor theory of value. This criticism is completely beside the point. It was not Marx's purpose to explain price change – as Böhm-Bawerk believed.

Marx was a scholar, but one not solely interested in scholarly matters. He was also interested in promoting change in society. This does not necessarily follow from his dialectics, but from *facts*. The harsh facts in society are that no class in power will ever give up its position; it will hold on to its privileges. They will only relinquish their power by revolution according to Marx. It is my impression that Marxian dialectics was a series of revolutionary developments where the contradictions between the forces and relations of production created the revolution – thesis, antithesis, and synthesis. Revolution is sudden change, but violence and bloodshed occur only because the old class in power will not give up its power, according to Marx. In fact the Russian Revolution was not very bloody; the system simply collapsed. The bloodshed occurred when the counter-revolution was started by the 'white guard' with Western support.

I have always been of the opinion that Veblen departed from dialectics because he was a 'graduationist'. In the Marxian scheme the thesis and antithesis of 'technology' and 'institutions' will only be corrected by revolution and the synthesis – the classless society. Marx believes that he relied solely on Hegel – drawing Hegelian concepts, which had relation to the development of ideas, and applying them in a dialectics of materialism.

In the Veblenian scheme, the process is something like

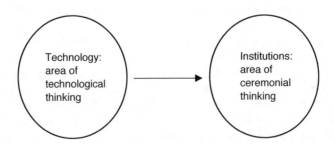

Technology becomes effective in social development by its impact on thinking. As people become influenced by technology, old customs, traditions, mores and superstitions are given up. Witness effect of printing on general scientific and educational standards.

In the Marxian theory change in society does not take place as a result of a change in ideas but because of class struggle – the vehicle for revolutionary social change.

A 'commodity' is unique to a capitalist economy; 'Value' is dependent on the institutional framework of society. This concept of Value would have no significance in a socialist economy. This was Böhm-Bawerk's mistake, in assuming Marx's Value to be simply exchange value, which it is not.

Marx differs from the utopian socialists, who posed social problems in the ethical sense of 'should be'. Ethical considerations play no part in Marx's theory (which is not to say that he had no ethical standards). The capitalist economy, according to Marx, will break down simply because it develops contradictions, not because it offends our moral senses; the trouble with capitalism lies in its functions, not in its morals. So with Keynes. The trouble with the maldistribution of income originates not in the fact that it is immoral or unethical, but because it prevents the economy from working properly.

Marxian value theory can only be applied to a capitalist economy, *because in a socialist economy there would be no commodities as defined by Marx*. When Marx abstracts in order to arrive at labor, it does not mean he abstracts from the universe. It simply means that he abstracts from the particular kinds of labor in existence; from the *qualitative* aspects of labor, leaving the *quantitative* – the ability to utilize muscles and brains.

The real point in this connection is that labor will be expended on any product, both under capitalism and socialism, but embodied labor has no significance in the socialist economy, even if it may exist, because only in the capitalist economy are 'commodities' to be found. The only goods with significance under capitalism are goods produced and sold – goods produced for sale. You could still have Value in a socialist economy, but it will not affect the functioning of the economy. The production of goods for sale in fact *defines* capitalism, according to Marx.

Marx is not criticizing the capitalist economy, he is analyzing it; and he concludes that forces are at work which will result in the system's own collapse, a collapse he will help to bring about by 'marching in the parade waving the banner'.

Some confusion may have resulted so far from the fact that we have not yet considered what Marx means by labor. Let us think of labor in connection with a specific commodity. How do we measure the quantity of labor? How do we measure the amount of labor power expended in the production of a commodity? According to Marx – *solely in units of time* – with clock hours, as Ricardo.

With respect to commodities, this raises the question of how to measure the embodied labor. In any line of production in modern society, in which a large number of workers are employed, some will work rapidly, others more slowly. Some workers use new and modern tools and devices, others use old and less efficient tools. Marx solved this problem by using a *modal average,* which he calls 'socially necessary labor'. Socially necessary labor determines, equals Value.

Socially necessary labor is the amount of labor time required by an average worker of average skill, using the prevailing techniques, to produce a commodity. I assume this to be an arithmetic average arrived at, if possible, by adding up the skills of all workers and dividing this pile of skills by the number of workers. The prevalent technique is the technique used in the production of the bulk of the output in the economy; this is a sort of mode. If most commodities are produced by a machine, then the labor time required by the handicraftsman is not 'socially necessary labor time'. Marx himself says:

> The introduction of power looms into England probably reduced by one half the labor required to weave a given quantity of yarn into cloth. The hand-loom weavers, as a matter of fact, continued to require the same time as before; but for all that the product of one hour of their labor represented after the change only one half an hour's social labor, and consequently fell to one half its former value. *Capital* (Modern Library edition) p. 46.

This has no reference to use value; thus you cannot evaluate the use value of a commodity produced. Use values are assigned by society to the product in question; it is institutionally determined. Marx regards wants as socially conditioned, whereas the marginal utility school takes wants as the result of 'human nature'.

The total labor required or devoted to the production of the commodity in question must not be a disproportionate part of the total labor supply in the economy. For example, the value of the aggregate labor may be greater than the volume of the commodity produced, because too much labor has been expended on the production of that particular commodity. So you must take into consideration total *demand*, which depends on the desirability of various goods.

Demand is expressed in the market and obviously depends on the distribution of income and purchasing power in society; and distribution of income is a matter of the institutional framework of society and the relation among the various groups in society in the processes of production. Marx does not pay much attention to demand; the same is the case with the writers of the classical school, for different reasons. I think the classical school failed to emphasize demand because of their assumption of perfect competition and mobility of the factors of production, and because of their acceptance of Say's law of markets. Marx neglects demand for totally different reasons. For him economics is the study of human relations and human activity – relations among men and men, not men and things. The psychological school considered relations between men and things. For Marx, demand is not something that exists independently of society; it is a dependent variable; demand is conditioned by society. The subject matter of economics for Marx was social relationships. Demand is much more a result in society than a cause.

The Marxian concept of 'socially necessary labor time' thus rules out, as having no value creating power, any labor which is not socially necessary, so defined; e.g. labor power expended on goods not entering the market. Embodied labor is the socially necessary labor, the labor necessary to produce a 'commodity'. Value is not something which exists in the universe; it exists only in certain relations. Exchange value is the phenomenal form which expresses Value (*Capital*, p. 43).

Another problem arises in connection with the labor theory of value – the problem of skilled labor. In the Smithian system there were different degrees of skill and hardship and ingenuity which Smith was unable to reduce to a common denominator. Paul Sweezy tries to solve this problem by assuming that different skills of labor are somewhat interchangeable.

For Marx the problem does not have to be solved because his theory is not a theory of specific prices; it is an aggregate theory; it is macroeconomics like Keynesian economics. Marx's theory was not intended to solve the problem of market prices; Marx's labor theory is intended to reveal the sources of aggregate value of production, not to show how specific prices are determined. Some goods sell above their value, some below, but the average of all of them will be equal to Value. If a good sells below its particular Value, it is because more than the 'socially necessary labor time' has been expended on its production, in which case the aggregate amount of Value in society decreases.

Marx avoids tautology by assuming that goods are exchanged at their Value, while remaining aware that particular goods almost never do so. All goods do exchange *on the average* at their Value. It may be that the market value is not equal to the 'natural' value, as in the Smithian system (with respect to specific commodities); but if Marx is talking in the same sense as Smith with respect to market price, it is because he is interested in *surplus value*, which we shall discuss later on.

Social Relations

In the absence of social relations, Value is not created. Man's labor, human labor, is the active agent operating on external things; other things have meaning only when man does something to them. All other things are passive; the only active want is human labor. So the source of Value must be found in human labor; it cannot lie in raw materials, as they themselves are created by man, by labor. Natural resources are functionally defined by technology. The creative agent, human labor, is portioned out in different things, so each thing (commodity) has Value in proportion to the amount of labor expended on it. This is the basis of *any* labor theory of value, not just Marx's.

Marx would say that those thinking in terms of marginal utility abstract from social relations and from the productive process as a *social process*. Want-satisfaction is a social function, because wants are culturally determined. Production is also a social process for the older classical economists.

The first use to which Marx puts his labor theory of value is to explain the source of property income. In the Marxian theory the active agent is labor, therefore all Value is the result of labor. If this is the case, it should be impossible for anyone to derive property income.[3]

The capitalist purchases various things such as machines, raw materials, etc. at their true Value. After the productive process the finished products are sold at their true Value, which is now higher because of the additional labor embodied. No surplus value seems to have been created in this process. Even if the assumption is dropped that all goods exchange at their Value, no surplus value would necessarily result, because the entrepreneur is both buyer and seller. The advantage he would gain as a buyer would be lost when he sells. The individual entrepreneur may benefit from buying cheap, but the capitalists as a class could not, because they are all buying and selling to each other. The capitalists as a class could not obtain surplus value or property income.

The solution to this problem is that there is one peculiar commodity which, when used in the process of production, creates value; this commodity is labor power. The capitalists buy labor power at its full Value; i.e., he purchases the use value of the laborer for a certain period of time. During this time labor power is capable of producing more than its own true Value; labor power produces more Value than was bought in the form of labor power. The difference accrues to the capitalist as surplus value.

The Marxian Theory of Surplus Value

Marx states that the capitalist, when investing his capital in production, finds it necessary to purchase two completely different kinds of factors of production: (1) raw materials, plant, machinery, etc. which Marx calls *Constant Capital* (C); and labor power, or *Variable Capital* (V). These two concepts are not the same as fixed and circulating capital to be found in classical writings.

Constant Capital is so called, not because it is long lasting but because it is not a source of surplus value of profit. Its Value is not altered in the course of production; it will have a Value determined by the quantity of labor socially necessary to product it. That value will be transferred to the final product, as the Value of the constant capital is used up in the processes of production. The capitalist merely replenishes, by the sale of the final commodity, the Value of the constant capital used up in the process of production.

Variable Capital. The case is completely different with respect to variable capital, or human labor power. This is a commodity which has use value because it produces useful goods. It is separable from the laborer (in the capitalist economy), who sells his labor power, his ability to work for a period of time. It does not necessarily have to be produced for sale in the market; people do not raise children in order to sell their labor power. But labor power is sold in the market, because it is the only way open to laborers to earn a living. The capitalist buys labor power at its true Value. The Value of labor power is determined by the socially necessarily labor required to produce labor power, as with any other commodity. In other words, the Value of labor power is determined by the labor power socially necessary to produce the real wage which is sufficient to maintain the worker's health, strength, etc. and allow him to reproduce himself. This is the old standard of living theory of wages, the one expressed by David Ricardo. *Labor power, however, has a unique character; i.e., the ability to create value when it is used in the processes of production.*

The value created by labor in the processes of production will be determined by the socially necessary labor time expended in the production of the output. The capitalist purchases this Value creating labor time at its own real value. The labor power is capable of producing commodities (output) which have more value than the labor itself. This additional Value (the difference between the labor power used in the process of production and the Value of the output) is what Marx calls *surplus value*. Surplus value is property income.

Nobody is cheated in this process according to Marx. The worker received full payment for his labor power; i.e., for the Value of his labor power. Everyone gets value received for value given. It just happens that this use value of labor power is capable of producing more value than it has itself when applied to the processes of production. This is true of no other commodity. There are two requisites for this condition: (1) political revolution and (2) industrial revolution.

(1) It is necessary to have the laborer free from the bonds of serfdom and slavery. He must be legally free to sell his labor power. When this was accomplished by *political revolution* one necessary condition was created, necessary but not sufficient. The other condition was met by:

(2) *The industrial revolution*. Having made the worker legally free by political revolution, how could you be sure that he would be willing to sell his working ability to the capitalist? *Why did the worker not work for himself?* Marx says that this was done by freeing the worker in another way – freeing him from ownership of the means of production, without which the productive processes cannot be carried on. This was accomplished by the industrial revolution. In the first place, it

made it more profitable to raise sheep and wool rather than other types of farm products. The enclosure movement resulted from this fact, which forced people off the land. Also the industrial revolution separated the worker from ownership of the means of production by making them too expensive. During the handicraft stage it was possible for the workers to own their own tools of production; not so after the industrial revolution. This left the laborer with nothing to sell but his labor power. Under capitalism, the worker does not own the means of production; he does not own the output created by his own labor power. He is unable to produce unless the capitalist furnishes him with the means of production – raw materials, plant, machinery, tools, etc.

Now if the production of the real wage of the worker will require 5 hours of labor a day, then these 5 hours labor is what Marx calls the 'necessary working time', or the time required to produce labor power. But if the actual length of time the worker spends on the job is 10 hours a day, then you have 5 hours of 'surplus working time'.

Actual Working Time: 10 hours
less Necessary Working Time: 5 hours
equals Surplus Working Time: 5 hours

When, as in this example, the worker can produce his real wage by producing commodities having an equal value to his real wage for one day in 5 hours, but he actually works 10 hours, then he produces *surplus value* for the capitalist in the remaining 5 hours. The difference between output produced during a given time and the value of the labor power used during this time is then the surplus value.

According to Marx, the laborer receives full payment for his labor power; he has no claim on the value of the final product. When the workers revolt, it will be because of the contradictions between the forces and relations of production. If the worker receives the full value of the finished product, there would be no property incomes – no capitalism – and no reason for revolt. This is *no* exploitation theory. The workers simply cannot make use of the use value of their labor power by working for themselves, so they must sell their labor power to the capitalists who use this labor power to create surplus value. Labor power is capable of creating value that is greater than itself.

What would result from minimum wage laws that reduced the working time to the 5 hours of daily work necessary to create the workers' real wage? No laborers would be hired because in this case no surplus value would be created, capitalists could obtain no profits, no property income. Capitalism would cease to function. In fact, Marx's surplus value is very similar to Senior's 'last tenth hour of working', the concept Marx himself ridiculed so much![4]

Marx's theory then is a labor cost theory of value. The fact that value is counted in monetary terms does not change anything with respect to the theory; e.g., if the wage is $0.50 an hour and the worker works 10 hours a day, the daily wage is $5.00. If the value of the output is $10.00, then in monetary terms, the surplus value is $5.00.

Marx did not have to go outside classical theory to get his theory of value. What was revolutionary was what Marx did to the theory. The reason why the classicists did not draw the logical conclusions from the theory was the Malthusian theory of population.[5] According to this, the population would maintain the real wage at the standard level of living. Marx ascribes this fact to the superior position of the owners of the means of production and to institutional factors which can be changed, whereas the classicists ascribed it to the natural propensities of man.

Additional Concepts of the Theory

The rate of surplus value is equal to the ratio of the surplus value of the output produced to the value of labor power which produced it; i.e., if we designate surplus value by s', value of output which is surplus by s, and the value of the labor power by v, then we have

$$s' = s/v \qquad (1)$$

or what is the same,

$$s' = \text{surplus working time/necessary working time} \qquad (1')$$

This is the ratio of the exploitation of labor; the ratio the capitalist is interested in, however, is the rate of profit, or the rate of return on his total investment, (or constant capital (c) plus variable capital (v) rather than the above rate of return on variable capital alone). When we designate profit by p', we then have

$$p' = s/(c+v) \qquad (2)$$

When constant capital (c) is used in the process of production the rate of profit will be less than the rate of surplus value(s') and shows the rate of exploitation of total capital.

Marx had a further concept which he called the 'organic composition of capital'. This is the ratio of constant capital to total capital (c plus v). If we designate [individual capitalist firm] organic composition of capital by o we have

$$o = c/(c+v) \qquad (3)$$

In the example we assumed that surplus (s) was 5 and that variable capital was also 5. In this case the rate of surplus value would be

$$5/5 = 100\%$$

When s' is 100% it would seem that the organic composition of capital would vary inversely with the rate of surplus value, because constant capital (c) increases relatively to variable capital (v), the organic composition decreases.

In this connection Marx's so-called 'great contradiction' develops in his labor theory of value. First he assumes competition and therefore uniform rates of profits in all lines of business. If profit should decline in one line of business, capital would move to more profitable lines of pursuit, which would decrease the excess profit in this latter line, and increase it in the former. A uniform rate of profit must therefore result from the assumption of competition. However, as Marx defines organic composition of capital, profit will vary from industry to industry, because the organic composition of capital varies from industry to industry. If we assume, as above, s' to be 100%, we have the following.

Taking two industries, cotton and steel, and assuming the following relations.

Cotton: variable capital (V) is 75% and constant capital (C) is 25% then the organic composition of capital is $c/(c+v) = 25\%$

In *Steel*, since there is to be found more constant capital,

variable capital (V) is 25%

constant capital (C) is 75%

Thus the rate of profit, with s' is 100% and therefore uniform, will be in *cotton*:

$$p' = s/(c+v) = (s/v)/((c+v)/v) = 100\%/(1/75\%) = 75\%$$

and in *steel*:

$$p' = 1/((1/1-0.75)) = 25\%$$

This indicates that Marx's theory would require varying rates of profit when you have varying composition of capital from industry to industry; i.e., the rate of profit will vary directly with the rate of surplus value, and inversely with organic composition of capital. On the other hand, Marx assumes *as a fact* full competition, which creates a uniform rate of profit in all lines of business, not a varying rate, as according to his *theory*. This is a contradiction between fact and theory, as in the Ricardian scheme. (Ricardo found that variations in wages would cause variations in profit.) There are two things to be done when theory does not agree with fact: disregard the facts (as Ricardo did); or formulate a new theory which accords with fact.

Engels called attention to the contradiction in the preface to the first volume; he challenged anyone to solve the problem and promised a solution in vol. III, which was published 21 years later. Marx's solution is simple and throws light on his labor theory of value. If Marx had been interested in specific prices, then there would have been a contradiction. In vol. III he says that all surplus value derives from the purchase and employment of labor power. Aggregate surplus value is the aggregate property income; thus the surplus value accrues to the capitalists as a class. It is distributed among them, not in proportion to the variable capital, but in proportion to each capitalist's total capital invested.

The Great Contradiction

Marx solves his great contradiction with the thesis that aggregate surplus value (S) during any given period of time is the difference between aggregate value of output produced during this period and the aggregate value of labor power expended during this period on the production of the output. Then the rate of profit in the economy as a whole (P) would be the ratio of the aggregate surplus value to the aggregate value of labor expended, which again would be aggregate constant capital (C) used up plus aggregate variable capital (V).

$$P = S/(C + V) \tag{4}$$

That is, aggregate surplus value (S) is equal to aggregate income (W) minus the aggregate investment during the period in total capital, or variable capital plus constant capital (V + C). The rate of profit is then

$$P' = (W–C–V)/ (C + V) \tag{5}$$

Now total property income or aggregate surplus value (S) is distributed among all the capitalists in the economy, so each capitalist receives the proportion of aggregate surplus value (s_i) that his individual total capital (v + c) is to the aggregate capital in the economy (V + C), or the individual capitalist's share of aggregate surplus value (S) equals

$$s_i/S \tag{6}$$

The distribution of aggregate surplus value among the capitalists is effected through the price system, so that each entrepreneur sells his individual output at the price which equals his total capital expenditure (c) plus this uniform rate of profit (p'); then each individual capitalist will receive the proportion of aggregate surplus (S) which equals the proportion that his own total capital expenditures (v+c) is of the aggregate capital expenditures in the economy (V + C).

If aggregate surplus (S) is 100% for the entire economy, and if the aggregate constant capital (C) used up is 500 and aggregate variable capital (V) used up is 100, then

$$P' = S/(C + V) = 100/(500 + 100) = 1/6$$

If a given capitalist produced output during a given period which cost him c in the amount of 5 and v in the amount of 1, then his output will sell at

$$5 + 1 + (1/6)(6) = 7$$

His individual total capital is 6 or c + v = 6.

If then, the individual capitalist's shares in total aggregate profit is deduced from (6) above, and we have assumed that aggregate capital, (c + v), was 600, then the individual capitalist's proportion of total profit will be

$$(6/600) \ S = (1/100)(100) = 1$$

Which is the last '1' in the equation

$$Price = (1 + P'')c + v$$

The sales price of the commodity equals the cost of production plus profit. It is an entrepreneur's cost theory.

All property income (surplus value or profit) is derived from production and utilization of labor power, and each capitalist gets a proportion of total property income which is determined by aggregate organic composition of capital in the economy, *not* by the individual organic composition of capital. The market does not determine the rate of profit; the price system is merely a device which determines the distribution of income, including the distribution of surplus value among the capitalists. The market does not create the profit; profit is determined by the productive process. Marx's labor theory is a theory of macroeconomics; his theory of prices microeconomics. The latter does not contradict his value theory but is derived from it. The theory of value is basic, the price theory derivative.

Marx uses his theory of value and theory of surplus value to discover the so-called *laws of capitalist development*, laws which control capitalist development through time. These laws will disclose the fundamental contradictions between the forces and relations of production which develop through time. I find five of these laws implicit in Marx; they are:

(A) The law of the falling tendency of the rate of profit.
(B) The law of concentration and centralization.
(C) The law of the 'industrial reserve army' or the Marxian theory of unemployment.
(D) The law of the increasing misery of the proletariat.
(E) The law of crises and depressions.

Let us take a look at each of these laws.

A. The Tendency of the Rate of Profit to Fall Continuously.

All economists since the 'creation' of capitalism have been of the opinion that the rate of profit will fall during capitalist development – Smith, Ricardo, Mill, Keynes et. al. However, they differ with respect to the causes which bring about this decline in the rate of profit. Smith attributes the falling rate of profit variously to competition in the commodity market, competition in the labor market and competition in the market for investments. Ricardo and the orthodox theorists after him attributed the phenomenon almost exclusively to the limited quantity of land and diminishing returns. Ricardo said that Smith's first two reasons (competition in the labor and commodity markets) could not be responsible for falling profits. *He refuted competition in the commodity market as a cause, because of his (Ricardo's) acceptance of Say's Law,* according to which *demand increases as output increases.* Neither is competition in the labor market responsible, according to Ricardo, because of the Malthusian theory of population, which is really Say's Law extended to the market for labor; i.e., as capital accumulation increases, demand for labor increases, which causes wages to increase *temporarily.* But as wages increase 'the laborers as a race will increase their numbers'; this increase in the labor supply will again force wages down to the standard of living level, the long run level of real wages. The only reason, according to Ricardo, for the falling rate of profits was the "niggardliness of nature," the declining return per unit of labor and capital as the margin is forced down. The resort to lower grades of land as population increases will cause per capita productivity to decline, but real wages cannot fall below the standard of living level, so the total share of the total output going to the workers as a class increases; and the total share of total produce going to the capitalists as a class decreases. In the Ricardian scheme, therefore, the causes for the declining rate of profit are to be found outside the economy; i.e., in the physical fact that the return per worker and per unit of capital decreases as resort is taken to lower quality land. Under such a theory institutional change could not overcome the scarcity of land and diminishing returns resulting from this scarcity.

Marx had a completely different explanation. He starts with his thesis that social change results from the contradiction between the forces and relations of production; so by the very nature of his theory, *he is forced to admit that the falling rate of profits could not be due to outside forces* – the 'niggardliness of nature'. To Marx the falling rate of profits is inherent in the capitalist system, and contributes this secular *tendency to the fact that capitalism by its very nature and function increases the organic composition of capital.* During economic development this ratio will increase, i.e., constant capital increases relatively to variable capital; this is brought about by the introduction of new machinery, etc. This increase in the organic composition of capital Marx attributes to two facts (similar to Smith's): (1) competition in the commodity market, and (2) competition in the labor market.

Competition in the Commodity Market. Marx's theory of surplus value and prices relates to an equilibrium situation; prices are related to, or equal to cost of production only in equilibrium. There is nothing the individual entrepreneur can do about the price given competition and the labor theory of value; the price of his output per unit will be determined by the labor time socially necessary for its production per unit. This does not mean, however, that the individual producer necessarily will have costs which will be related to price in equilibrium. If the individual producer avails himself of any improved technique, he may produce a larger output per worker (i.e., same total cost, but expanded output). When he has reduced the labor time required to produce the output in his establishment below the socially necessary labor in the economy as a whole, he will not thereby depress the value of his own output, but will reduce his cost, by increasing the output of laborer per unit of time. So it is an advantage to each producer to introduce as soon as he can a new technique, and increase his own profit. In terms of the labor theory of value, it means that the value of the output will be determined by the socially necessary labor; and in the individual capitalist's establishment, he uses less than the socially necessary labor, thereby obtaining a larger profit, or larger surplus value than is obtained in the economy as a whole. Of course what is an advantage to each capitalist will be an advantage to any other capitalist, and they will all begin to use the new technique, which is introduced only because it increases the productivity of labor. When all entrepreneurs are using the new technique, the socially necessary labor will now be determined by the new technique, not by the old. The introduction of the new machinery means relatively more constant capital per worker; thus the whole society ends up with a higher rate of organic composition of capital. *With the rate of surplus value the same, the rate of profit will fall.*

If, for example, we assume S to be equal to V, therefore S' is 100%; C is 75; and V is 25; then $75/(75 + 25) = 75$ and $P' = 25/(75 + 25) = 25$.

Then the new technique is introduced, i.e. constant capital increases in relation to total capital. Assume that C is now 80. Now, $80/(80 + 20) = 80$ and $P' = 20/(80 + 20) = 20$.

The rate of profit has fallen, assuming no change in the rate of surplus value, as a result of the new technique – and this process goes on without limit. So the technological process itself tends to reduce the rate of profit, as the capitalists try to increase profits by using new technology. Marx says himself that capitalism has increased technology more than all preceding ages, so capitalism provides a stimulus to the development of new techniques, which when universally adapted result in pulling down the rate of profit.

The fall in the rate of profit in a profit economy is, of course, a tremendous and fundamental contradiction, one of the insoluble contradictions of capitalism which will eventually destroy it. What is to the advantage of the individual capitalist is to the disadvantage of the capitalists as a class. (Note that this proposition denies the Smithian thesis that total social wealth is equal to the sum total of all individual wealth.)

We will for the time being put aside (2) competition in the labor force, to be considered under (C) 'the industrial reserve army'.

This theory is a theory of constant depression or a theory of economic maturity, but it is also a theory of economic collapse. When profits cease to exist, capitalism will cease to exit. It is not a theory of a stationary state as in the classical school proper. Ricardo assumed that profit would eventually drop to a minimum level where the real wage per worker would be maintained at the standard of living level; and that the economy would go on forever in this state. Marx's is *a theory of collapse, brought on by the cessation of profits.*

B. The Law of Concentration and Centralization.

In the development of capitalism, ownership becomes concentrated in fewer and fewer hands, and production becomes centralized in fewer and larger enterprises. This tendency results from forces in the economy itself, not from the outside.

The tendency for profit to fall tends to further this concentration and centralization. Any one capitalist, Marx states, is interested in maximizing his profits; he wants to accumulate more and more capital by re-investing his surplus value (profits). The absolute profit of the capitalist will depend on the rate of profit and the amount of capital on which he realizes that profit; so absolute profit can be increased by either: (a) increasing the rate of profit, or (b) increasing the amount of capital. The individual capitalist cannot control the rate of profit, but he can, within limits, control his capital. This will lead the individual to seek to increase his capital; and as the rate of profit falls, the capitalist is under a strain to accumulate more and more capital. In this process, some have an advantage and the more fortunate, and the faster ones, gain on the smaller capitalist who is pushed out, his firm absorbed by the larger ones. Any capitalist who grows faster than others has an advantage in large scale production; the expansion of the firm reduces the cost of production: and in each line of production there will be a tendency towards centralization of production in greater and greater establishments.

The actual development of the capitalist economy in the 19th century caused many people to question the validity of this law. Among the critics were those who today would be branded 'right-wing socialists'. These critics emphasized especially two points in the actual economic development of capitalism.

1. *The persistent maintenance of small-scale enterprise*, particularly in the fields of agriculture and handicrafts. In fact the development of agriculture in the 19th century was in the opposite direction to a large extent. Large manors and estates were divided into smaller farms; and there was no great concentration and centralization in handicrafts; retailing was still carried on by small establishments.
2. *The development of the corporate form of organization* as the most important form of business organization – in terms of production, investment, return on capital and number of workers employed – has prevented the concentration of ownership in few hands, as Marx predicted.

During the 19th century, at the time of Marx's writing the leading forms of business organization were the proprietorship and the partnership, not the corporation. For that reason, Marx assumed that development of large scale enterprise would be accompanied by a reduction in the number of owners, due to the unlimited liability, which could be met only by people who had the necessary financial resources. The development of large scale enterprise would therefore be accompanied by concentration of ownership.

The development of the corporation was assumed to undermine Marx's law of concentration and centralization, because it made large diffusion of ownership possible along with the development of large-scale enterprise. The corporation made *centralization of production* possible without concentration of *ownership*. The development of the corporation created an entirely new middle class, different from the old Marxian 'petite bourgeois'.

The following may be said, however, with respect to the alleged diffusion of ownership resulting from the corporation. Technically, it would be true that the corporation permits the centralization of production without the concentration of ownership. However – and this is essential – the corporation has completely changed the nature of private property and has deprived owners of their fundamental rights of private ownership, i.e., the right to *control,* and has left them only with the *right* to receive income. In point of fact, the share-holder hasn't even the right to receive an income, they have only the *opportunity*, which will be realized only if those in control of the corporation decide to distribute dividends. This development has reduced the owner of property to a completely functionless class; they are merely *rentiers* without the fundamental right associated with ownership; they do not own physical objects, only paper.

So in spite of the criticism leveled at Marx's law of concentration (of ownership) accompanying centralization (of production), concentration of control (which is the essential matter) *has* taken place, a concentration which has completely undermined the institution of private property, i.e., the appropriation of private property rights of private owners by those in control.

This is a very important development; it has in fact removed the justification for private ownership. The only difference between the Post Office Dept. and a large corporation is that the owner of the former (U.S. citizens) have more control over their property than the owners of the corporation. The development of the corporate structure makes the transition to socialism easy. We have seen that when the U.S. Government, during wars and other emergencies takes over the railroads, and outsiders can see no difference; the trains run as always. Adam Smith argued that private initiative would secure the most efficient production; but with respect to corporate property, this concept has no meaning at all.

The extent of corporate power is beautifully illustrated in Walter Prescott Webb's *Divided We Stand: the Crisis of a Frontierless Democracy* [New York, Toronto, Farrar & Rinehart, Inc. 1937]. The bottle monopoly, after the destruction (financial) of an independent Texas producer, destroyed (physically) the plant of the latter. And then the local Chamber of Commerce comes along and erects a sign at the location of the destroyed plant advertising the wonderful force of private initiative.

Even Kaiser cannot start today without the support of the government-owned R.F.C.; and once started, he discovered that he had such a small part of the total market he had to merge with another small producer (Willys) in order to survive in the battle with the giants of the industry.

The idea that private enterprise is more efficient than government operation is also a fiction. I have once had an arbitration case involving a plumber from a large Texas corporation. Arriving to repair some pipes at 7 o'clock in the morning, he stood around talking to guards until 10 o'clock when he started to work. The men who were to dig the ditches for this pipe had not finished until then. The plumber was paid $2.50 an hour during this whole period. There is waste in other quarters than government.

An illustration of the concentration of control in a corporation is Standard Oil of NJ Out of a total of 106,520 stockholders, the record number of 600 attended the annual stockholders meeting in the small town of Bloomington, NJ in 1947 (according to the stenographic report of the meeting, July 3, 1947). This billion dollar corporation expressed, through its chairman of the board, its gratitude because the Presbyterian Church, the Methodist church and the Baptist Church of Bloomington served dinner for the stockholders without which the meeting could not have taken place (according to the chairman). The board of directors was elected in one motion – 30 seconds; most of the people elected were not present.

C. The Law of the 'Industrial Reserve Army' of the Unemployed.

This is the second major reason why the rate of profit tends to decline under capitalism; i.e., competition in the labor market. (See above *A. The tendency of the rate of profit to fall continuously*).

Capitalist accumulation presents a problem or dilemma in that it increases the demand for labor, increasing wages, and cost, and thereby decreasing profits. The orthodox economists escaped the dilemma through the Malthusian theory of population, which in fact is an application of Say's Law to the labor market. In this scheme the labor supply will adjust itself to demand; increase in demand increasing real wages; increased real wage resulting in increased population and labor supply, forcing the real wage back down to the standard of living level, below which they cannot go. (If they do fall below this, population will decrease and wages will rise.) So in the orthodox scheme wages will fluctuate around the standard of living level; this process can never be stopped; labor supply will always adjust itself to demand. Therefore the classicists assumed that capitalism does not evolve towards collapse, but towards a stationary state, where wages are at the standard of living level and profits are at the minimum.

Marx could not accept the Malthusian theory of population. He rejected it on the theoretical grounds by maintaining that population increase is socially determined. There is nothing in the nature of the universe that brings about changes in population; change is determined by custom, etc. Each institutional arrangement or order has its own 'law' of population; it is not a universal, natural order. Marx pointed out that even in a capitalist economy, children are not produced for sale in the market in the way fixed capital is, so there is no reason to believe that an increased stability of labor power would itself induce an increased production of labor power.

This left Marx with the problem of accounting for the fact that capital accumulation has gone on without decreasing the profit level below a tolerable level. He solves this problem by saying that there must be from time to time, if not continuously, surplus labor, which serves to hold down wages as demand for labor increases. He emphasizes that the capitalist economy requires such an 'industrial reserve army' because the economy works during periods of cycles; it is not an economy which functions continuously at a uniform rate. There must be a reserve of workers ready to enter production during periods of prosperity. The reserve army is simply the unemployed part of the workers. What occurs is not absolute overpopulation, as with Malthus, but relative oversupply of labor, created by the very functioning of the system itself – not by universal natural law.

Marx argues furthermore that capital accumulation increases the demand for labor which will tend to increase wage rate; however, the capitalist have an expedient which can relieve the pressure of the wage rate by decreasing the demand for labor (or more correct, an expedient which prevents the demand for labor from increasing). This expedient is the *substitution of machinery for labor*.[6] As wages increase the capitalist will see an advantage in introducing machinery instead of hiring labor. This introduction of machinery is made possible by the continuous development of technology. It is a theory of technological unemployment. This is one way the industrial reserve army is recruited; another is through depression and crises.

Classical theorists, using Say's Law, said that demand was only limited by supply; so for them introduction of machinery would lower demand for labor, which would lower wages, and prices. With commodities for which the demand is elastic, when prices are lowered, a greater total amount of money will be spent on these than before; this will expand production, which will mean increased demand for, and employment of, labor (more employed than before the introduction of machinery). In the commodities for which demand is inelastic, price decreases will result in a smaller total amount being spent on these; consumers have surplus funds to spend on other things, increasing employment in these lines. Workers will be transferred from the sectors where unemployment resulted from the introduction of labor-saving machinery.

Marx, however, rejected Say's Law.

[*The Great Contradiction (concluded)*]
As mentioned earlier, Marx gives two reasons for the falling rate of profit in the capitalist economy: *competition in the commodity market* in combination with the profit motive leads to the introduction of new machinery, increasing the organic composition of capital, which leads to a decline in the rate of profit; and *competition in the labor market*.

The substitution of machinery for labor tends to relieve the pressure on wages, preventing wages from rising and decreasing profits. However, the introduction of machinery increases the organic composition of capital, and with a given rate of surplus value (S') the rate of profit will fall. This is another contradiction in the capitalist economy. In the absence of the introduction of new machinery, increased accumulation would increase the demand for labor, raise wages, force down profits. But the capitalist can introduce new machinery in attempting to overcome this, thereby increasing the organic composition of capital, which lowers the rate of profit, given a constant rate of surplus value. So, both competition in the commodity market and competition in the labor market tends to lower the rate of profit.

Until now we have assumed a given, constant rate of surplus value, which is of course unrealistic. According to Marx there are five ways open to the capitalist by which he can increase the rate of surplus value. The capitalist is always under pressure to use these five means; if he does not, the organic composition of capital increases, and profits fall. However, if the capitalist offsets the increase of organic composition of capital by increasing the rate of surplus value, he may prevent the rate of profit from falling. Before we discuss these five methods by which the capitalist may increase the rate of surplus value, let us briefly consider how an increased rate of surplus value may effect the rate of profit, according to Marx.

Remember the formulae for the rate of surplus value (S'); the organic composition of capital (O) and the rate of profit (P') when surplus is S, constant capital is C, and variable capital is V:

$$S' = S/V \quad O = C/(C + V) \quad P' = S/(C + V) = S'[V/(C + V)] = S'(1-O)$$

If, then S' is 50%, C is 50 and V is 50 then

$$C/(C + V) + V(C + V) = 1$$

$$O = 50/(50+50)$$
and
$$P' = 0.5(1-0)$$

$$= 0.5(0.5) = 0.25$$

(S must be 25, i.e., 1/2 of V which is given as 50)

Now if because of the introduction of more machinery, the organic composition of capital is changed, then we have the following; assuming C as 75, and V as 25:

$$S' = 50\% \quad O = 75/100 = 75\%$$

and

$$P' = 0.5(1-0.75) = 0.125$$

Or, as a result of the increase in the organic composition of capital, the profit rate has decreased to 12.5%. If we now assume that the capitalists have been able to increase the rate of surplus value by one of the five means at the same time the organic composition of capital has increased, they will be able to maintain the rate of profit. That is the rate of surplus value is now 50% since $S = 25$, $V = 50$, and $C = 50$. Then, in the second case, when C is 75 and V is 25,

$$S/V = 25/25 = 100\%$$

(S is now 25 because of the new formula for S′ according to which S is 100% of V, which is now 25.)

So, it is possible to maintain a constant rate of profit even when the organic composition of capital is increasing. P′ varies inversely with O and directly with S′. Dacy has developed a combined formula for the rate of profit, which in all its simplicity is:

Now we will look at the five methods by which the capitalist can increase the rate of surplus value and thereby offset the increased organic composition of capital.

The first method is lengthening the working day. When this occurs, more absolute surplus value is created, which of course will increase the rate of surplus value, since this is the ratio of total value to variable capital. (Variable capital consists of the price the capitalist pays for the value of labor power purchased at its true value.) When therefore the working day is increased, but the price paid for labor is the same, more absolute surplus is created. The working day of child labor (they were often chained to the machines) was mostly 16 hours a day in British industry at the time Marx was writing; so the capitalists took advantage of the absence of minimum working hours for children as well as for adults.

The second method is speeding up production (increasing output per unit of time). If the workers are 'speeded up' so they produce more per hour, more absolute surplus value is created, and the rate will be increased. And, especially, if the workers can be speeded up in the wage goods industries, it means that the socially necessary labor time required to maintain the workers (and which is equal to the Value of labor) will be decreased. Then of course the surplus value is increased in the economy as a whole, even if the workers are not speeded up in other lines of industry, because the Value of labor is decreased.

The third method is to reduce wages. Marx's theory of a static economy does not rule out this method because the actual wages may fluctuate about the standard of living level. To the extent that the actual wage is above the standard of living level, they can be reduced; furthermore, any given employer takes a rather short run view; he does not concern himself with the necessity of maintaining the workers living standard, which can therefore be reduced, temporarily at least, below this level. Thirdly, there is a method by which the wages of workers can be reduced *permanently* below the standard of living level. This method is the utilization of child labor and the labor of women. This in itself is cheap labor, because women and children are forced into industry in order to supplement the income of the family head. In this case husband, wife, and children all work at wages which will be below the standard of living level; when all the sub-standard wages are pooled, they will be able to maintain the family's standard of living, impossible for a single family breadwinner.

This is why the capitalists utilize the labor of children and women. It depresses the general level of wages below the standard of living level, thereby creating surplus value. Marx was, of course, not the only one who called attention to the gruesome and terrible conditions in English industry in his day. Marx did not paint an exaggerated picture of these condition; the facts are revealed in the 'white paper' on British labor condition, resulting from Parliamentary investigations. The British *laissez faire* economy was the most cruel system in the history of mankind – worse than any slave system ever developed. A slave owner is necessarily interested in the upkeep of his slaves, as they constitute his assets, his property.

An industrial economy cannot be based on slave labor; it would be too expensive for the capitalist. If, e.g., U.S. Steel should have the responsibility of maintaining its workers as slaves, it could not operate. The costs in periods of decreasing demand and therefore decreasing income would be so large that the corporation could not stand it. Under a system of 'free' workers, the capitalists simply fire the workers when production declines; if the capitalist employed slave labor they would have to maintain the slaves during the slack period, otherwise they would lose part of their investment. It was not solely on humanitarian grounds that the Northern States in 'God's own country of the United States' were opposed to the slave system; economic considerations played a decisive role. The industrialized northern states could not operate on slave labor. In the golden days of British *laissez faire* capitalism, entrepreneurs were not hindered by child labor laws, maximum working hours, safely measures, etc.; they had no responsibility for their hired workers. They were forbidden to organize (which was called 'conspiracy'), so they chained children to machines, utilized women workers, and depressed by these means the wages of the male workers also.

The fourth method is increased mechanization in the consumer goods industries (or wage goods industries). This will increase the output per worker per unit of time, decreasing the socially necessary labor time for maintaining the workers, and thereby increasing the surplus value in the economy as a whole. The Value of labor decreases. (This involves a contradiction, which will be discussed later.) The improved technique in the wage goods industry does not worsen the condition of the individual worker, who will be able to maintain his job; but it may harm the laboring class as a whole, because some of them may be fired.

The first three methods are effective only within certain limits. There are limitations to the working day; after a certain point there will be diminishing returns. There is a maximum limit to the speed up process; workers can only turn out a certain amount per hour. And there is an absolute limit to the lowering of wages, even if breadwinners, wives, and children work long hours.

The golf links lie so near the mill
That almost every day
The laboring children can look out
And see the men at play.

(Sarah N. Cleghorn)

The fourth method however is unlimited in its effect on increasing the rate of surplus value. However, it implies a contradiction. Technology may be increased so the wages (Value of labor) are depressed. The wage goods necessary to sustain a worker one day (say formerly produced in 6 hours) may after the introduction of machinery be decreased to 30 min. This will of course increase the rate of surplus value in the economy as a whole. *But this very method of introducing new machinery in the wage goods industries increased the organic composition of capital which reduces the rate of profit.* So there develops a question. Does the increased technique lower the socially necessary working time so much that it offsets the effect on profit resulting from the increased organic composition of capital brought about by the same introduction of the technique? It is impossible to solve.

The fifth method is the importation of cheap food from foreign countries. This was the method favored by David Ricardo. Great Britain took advantage of importing cheap colonial products, and agricultural products from Poland where the wages were low. When this cheap food was imported into Great Britain, it reduced the socially necessary labor time to maintain workers. There is of course an absolute limit to this method at any time, and as other countries become more and more capitalistic, the spread between the labor costs in the colonies (and underdeveloped countries) and Great Britain becomes smaller and smaller.

D. The Law of the Increased Misery of the Proletariat.

This law has been the most severely criticized of all the Marxian concepts. Criticism for the most part however has been irrelevant due to a failure to take into account the level of abstraction that Marx is working on in Vol. I. He is assuming *laissez faire* economics conditions and his ideas developed after close and long examination of the British capitalism in the latter 18th and early 19th centuries. He constructs his model on the basis of that type of economy, one in which there was no interference by the state, nor by organized workers, in the affairs of capitalists.

Given this model, there can be no question that the lot of the working class would have deteriorated until it would have reached the worst conditions possible. But the rise of consumer co-ops, labor unions, wage and hour legislation, etc., had materially changed the structure of capitalist economy. If conditions had remained as they were when Marx was writing, then his predictions regarding the increased misery of the proletariat might well have materialized.

E. The Law of Crises and Depressions.

Marx's theory is one of cyclical depression and permanent depression. Especially with respect to the cyclical depressions his theory is a departure from classical theory – to a larger degree than any of his other economic theories. The reason for this is that Marx denies Say's Law. Relying on Say's Law, classical theory cannot account for cyclical fluctuations in terms of the functioning of the capitalist economy itself. According to Say's Law there is no reason why cyclical fluctuations should occur because of the functioning of the economy, as well as no reason for a tendency towards permanent depression. The classical economists could not, however, close their eyes to the facts; they attributed the fluctuations to non-economic causes. For the classicists the factors that threw the economy out of equilibrium were external – Jevon's sun spots, or psychological factors, etc. Also included in these external factors was the tampering with the economy by government agencies, e.g., the monetary authority's interference in monetary matters. Marx said that classical theory misconceived the nature of the capitalist economy, did not understand its basic nature. Classical theory, Say's Law, pictured the economy as a 'simple commodity producing economy' – an economy in which goods are produced for *use*, the producer requires *use-value*. Such an economy is not capitalist according to Marx. It may be a market economy, but the object of producers is to acquire goods; people sell their own produce to acquire money to buy other people's products, i.e. Commodity – Money – Commodity (the classical concept)

This process follows, of course, Say's Law; Say's Law is applicable to a 'simple commodity-producing economy'. People do not produce for any other purpose than to consume. As in Ricardo, 'people do not lock their money up in a chest'. In such an economy, money's chief function is a medium of exchange (and in a limited degree, a measure of value). Since no one withholds money; no one withholds goods either; for as long as there are unsatisfied human wants, there is no reason why the economy should not function at full employment, except when external non-economic factors interfere – droughts, tornadoes, wars, major disasters, and government interference. Such disasters may make it physically impossible to carry on production, but nothing in the economy itself slows down the process.

According to Karl Marx, however, the capitalist economy is *not* a simple commodity producing economy. A capitalist economy is one in which production is controlled by the capitalist owners of the means of production; their objective is not to acquire goods for consumption, but to accumulate capital in order to obtain a profit. The capitalist wants *exchange-value*, not use-vale; he wants to increase his wealth, not his consumption. So in the capitalist economy, as contrasted with the commodity-producing economy, the capitalist starts with money (M); he purchases required materials, labor power, machinery, etc., and sells products for money, i.e.,

$$M - C - M'$$

But this process would have no meaning if the final sum of money does not exceed the original sum, for money is money, there is no qualitative difference. For the process to have meaning there must be a *quantitative difference* between the original and final sums of money, so the process is:

A capitalist desires to maximize profits, and so to accumulate capital. To the extent that the purpose of production is *not* to maximize profits, to that extent, the economy ceases to be capitalistic; to the degree that the modern, impersonal corporation is less motivated by profit than the old-fashioned proprietor, to that degree the corporation is less capitalist.

If the capitalist anticipates that he will not realize surplus value, he will not invest, and the economic process breaks down. The process goes on only in terms of profit expectations, not according to use-value. Use-value as a determinant in the working of the economy comes into the picture only when the person who wants use-value has the money (or does not have the money) by which to acquire this use-value – this is the fact stressed by the underconsumptionist.

At the end of any given period, the amount of capital is greater than at the beginning of the period, because the capitalist has accumulated capital on the basis of the surplus value he has obtained in the course of the economic process.

The fact that classical theory assumed the economy to be a simple commodity producing economy (C–M–C), a system under which profit is not the vehicle for accumulation may be the reason why Paul Sweezy declares the classical theory in fact a theory of socialism. In the capitalist economy it is the drive for profit which leads the capitalist to produce, hire workers, and sell commodities; when this element is absent, the theory is not truly capitalistic.[7]

In the Marxian formula anything which affects profit expectations will upset the economy. For Marx there are two processes explaining the decline in profit rate – cyclical change and constant decline or constant depression.

A cycle is constituted of fluctuations which form a pattern, prosperity followed by depression. Economic theory must offer some explanation for these more or less regular fluctuations.

In the Marxian scheme it is the law of the industrial reserve army. Fluctuations would *not* occur if the following conditions were met: (a) technological progress proceeding smoothly at a uniform rate, and (b) technological progress must be such that it displaces labor at a rate sufficient to permit the capitalist to accumulate capital without any upward pressure on wages; i.e., increases in technique proceed in such a way that the demand for labor to produce the new means of production does not increase faster than the reduction in the amount of workers resulting from the use of the new labor saving equipment. If these conditions were met the profit rate would not decline.

In the capitalist economy, these conditions are not met. Technological progress does not proceed at a smooth and uniform rate; it is highly irregular. Technological developments occur in 'bursts', followed by periods of slower development. One of the wildest bursts was the so called 'industrial revolution'; in this period the whole productive process in the important industries such as textile and transportation changed rapidly; this gave raise to specific demands for steel, various kinds of machinery; this induced the introduction of a whole range of new machines, tools, devices, etc.

Whenever there is a burst in technological development, the pressure on the capitalists to utilize the new inventions is great and increasing, which results in a sudden increase in capital accumulation. *Each individual capitalist will seek to improve his profit by introducing the new equipment, so all capitalists will be compelled to introduce the new machinery.* So the second condition (b) is not met. *The production and installment of the new machinery increases the immediate demand for labor; at the same time, the new machinery will not be able to release workers immediately because it takes time to produce the new devices. During this period the total demand for labor is increased, depleting the industrial reserve army, and raising the wage level. Surplus value and profits decline.* There is an increase in employment without a corresponding increase in productivity. When profits reach such a low level that they do not have an attractive effect on capitalists anymore, they will discontinue investments. Then the crisis develops, followed by depression; the industrial reserve army is rebuilt. Depression is not then an abnormal aspect of the capitalist economy, but a normal consequence of the system. Marx says that depressions are necessary for the working of capitalism because it is a prerequisite for the creation of the industrial reserve army, without which the prosperity phase, the 'burst' of new inventions, could not take place.

The industrial reserve army has two sources of supply: depressions and the introduction of new machinery. The sequence during the cycle is: a significant improvement in technique leading to an accumulation of capital; the increased total demand for labor *immediately*; wages rise, and profits fall; low profits result in crisis and depression, during which the industrial reserve army is rebuilt. As a reserve army is built up during the depression, marked by falling wages and falling value of capital equipment, the state is set for a new revival. However, the depression in itself does not bring about prosperity, which is the result of new 'bursts' of invention, opening up new markets, etc. The factors, i.e., inventions, may seem just as external as in the classical scheme; but it is not invention, but the *internal response* of the economy to invention which brings about crisis and depression. The reaction of entrepreneurs, the real factor, to external forces is a purely institutional factor, absent in a simple commodity producing economy, as well as in a socialist economy.

Marx's Underconsumption Theory

What we have left to consider is Marx's underconsumption theory. According to Marx, a crisis may occur for two reasons. One is significant technological progress, as we have seen. The second reason is a more permanent factor – underconsumption, or lack of purchasing power among the proletariat.

If and when the capitalists find it impossible to sell their output at prices which represent the value of the output, determined by entrepreneur's cost of production, a 'realization crisis' (as Paul Sweezy calls it) takes place. It is the inability of the capitalist to realize the value of output resulting from the failure of the market to absorb the output. The workers have received in wages less than the value of the output, so they are unable to buy the whole of the produce; that part which is not bought by the workers must be purchased by the capitalists; but the capitalists are not primarily interested in consumption; and so on according to the familiar underconsumption theory. Marx added nothing to the theory, his is similar to that of Rev. Malthus. It is because of the difference between the value of labor and the value of output that surplus value exists; this surplus value accruing to the capitalists makes it impossible for the workers to buy the full output. This is a contradiction inherent in capitalism; the system cannot function without profit, but this very profit creates permanent depression.

The difference between Malthus and Marx is that Marx has no 'unproductive consumers' who solved Malthus' dilemma. There is no escaping the Marxian scheme – no unproductive consumers to compensate for the lack of workers' purchasing power, to bring the propensity to consume to unity.

The object of any economic system must be to produce goods for final consumption, irrespective of institutional arrangements directing the process of production. From a technological point of view, the object of production is consumption; machines are not produced for their own sake, they are means to produce other goods, consumer goods, or use-value. In the capitalist economy, however, production is controlled by capitalists whose objective is accumulation of capital and creation of exchange-value, not use-value. The process of production from an institutional point of view, on the one hand, with the capitalist producing to obtain surplus value and realize profit; and on the other, from a technological point of view, with production for consumer goods, use-value. This is the inherent contradiction in capitalism. The failure of the market to absorb production, evidenced by excess capacity, will lead to the final break-down of the capitalist system, according to Marx.

As mentioned earlier, Marx assumes full competition, but the appearance of monopoly would make no difference. Its effect would be to redistribute surplus value among the capitalists.

A student raised the question of whether or not it would be to the advantage of the capitalists to invest mainly in variable capital instead of increasing their constant capital. This would prevent the organic composition from increasing and reducing profits.

If capitalists invested in mainly variable capital, wages would be forced up; furthermore, if manual labor was used exclusively in the wage goods industry it would increase the socially necessary labor, decreasing the rate of surplus value in the economy as a whole. In order to escape labor costs, the individual capitalist will utilize new inventions as soon as they appear, because it will increase their individual rate of profit. But as all capitalists are utilizing the new technique, the rate of profit as a whole will be lowered.

Lord Keynes thought the basic contradiction in the capitalist economy could be solved without complete institutional change. He thought that private enterprise did a pretty good job in allocating resources; the only trouble was the tendency towards the development of underemployment situations. Keynes' primary concern is the creation of full employment; after that is achieved the allocation function will go on.

However, Keynes did not solve the basic contradiction in the capitalist economy; the logical conclusion of his theory is total government planning of investment. In the beginning roads, schools, power dams, etc. are objects of public investment; but there is no need, for government investment will still be needed after all necessary roads, schools and dams have been built. A further necessary conclusion of Keynesian theory is nationalization of the banking system, when the interest rate has sunk to zero. The world has not yet seen bankers willing to lend money at a zero rate of interest. And when the marginal efficiency of capital has reached zero, there will be no capitalist class. Keynes tries to remedy capitalism, but his remedies kill the patient a little at a time, whereas Marx levels the system in one powerful blow.

When the government takes one step, people discover that government can create employment; they will be under constant pressure to take further steps.

APPENDIX

'Halian Economic Theory'

In the concluding remarks of his paper, *Some Implications of Keynes' General Theory of Employment, Interest and Money,* in a treatment of the crisis of Keynes, E.E. Hale has this to say:

> Professor Knight was equally bitter in 1937: "Unfortunately [he said] that which is true [in the *General Theory*] is not new and that which is new is not true."
>
> There were many other reviews of like tenor, they sound somewhat juvenile and somewhat archaic today, just 12 or 13 years later. But one should not be too critical of them, for they represent the first startled and angry reactions of the orthodox who sensed that the renegade was despoiling the temple. Professors Habeler and Schumpeter do much to better jobs, as they should after a decade in which to marshal forces and determine strategy and tactics. Nevertheless it is a losing battle. In fact it is already lost. The damage has been done and it is irreparable. What the bushy-bearded, heavy-handed German revolutionary did with malice aforethought and by frontal attack, the English aristocrat, a scholar of Eton and King's College, Cambridge, a director of the Bank of England, an advisor to the Chancellor of the Exchequer, a peer of the Realm, performed neatly, skillfully, and *unconsciously* by flank attack.

Keynes' theory has thrown some new light on the underconsumptionist theory. The essential difference, it seems to Mr. Hale, between underconsumptionism and Keynesian underinvestment theory results from the way that he looks upon the economic system. The underconsumptionists seem to be viewing the system primarily from the point of view of its universal objective – producing of goods for consumption so consumption is the active variable in the functioning of the economy. The institutional framework comes into the picture through the effect the particular type of organization has on the relation of this ultimate objective of any economy.

The Keynesian point of view is somewhat different. Keynes fixes his attention almost exclusively upon the particular economic structure or particular kind of economic organization in existence – upon the capitalist system. Although it is true that the capitalist economy like any other exists ultimately to produce goods and services for consumption, this is not the immediate objective of those who control the economic processes. Rather, they are interested in making profit. Therefore the active variables in the capitalist economy is not the volume of consumption, but the level of investment; fluctuations in the level of activity result not from fluctuations in consumption but from variations in investment.

In the underconsumption theory, the level of economic activity depends on the level of consumption and varies as consumption expenditures vary; in the

Keynesian theory, the level of economic activity depends on the level of investment and varies as investment varies.

This brings us to the question of the relation of the theories of Marx and Keynes. The investment process, that is, the process of accumulation of capital, necessarily involves or is involved in, a fundamental contradiction with the ultimate objective of the economy, the production of goods for consumption. Almost the whole of the Marxian analysis is devoted to the contradictions that arise from the process of capital accumulation; Keynes finds precisely the same contradictions. The contention of the underconsumptionists that ultimately the level of economic activity must depend upon the extent of consumption expenditures or the extent of the market in which goods are sold to ultimate consumers, seems to Hale undeniable. Investment itself must depend upon the prospects of markets in which the resulting increased output can be sold at profitable prices, and the final market must be the final buyer – the consumer. Thus consumption becomes the variable that in the final analysis must determine the level of investment. Underconsumption takes the long-run view; Keynes the short-run.

If investment ultimately depends upon the extent of consumption expenditures, how then is it possible for any investment ever to be profitable? For whatever the level of consumption at any one time, no additional investment is required to produce the output of goods then being consumed. Keynes solved the problem by having investment decisions depend, not on current results, but on anticipated future returns on investment or upon anticipated future markets – the marginal efficiency of capital. This investment is independent of the current level of consumption, but dependent upon the expected future level. It is this anticipation of future markets that expands investment in the present.

The underconsumptionists have generally overlooked the fact that entrepreneurial decisions are based upon anticipation of the future, and have assumed incorrectly that they are based on past realized results. Mr. Hale finds this true of all underconsumptionists with whom he is familiar – Malthus for example. Adam Smith and the other classicists depend upon the quantity and efficiency of the productive resources to increase the wealth of the nation, and an increase in the wealth of the nation depends upon an increase in the quantity and efficiency of the productive resources. Malthus takes these and finds that they do not increase the wealth of the nation because none of these things of and by themselves expands consumer purchases; i.e., increased population does not of and by itself increase consumer demand. The same view is held by Hayes and Dobson.

Now then, from that point of view any saving of necessity becomes disastrous. The economy could not continue to function unless all income was consumed (provided there was no offsetting feature outside the economy providing additional markets). Malthus found the compensation feature in unproductive consumers. Hayes gets out of the dilemma with his concept of 'extraneous forces' – pushing out frontiers, etc.

Keynes solves the whole problem by bringing what Hayes calls the extraneous forces into the center of the stage and making the level of investment depend upon anticipated profits rather than on existing consumer expenditures. Despite this, however, the contradiction remains; i.e., the process of capital accumulation at one and the same time restricts consumer demand and increases the capacity to produce; it is self defeating. This is, for Hale, the element of unquestionable truth in underconsumptionists theory. For Keynes the inevitable day is only postponed, but not indefinitely. The conclusion is inescapable that capitalism can continue to function effectively only so long as the economy continues to expand; it cannot exist in the absence of an expanding economy. The stationary state of the classicists is impossible.

All – Marx, the underconsumptionists, and Keynes – find the essential contradiction of the capitalist economy, the insoluble contradiction of capital accumulation; and all find the solution outside the capitalist system.

THE JEVONS-AUSTRIAN THEORY OF VALUE

The Marginal Utility School

With the development of the psychological school of economics (marginal utility school) a shift took place in value theory from an objective approach to a subjective one. The marginal utility theory is almost wholly subjective, whereas, e.g., Ricardo's theory was objective. What are the implications of this development? What are the results of the shift?

In a subjective theory, the individual becomes the unit and the center of attention, not the social body; thus, the resulting economics will be individualistic rather than social. Although it is not correct to say that the individual played no part in the classical economics, nevertheless classical theory is primarily concerned with the functioning of the economy and the society as a whole and in its various parts, and not directly nor immediately with individual activity nor individual welfare. Marginal utility analysis is atomistic, economic laws are deduced from the psychology of the individual not from society. Economics becomes a kind of branch of psychology.

Now I do not think that this shift to subjective theory was made primarily in order to disprove Marx; to hold this opinion would amount to believing the marginal utility theorists were intellectually dishonest. They were biased, i.e., influenced by their environment, but this is not dishonesty; dishonesty is the fabrication of a theory to support preconceived notions known to be false. The great, i.e., well-known, economists were all biased. Ricardo was a free trader because he was convinced that free trade would increase profit, which to him was essential for capital accumulation and economic development. Ricardo developed a theory supporting free trade; but he did not develop a theory he did not believe; he was not intellectually dishonest.

Even in the case of Böhm-Bawerk I do not think intellectual dishonesty was involved. Of course, we do not know whether or not Böhm-Bawerk intentionally misrepresented Marx in order to disprove him, or whether he simply misunderstood Marx completely. I do not believe we are justified in labeling him dishonest. If one is not sympathetic to a theory, one may criticize it, but he is not justified in implying dishonesty to those who hold the theory. The marginal utility theorists were convinced of the validity of their theory.

The labor theory of value in Ricardo was seized upon by the so-called Ricardian socialists and later by Marx as a basis for socialism. This of course embarrassed all those who admired the capitalist economy and led them to scrutinize the theory. Ultimately alternative theories were developed. Senior, for example, developed his abstinence theory as an answer to socialist labor theory of value, but Senior's was not necessarily a dishonest theory, a fabricated or 'cooked-up' theory in which he did not believe.

It is just as reasonable to assume that the marginal utility theory was developed because of an increasing belief that the cost theory of the classicists was inadequate. As a matter of fact, marginal utility did not provide the ultimate answer to socialism. If you carry marginal utility analysis to its logical conclusion, you can support a communist economy and condemn capitalism. The psychological school takes *the* economic problem to be the allocation of scarce means among alternative, competing uses. There is no other economic problem. To the degree that this problem is solved depends on the degree scarce means are distributed among competing ends; the ideal is the distribution of resources in such a manner that want-satisfactions are maximized. In the solution of this problem the way is open, according to the marginal utility school, to permit each individual to utilize his own productive resources as he sees fit. This follows the assumption of the Jevonian pleasure-pain hedonistic concept of human behavior.

The second assumption is that the individual knows better than anyone else how to manage his economic affairs – how to invest his money, in what line of business to take a job, when to sell or buy, etc. If the individual is left alone to spend his income, he will buy goods on the basis of the relative utility of the goods available; he will weigh the satisfaction attainable from each good and service. For example, as the purchase of any particular good is increased the utility of each additional (marginal) unit is diminished; so the individual will spend his income on other commodities from each unit of which he will get more satisfaction. In the end each individual will allocate his income in such a way that all units of the various goods have the same utility.

When the individual allocates his income in such a manner that all units of the variable goods have the same utility, want-satisfaction is maximized – utilities are in reverse relation to price. Capitalists will produce goods which command the highest price in the market in order to obtain the highest profit, but the consumers will buy those goods which have the highest want-satisfaction, so in the final analysis the consumer makes the allocation of resources; they will run the economy by their 'dollar vote'. So far, the theory relies on private enterprise. Only in such a system will the individual be able to maximize his wants, because the individual is the best judge of his own want-satisfaction.

But here a problem develops. Since the utility per unit diminishes at the margin, it would seem to follow that the final utility acquired by high-income receivers would be lower than the utility of the last unit acquired by low-income receivers. This calls for a redistribution of income, since the logical conclusion would be that only equal distribution of income would maximize want-satisfaction, then it would seem that distribution of income according to need would maximize want-satisfaction. This is not closely connected to capitalism.

This fact has been pointed out by von Wieser, Marshall and others. Marshall himself says that inequality of the distribution of income is one of the factors that makes it impossible for *laissez faire* to maximize want-satisfaction. The other factor, according to Marshall, is the existence of increasing and decreasing cost industries. Von Wieser in his *Natural Value* argues that the maximization of want satisfaction would only be realized in a communist society. It would seem then that those who developed the marginal utility theory did not do so to refute Marx; it can be used as well against capitalism as it can against Marxian Value theory. G.B. Shaw argued in the 1880s that the socialists should replace Marxian Value theory with the newer marginal utility analysis, which was then influential in academic circles.

It is not easy to fit the psychological theory into my thesis that economic theory is an intellectual reflection of the period in which it is developed, an intellectual reflection of the economic problems of reality. Certainly it does not fit the thesis in the sense that the theories of Smith, Ricardo and Malthus do. Perhaps we can say that psychological economics is a reflection of the problems of the real world in a negative sort of way. During the period of the older English classical theorists, economic problems were pressing – problems of economic policy, free trade vs. tariff, population pressures, etc. So everybody was interested in economic problems, not just professors in the department of economics. Economics was discussed in magazines, newspapers, by men of affairs, in Parliament, all over the place. Not so after 1850–60. Then economics retired into academic halls; from 1860 until 1930, it was cultivated only by professors. Economics was without general interest in this period; its language and technique were esoteric. Anyone who discussed economics must learn its language. What caused this development?

There were no great economic problems demanding attention. From 1860 until about 1920 the capitalist economy enjoyed its greatest success; it embraced the world, so to speak, and operated with great success. There was a vast expansion in production and standard of living in the major capitalist countries of the world – Great Britain, Germany, the United States and France. The capitalist system and *laissez faire* seemed to produce satisfactory results; even the wage earners gained from the increased cake, not however from the functioning of the system but through legislation. The system seemed to work and the future looked rosy.

> And while the house of Peers withholds
> Its legislative hand,
> and noble statesmen do not itch
> To interfere with matters which
> They do not understand,
> As bright will shine Great Britain's rays
> As in King George's glorious days.
>
> (W.S. Gilbert, Iolanthe)

There were some few short depressions, but prosperity covered more time than did recessions, and each peak of prosperity was higher than the last. This may account for the lack of interest on the part of the public in economic matters.

Economic matters were left to the learned professors in the quiet halls of the universities; and they could spin out their subtle theories in intricate mathematics, as they did not have great problems to occupy their minds. In the great depression of the 20th century economics was again drawn from the academic halls to the wild life of the town square, the turbulent life of the market place. Marginal utility analysis lost out, except in the academic halls, because marginal utility analysis was useless for touching and solving the economic problems of depression and war.

So it was the absence of problems that, in a negative way, developed marginal utility analysis from 1860 to 1920–30. The professors had time to resolve theories incapable of solving problems because there were no problems to solve.[8]

The Psychological Theory of Value

A normative science passes value judgments; a positive science does not. The economist of the marginal utility school considered economics a positive science.

The psychological theory of value is generally regarded as having been originated by Jevons (England, 1871), Menger (Austria, 1871), and Walras (Switzerland, 1874). Like most theorists however, they had forerunners.

The concept of productive services of the factors of production, including the services of entrepreneurs, had already been introduced by J. B. Say, the French economist who popularized Adam Smith. Say traced the value of labor, capital and entreprenuership from the services they produced; the value of the services he traced from the utility of the services. The same in Jevons who repeatedly says 'value depends on utility'. J. B. Say reached the same conclusions as the marginal utility school – the value of the productive factors derived from their services and the value of the services derived from the utility they create (the want-satisfying ability of the goods produced by the services).

The labor theory of value was rejected by Adam Smith, who saw it applicable only to the 'rude state of civilization', not to the modern economy. Smith therefore introduced the entrepreneurs cost as the source of value; Say popularized Smith and also traced entrepreneurs' cost as the cause of value. Say added something, however. Value flows from the utility of the goods to the services which produced the goods, and from the services to the factors of production which performed the services. *So value comes from the utility of goods*, which result from services performed by the factors of production utilized in production by the entrepreneur.

This sequence was not found in Adam Smith or other of the early economists of the classical school. Say anticipated the marginal utility school in finding that entrepreneurs' costs are determined by the value (utility) of the final product.

It is a shift of emphasis on supply as the controlling determinant of value to *demand*; this is the shift which characterizes the different emphasis of the classical and neo-classical schools. In fact it is a bit more than a change in emphasis. The older classical economists talked in terms of the economy as a whole, and about production as a social process; they looked at the economy as a whole in its function, not at the individuals who make up the economy. The marginal utility theorists on the other hand look exclusively at the individual and abstract him from society 100% – the social order could just as well be non-existent.

Talking in terms of supply means talking in terms of a co-operative process – production, the terms of older classical economists. The terms of the marginal utility analysis, the want-satisfying ability of goods considered by individuals, these are the atomistic terms of individual demand.[9]

It is because the marginal utility analysis takes the individual as a self-contained and self-sufficient unit abstracted from society that the theory can be so aptly illustrated by simple examples, i.e., the Robinson Crusoe example.

Jevons, although he does not mention Crusoe by name, never gets away from the individual. For this economics, the situation on Crusoe's island is not changed by the appearance of Friday. In the real world, the situation would be entirely different with Friday because rules and regulations by which to play the game are needed that are not necessary when Crusoe is alone. Marginal utility analysis models the economy in the same terms whether Crusoe is *alone,* or *whether* there is a Friday, or 65 million Fridays.

In marginal analysis, demand causes the productive process. In classical theory value resulted from production, from entrepreneurs' cost. In marginal theory value results from, and is determined by, the demand of the individual. Utility derives from the fact that human wants are insatiable and goods are scarce; 'free' goods have no 'marginal utility' say the marginal theorists, thereby avoiding Smith's dilemma regarding water and air. Scarcity can only be defined by utility; goods have utility only because they are scarce.

According to Jevons, there is no such thing as *average* utility. Jevons holds that utility cannot be measured absolutely, but only as a difference, as more or less. Because measurement of utility are made by the individual, and because one individual's mind is inscrutable to another, utility cannot be measured on an absolute scale; therefore *average* utility means nothing.

Marginal Utility Curve

If the curve determines the marginal utility of any quantity of the commodity, what would be the total utility? Would total utility be determined by adding marginal utilities, or must some adjustment be made in the marginal utilities of the first units as more units are added?

For example: a family lives in a five-room house; the weather is exceptionally severe – 40° below zero. The utility of heating one room would have a certain value, but if a second room is heated, this utility might be smaller than the utility of heating the first room, and will not the fact that two rooms are heated in and by itself reduce the utility of heating the first room?

According to Von Wieser the total utility consists of the marginal utility of each unit of a commodity multiplied by the number of units of that commodity. In the diagram overleaf, then, the total utility (according to Von Wieser) would be OQRM. Marshall introduces the concept of 'consumer surplus'; this exists when there is a difference between the total utility of the quantity Q (the total utility of which is area OQRM) and the total utility of the whole area OQRU. OQRU is the marginal utility of the last unit OM times the number of units OQ; OQRM is the sum of all the marginal utilities.

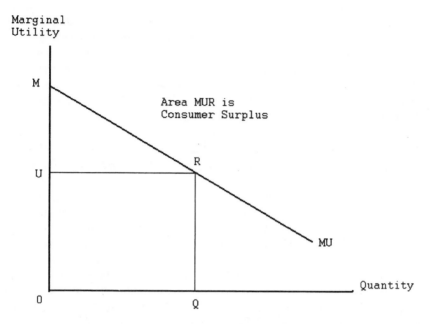

This implies that each individual can compare the quantity of the utility of one good with the quantity of utility of another good.

But back to our immediate subject. As mentioned, J. B. Say was one of the early forerunners of the marginal utility school, as were Richard Cantillon and Augustin Cournot. The major anticipatory contributions of Cournot were the mathematics he developed as a tool of economic analysis; he, however, rejected utility as a factor because he assumed utility could not be treated mathematically; he felt that economics was the study of relations between magnitudes not the magnitudes themselves (the same idea held by Jevons). Senior also anticipated the marginalists; he introduced the psychology of individuals – pain of working, the abstinence of capitalists' postponement of the use of their income, which gives rise to interest. Prices of commodities are determined by the prices paid to workers to induce them to undergo the pain of working, and by the prices paid to capitalists to induce them to undergo the pain of abstinence during the period of production.

The most notable of the forerunners of the marginal utility school was the German economist Herman Heinrich Gossen who in 1854 published his *Antwicklung der Gesetze des menschlichen Verkehrs und der daraus fliessenden Regeln fuer menschiches Handeln. (Development of the Laws of Human Activity and the Rules for Human Behavior Resulting from these Laws).* Gossen had all the concepts embodied in marginal utility analysis – protocol of the ratios between the marginal utility of the commodities traded, etc. Gossen commanded no attention whatsoever, and became so disgusted after the sale of about five copies of his book that he withdrew the remainder from circulation. Today there are only about three copies in existence. When Jevons in 1871 published his first edition he was totally unaware of Gossen's book; later when Gossen was called to his attention, he mentioned him in the preface to his second edition.

Why is it that marginal utility theory was in fact developed by Gossen in 1854, but commanded no attention until it was 'redeveloped' by Jevons in 1871, when it received great acclaim from academic economists. In fact Jevons created as much a stir in 1871 as Keynes did in 1936.

Possible causes for this are: (1) Gossen was relatively unknown, whereas Jevons was one of England's leading economists; Menger was well-known in Austria (because of the controversy between the German historic school and Menger's method of deductive analysis). (2) Germany in 1854 was not as advanced economically and industrially as Great Britain in 1871. It was not until after the Franco-Russian war of 1870–71 that Germany developed a modern industrial economy, so the situation was not so favorable for an appreciation of Gossen's work as was the situation in England 17 years later. (3) A more fundamental question may account for the shift from the older supply-cost of production approach to the newer demand-utility approach. This fact may be the realization of the significance of the extent of the market. In Great Britain during the time of the older classical economists, i.e., shortly after the industrial revolution, the problem seemed to be production. There seemed to be no problem in selling the final products. But at the end of the 18th century markets were no longer considered to be unlimited, so conditions of demand became important.

The history of economic thought shows a close relation between the theories developed and the conditions of the economy at the time of the formulation. Unconsciously, it might have been that marginal utility was developed as a rejection of Marxian theory, the labor theory of value.

More significant is the fact that there were forerunners. Then later on certain problems developed in the real world, problems on which the forerunners threw light – and new theories were developed, partly on the basis of the theories of the forerunners.

The Marginal Utility School (continued)

As mentioned the three important names in the marginal school are Jevons, Menger and Walras. There are some differences in their sources of inspiration. Walras is influenced by Cournot; Jevons stems from British utilitarianism. The basis of Jevon's economic theory is the hedonistic psychology of Bentham, but he was also influenced by the mathematics of Cournot. Jevons stated specifically that he would deal with quantities, quantities capable of variation in infinitesimal amounts. Menger stems from the German predecessors of utilitarianism; he was also influenced by Kant.

The second generation of the marginal utility school, especially Marshall, derived their theory from Senior, his abstinence theory and his theory of monopoly, and from J. S. Mill whose eclecticism and desire for compromise especially influenced Marshall. Marshall was a better mathematician than Jevons, but Marshall did not make use of the language of mathematics in his *Principles*. Marshall was also interested in ethics and welfare; he advocated the maximization of welfare.

Extreme individualism is the main characteristic of the marginal utility school. The individual is treated as a self-sufficient unit, he is independent of the society. Marginal utility analysis is a theory of the individual, an individual whose behavior is determined solely by individual psychology, not by environment. The marginalists considered their theory a universal theory, applicable to the behavior of any individual in any society. The institutional framework has no influence on economic behavior, according to this theory.

The second characteristic of the marginalists is the concept of the nature of economic problems. For the marginalists there is only one economic problem – the allocation of scarce means among alternative uses, i.e., the problem is the problem of economizing to maximize want-satisfaction. The economy of scarce means is realized to the extent that the satisfaction of wants is realized from the ends which the scarce means are capable of producing. A corollary assumption is the insatiability of human wants.

The solution of economizing scarce means is derived from an application of the law of diminishing marginal utility. Maximum want-satisfaction is realized if scarce means are so allocated among competing uses that the marginal utility derived from any one use is equal to the marginal utility derived from any other use. Marginal utilities are equalized in the different employment of the goods. Economizing consists in not using any scarce good for a use in which the marginal utility is less than in any other alternative use.

A third characteristic is that the marginalists hold that economics is a positive not a normative science. They consider the main business of economics to tell 'what is' not 'what ought to be'; economics should not concern itself with value judgments. The best modern exponent of this view is Lionel Robbins. (In point of fact, none of the 'positive' marginalists ever hesitated in making value judgments.)

The marginalists maintain and argue that their approach is superior, especially to the older classical cost approach. There are several reasons for this attitude:

(a) A theory which bases exchange value on cost of production can never give a final explanation because it cannot tell why costs were incurred in the first place. Any cost of production theory of value is circular in reasoning because it cannot explain the prices of these costs; it can only explain some prices in terms of other prices. On the other hand, the marginal utility school says, it is the utility of goods to consumers that explains the incurrence of costs and determines the costs of the factors of production, because these factors derive their value from final products.

(b) Marginal utility theory is a general theory of value (they argue), whereas cost-of-production theory is only a limited theory of value, applicable only under certain conditions. Ricardo excluded non-reproducible goods from his labor theory of value, stating that labor expended could not explain the value (price) of goods not reproducible. Marginal utilitists say that their theory is equally applicable to both non-reproducible and reproducible goods.

(c) The cost theory can only explain the exchange value of goods under conditions of free competition, whereas it is assumed that marginal utility theory can be used in any market situation.

(d) Marginal utility theory is claimed to be more realistic, because ultimately goods are produced only for consumption, and they are consumed only to satisfy wants; therefore it is conditions of demand that control and determine the productive process and the direction of production, not conditions of supply.

These are some of the chief characteristics of the marginal utility school. There are, however, some differences between individual members of the school.

First, in the case of Jevons, but not in the case of Menger and the Austrians, we find that the theory of distribution is independent of the theory of value. This is also true of the classicists. Note that Mill in his *Principles* treats production, value and distribution in three different parts.

Walras is the most positive of the marginal utilitists and the least normative. This is because of his mathematical approach; he used the method of general equilibrium analysis, the technique of simultaneous equations. This approach enabled him to determine the whole system of exchange. You have as many equations as you have exchanges; as many equations as known variables; the system is thus determined. Walras, however, like the others was not hesitant about making value judgments, particularly with respect to the functioning of *laissez faire*.

Menger developed the idea that utility is not measurable; it is a purely relative concept. Goods can be arranged in order of their utility, but it is impossible to measure in absolute terms the utility of one good. It is therefore impossible to compare the utilities of different goods; goods can only be arranged in order according to their ability to satisfy human wants. Menger does not use mathematical language, but his method established the foundations for the equilibrium approach, and he is the forerunner of indifference curves. Menger himself does not use the term *'utility'*, he uses *'bedeutung'* (which means significance).

Jevons uses the language of mathematics, but he is tied to the English utilitarian philosophy and uses this school's psychology of hedonism to a much greater extent than other members of the marginal utility school. Jevons employs hedonism as an extra-economic factor. He insists strongly on the 'basic psychology of the laws of pleasure-pain determining human behavior'. This has created many difficulties for his followers; for when an economic theory is based on psychological 'laws' which are subsequently proved wrong, the whole system is undermined; i.e., if hedonistic psychology is unrealistic, Jevons' economics is unrealistic.

With this theory there is in reality no economic problem; the free market takes care of the allocation of scarce means among competing uses. All that is necessary is to prevent other forces from interfering with the operation of the free market. However, strict impartiality demands that the interference of other forces not be condemned; this is a value judgment. They did, nevertheless, condemn government interference and thereby made value judgments, in contradiction of their solemn principles of non-valuation.

The psychology of hedonism holds that man is motivated by his desire to maximize pleasure and minimize pain; it follows that if he acts at all it is proof of the possibility of increasing pleasure by acting. Anything man does is intended to increase pleasure, and he selects his actions in such a way as to maximize pleasure. The individual is a very skillful calculator of results of any given action with respect to the balancing of pleasure and pain. The motivating force is taken to be desire for pleasure, that this is what causes man to act; but in fact all we know is that man has acted. This is taken as proof that man has obtained maximum satisfaction. The conclusion of the marginal utility analysts is included in the major premise.

Some Specific Problems not Solved by Marginal Utility.

The theory, simply stated, contends that exchange values – the ratio at which goods exchange or prices – are determined by the subjective valuation of individuals in the market, controlled by the fundamental law of diminishing marginal utility.

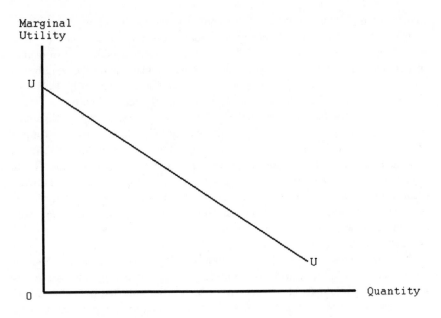

Diminishing marginal utility means simply that the utility of the last unit of a commodity is smaller than that of the preceding units; the final degree of utility, marginal utility, will be positive only if the quantity is insufficient to satisfy all demand for the particular commodity.

In the diagram, UU indicates the utility placed by any individual on the last unit of a commodity as a buyer. The buyer and seller are exchanging one good for another (money may be involved, but it serves only as a means of exchange, it has no utility in itself). The buyer comes into the market with a scale of diminishing utility which determines how much he will give up and how much he will acquire; the same with the seller. It is impossible to quantitatively measure utility, because utility is as the individual determines or evaluates the good, and since we cannot get inside the mind of the individual to examine the indicator on the scales by which he measures this utility, all the observer can do is to estimate the force of the motive by the resultant behavior. We determine the valuation which an individual places on a commodity, or how much he offers in exchange, or the price he is willing to pay. Jevons' theory does not require the comparison of quantities of pleasures and pains; it turns on those critical points where utility is a bit more or less, the final, marginal utility, not total utility.

Jevons failed to solve the problem of getting over from subjective evaluation of individuals to objective market prices, i.e., he is unsuccessful in explaining how the interaction of the behavior of all individuals in the market – as determined by the fundamental law of desire for maximization of pleasure and minimization of pain – acts to establish a competitive market price. He is unsuccessful in making the transition from the psychological feelings and valuations of individuals to objective prices. Jevons attempts the transition (unsuccessfully) by two devices: (1) the law of indifference and (2) the concept of a trading body.

(1) The law of indifference means that buyers do not discriminate among sellers of identical goods except on the basis of price; nor do sellers discriminate among buyers except on the basis of price. 'There can only be one price for a given commodity in a given market at any one time'. If the price quoted or charged by different sellers are different, the buyers will seek the lowest price; and if buyers offer different prices, sellers will sell at the highest price. This statement by Jevons does not, however, explain economic behavior; it is only a definition of competition; it does not explain or describe the forces at work in transferring subjective evaluation to objective market prices.

(2) By the concept of a trading body, Jevons means simply a body of sellers and buyers in the market. One trading body differs from another only with respect to numbers. A trading body can range from one buyer and one seller to thousands of buyers and sellers, and Jevons treats them all alike; to him the determination of prices is identical whether determined by a trading body of two or two thousand. In the case of an isolated exchange, where A has commodity X and B has commodity Y, Jevons assumes that each will continue to increase his want satisfaction by exchange until the final degree of utility of each commodity is the same for both participants. But what happens if the sellers' minimum price exceeds the buyers' maximum price? Jevons cannot tell us.

In the case of a trading body of many buyers and sellers, the price will settle at a point between the price the least eager seller will demand and the price the least eager buyer will offer. But this situation is entirely different from the case of a single buyer and a single seller; Jevons treats them alike.

The problem is to determine the market demand schedule; you must have the whole system of prices before the individual can make a decision; he must know the process before he sells or buys. But this is exactly what Jevons tries to establish at the beginning, that prices are determined by individual action. However, individuals only act within the framework of prices in existence.

The Jevonian attempts to bridge individual decision and markets' prices are unsuccessful both by the method of the law of indifference and by the concept of trading bodies.

Jevons on Exchange Value

[Böhm-Bawerk developed the theory of interest, but he is not considered an originator of marginal utility theory; he wrote later than Jevons. The Austrian School's great men are Böhm-Bawerk, Menger and Von Wieser.]

How does Jevons define exchange value?

He first complains of "the thoroughly ambiguous and unscientific character of the term value." (1911, p. 76) He then lists the various meanings which have been given to the term – *value in use and value in exchange,* but finds that value has been actually used in a third sense. He says (p. 80) "Thus I am led to think that the word value is often used in reality to mean *intensity of desire or esteem for a thing.*" For Smith use-value was a physical value, a quality in a commodity like heating power in coal; value in use increases in proportion to the volume of the commodity. In Jevons' theory value in use is a psychological concept; the utility of the second unit of the commodity is smaller than the utility of the first unit.

Jevons defines exchange value on p. 78: "*Value in exchange expresses nothing but a ratio.*" Marginal utility determines exchange value, or the exchange ratio, but is not itself exchange value.

Jevons denies intrinsic value. He says (p. 77) "Persons are led to speak of such a nonentity as *intrinsic value.* There are, doubtless, qualities inherent in such a substance as gold or iron which influence its value, but the word value, so far as it can be correctly used, merely expresses *the circumstance of its exchanging in a certain ratio for some other substance.*" Jevons proposes (p. 81) to "discontinue the use of the word value altogether, and when, as will be most often the case in the remainder of the book, I need to refer to the third meaning [1. Value in use, total utility; 2. esteem, final degree of utility; and 3. purchasing power, ratio of exchange], often called by economists exchange or exchangeable value. I shall substitute the wholly unequivocal expression *Ratio of Exchange*, specifying at the same time what are the two articles exchanged."

So exchange value for Jevons is simply a 'ratio of exchange'. When Jevons uses the word value in this sense 'its dimension will be zero'; value will be expressed, like angular magnitude and other ratios, by abstract numbers. But Jevons' ratio of exchange has terms too – they are: the ratio will be between the marginal utility of one commodity to the marginal utility of another commodity.

As an example, assume two individuals with two commodities. A has commodity X, and B has commodity Y; the marginal utility of X to A would depend on how much he has and would be less than the utility of Y. On the other hand, B would place a higher value of a unit of X than on a unit of Y. Each will benefit, then, from exchange. As they proceed, the marginal utility of Y to A and X to B will decrease, and they will continue until the final degrees of utility for the commodities are equal for both persons, and loss of utility will result from further exchange. This, according to Jevons, determines market value.

Jevons sums up his law of exchange in a neat sentence (p. 95) "The ratio of exchange value of any two commodities will be the reciprocal of the ratio of the final degrees of utility of the quantities of commodity available for consumption after the exchange is completed."

In other words, after the exchange is completed, each exchanger will have a quantity of goods and a degree of utility, and the ratio of the exchange will be the reciprocal of the final degrees of utility of the quantity each possesses.

Let us assume that at some point the marginal utility of a unit of X and Y are identical to A; he then would be unwilling to exchange any further at the ratio of one to one. Suppose that when that point is reached, the marginal utility of a unit of X to B should be twice as great as the marginal utility of a unit of Y; then B would be willing to offer any amount of Y up to two units for each unit of X. Now, since the utilities are the same for A, he would be willing to give up a unit of X for more of Y. This will continue until the ratio becomes the reciprocal of the final degree of utility of the quantities each has.

This is an illustration of barter. Money is used in the actual exchange, but it has no utility of its own. The marginal utilitists reach the same conclusion as members of the classical school, namely that money serves as a means of exchange, and is never hoarded.

Another example. Two persons, A and B, enter the market, A with 10 bushels of corn and B with 20 lbs. of beef. Each commodity will have a final degree of utility for each individual. If the utility of the tenth bushel of corn were greater to A than a lb. of beef, no exchange would take place. Exchange will only occur if the utility of one lb. of beef is greater than the utility of the tenth bushel of corn to A, and if one bushel of corn has greater utility than the twentieth lb. of beef to B. At what rate does exchange take place?

Suppose that exchange proceeds – one bushel of corn for one lb. of beef. What would be the relation between the marginal utility of corn and beef to A and B? The marginal utility of corn will increase for A, who now has one unit less, and the marginal utility of beef will decrease for A, who now has one unit more; the marginal utility of beef will increase for B, and the marginal utility of corn will decrease. Exchange continues until the marginal utilities of both commodities are the same. According to Jevons,

> This point of equilibrium will be known by the criterion, that an infinitely small amount of commodity exchanged in addition, at the same rate, will bring neither gain nor loss of utility. In other words, if increments of commodities be exchanged at the established ratio, their utilities will be equal for both parties. Thus, if ten pounds of corn were of exactly the same utility as one pound of beef, there would be neither harm nor good in further exchange at this ratio. (p. 97)

However, it might well be that the marginal utility of two pounds of beef is such that it will exchange for one bushel of wheat. So long as the parties in the market place different values on commodities, exchange occurs. But note that the parties were exchanging before the ratio of exchange of the final unit had ever been established. How did the first units ever get exchanged?

Another problem. When you have more than two people exchanging how can we derive the market price? Jevons solved this by his trading body, which might be of any size, and Jevons assumed the process to be the same irrespective of the size of the trading body. (see Roll's criticism of the concept of the trading body)

And another. We have assumed that commodities are infinitely divisible. This is contrary to fact; there are minimum units into which commodities may be divided. The problem becomes indeterminate.

If a dealer is willing to sell a Ford [automobile] for $800, but a buyer will pay $1000. What is the exchange ratio? It cannot be determined – only the limits are set. Determination requires perfect knowledge of the schedules of marginal utility. Jevons himself says that each mind is inscrutable to another; thus the condition – perfect knowledge – essential to the theory is impossible by admission. Jevons assumed that exchange ratios are constant, but that utility changes as exchange takes place.

What happens if some of the goods exchanged at a ratio other than the equilibrium rate? If we assume the equilibrium rate to be one bushel of corn to two pounds of beef, if there are many buyers and sellers, this means that the market will be cleared at that exchange ratio: or if money is used, it may be that the equilibrium price is $2 a bushel for corn, established before and maintained during the market period. The first buyer will pay that price, and the final seller will sell at that price. But suppose that before the period the price had been $3 a bushel, then $2 would not be the equilibrium price.

Assume, for example, that a buyer is willing to pay

$0.50 @lb. for 20 lbs.
0.75 @lb. for 15 lbs.

1.00 @lb. for10 lbs.
1.50 @lb. for 5 lbs.
2.1 @lb. for 1 lbs.

But after having bought one lb. for $2.00, would he then be willing to pay $10.00 for 20 lbs? Obviously not, so, if a change in price takes place, it must mean that the equilibrium price has changed. If homogenous goods sell for more than the normal price, normal price is not normal.

How is the transition made from subjective price to the equilibrium market price. Jevons did not solve this problem; he evidently assumed that no exchange takes place at any but the equilibrium price. His concept of indifference merely defines a competitive market; and with the concept of the trading body, it is necessary to assume all other prices fixed in order to know what one individual will pay for an additional unit of any given good.

Walras uses a different technique to solve the same problem. He called it *prix crie*; this is a kind of auction, with prices called out and adjustments made until the equilibrium price is reached, at which time exchange takes place. Buyer and seller are aware of the offer before exchange occurs, then when the price is called out, the seller knows the demand curve and the buyer the supply curve. This is a clever solution, but it happens not to be the way the economy operates.

There are many unsolved problems in marginal analysis. What, e.g., will be the value of a good which has no utility of its own, but acquires utility when added to another? What is the utility of a single shoe? Suppose one good is composed of three other goods—sugar, flour and cherries to make up a cherry pie: what then is the utility of each ingredient? Menger says that to establish the utility of each single ingredient, you have to take the value of the consumer good produced (the pie) and subtract a unit of the factor, the utility of which is sought, and ascertain the loss of value incurred thereby; the loss of value is the value of that factor.

Von Wieser solved the problems by use of simultaneous equations. Taking land, labor and capital as the factors of production, you have three variables combined in different proportions in different lines of production, so that if you pick up any three lines in which the proportions vary, then find the value of the output in any combination of factors, you have three equations by which to determine the amount of value to be imputed to each of the three factors.

Jevons (continued)

The marginal utility theory is offered as an explanation of the determinants of demand in the market. What then is Jevons' idea with regard to the part played by supply in determining value (if any), and with respect to the part played by cost of production (if any)?

Jevons begins by saying that value depends entirely on utility. In chapter IV, Jevons states that it is a prevailing opinion among economists that labor is the cause of value, 'asserting that all objects derive their value from the fact that labor has been expended on them; and it is thus implied, if not stated, that value will be proportional to labor. This is a doctrine which cannot stand for a moment, being directly opposed to facts'. (1911, p. 163)

Thus it seems to be Jevons' opinion that cost, especially labor cost, cannot determine value. He says that Ricardo disposes of the doctrine of labor as a factor determining value when he says:

> There are some commodities, the value of which is determined by their scarcity alone. No labor cost can increase the quantity of such goods, and therefore their value cannot be lowered by an increased supply. Some rare statues and pictures, scarce books and coins, wines of peculiar quality, which can be made from grapes only grown on peculiar soil. Their value is wholly independent of the quantity of labor originally necessary to produce them, and varies with the varying wealth and inclinations of those who are desirous to posses them.

Jevons continues, after this citation of Ricardo, "The mere fact that there are may things, such as rare books, coin, antiquities, etc., which have high value, and which are absolutely incapable of production now, *disperses the notion that value depends on labor.*"

In his reference to Ricardo, Jevons hits below the belt, because Ricardo in his treatment of value as determined by labor explicitly excepts all the things quoted by Jevons. Ricardo's value theory applies *only* to reproducible goods.

On p. 164, Jevons says, "The fact is that, labour once spent has no influence on the future value of any article; it is gone and lost forever." This is no argument against the labor theory of value. On p. 165, Jevons states that although

> labor is never the cause of value, it is in a large proportion of cases the *determining circumstance*, and in the following way: Value depends solely on the final degree of utility. How can we vary this degree of utility? – By having more or less of the commodity to consume. And how shall we get more of less of it? – By spending more or less labor in obtaining supply. According to this view then, there are two steps between labor and value. Labor affects supply, and supply affects the degree of utility which governs value, or the ratio of exchange. In order that there may be no possible mistake about this all-important series of relations, I will restate it in a tabular form, as follows:–
> (a) Cost of production determines supply;
> (b) Supply determines final degree of utility;
> (c) Final degree of utility determines value.

If x determines y determines z, then x determines z; so in spite of all his elaborate explanations, Jevons is right back to where the classical economists were

– value depends upon the cost of production. Here Jevons yields completely to the cost of production theory.

Jevons' entire analysis applies to the valuation of consumers goods; he says nothing about the valuation of capital goods or labor. Thus, he does not derive his theory of distribution from his theory of value. In the case of producers' goods, they have no utility themselves; they do not directly satisfy human wants. Jevons thus left a big gap in the theory which was filled by the Austrians' analysis through the concept of derived utility, i.e., the utility of the means of production is derived from the utility of the consumer goods which they produce. The Austrians say that cost depends on the final value of output; so marginal utility of the final goods determines cost.

This left the question of determining the value of the three factors of production – land, labor and capital – used in the production of any given commodity. How much of the value of the final product is to be imputed to each of the three factors. Menger attempted to solve the problem in the following manner:

> Take the value of the final product produced by the combination of the factors of production; then subtract a unit of the factor being evaluated; you may thereby ascertain the loss of value incurred. This loss of value is the value of the unit of the factor subtracted. In other words the value of the factor of production is computed by negative imputation.

This solution is not satisfactory; Von Wieser pointed out that if the final result depends upon the co-operation of two or more factors, the economical use of the factors demands that they be combined in the most efficacious proportions in order to maximize the value of the output; and that if you vary the quantity of any one of them you will affect the final outcome by a greater amount than the variation of any one factor. Take an extreme example. Assume that a good is produced by the combination of land and labor. To use Menger's method, if the whole of the labor is subtracted, then the value of the product equals zero; you may then say that the whole of the value of the final product is produced by labor; but the same would result by abstracting the land, then the conclusion would be that the entire value of the product is the result of land. Von Wieser proposed another solution.

He noted that in different lines of production the factors are combined in different proportions. In agriculture, e.g., a relatively larger amount of land is used than in steel production. Taking land, labor and capital as the factors of production, Von Wieser says that you have three variables combined in different proportions in different line of production. So if you select any three lines in which the proportions vary, then find the value of the output in any combination of the factors, you then have three equations by which to determine the amount of value to be imputed to each of the three factors. That is, the method of solving simultaneous equations.

For example, land, labor and capital are used in the production of shoes; and these three factor have their value determined by the value of the final product. Von Wieser takes the *fact* that certain quantities of factors of production produce shoes, which will sell at a certain price, a price determined by the final degree of utility. At this point other commodities enter the picture because the same factors of production are used in the production of these other commodities. The enterprises competing for the factors of production of the greatest value will be able to purchase them because of the greater value of their final products. In fact producing any commodity involves an opportunity cost; it can only be done by foregoing the production of other commodities, in the production of which the factors of production could have been used.

Let us assume three producers all using land (x), labor (y), and capital (z). A produces shoes at a value of 20, B produces flour at a value of 30, C produces barrels at a value of 40 (values are per unit); we may then derive the following equations:

$$1 \text{ shoe} = 1\frac{1}{2} \text{ flour} = 2 \text{ barrels}$$

In this system, wages are determined by the marginal productivity of labor, a concept which Keynes accepts.

The great weakness in Jevons' theory is his hedonistic psychology. The Austrians and Marshall tried to escape but did not succeed. Hedonism is wholly discredited today. In the first place, people are uninformed and ignorant of the quality of different products. Furthermore, man's behavior is determined by custom and habit, not by individual psychology. The customer does not enter a store, evaluate the different prices and equalize the marginal utility between sugar, flour, etc. Furthermore wants are not universal and given, as the marginalists assumed; wants are socially derived.

The marginal utilitists maintained that human nature does not change. You begin with given wants and scarce resources, so the only problem is allocation of the resources among the competing ends, determined by given natural wants. The only policy is a negative one. Another shortcoming of the theory is that a free market cannot result in maximizing want satisfactions, because of the unequal distribution of income. This theory, a defense of *laissez faire*, ends by justifying communism as the only means of maximizing want-satisfaction. Jevons escapes this dilemma by incomparability of wants, i.e. the want satisfaction of the poor cannot be compared to the want satisfaction of the rich.

I believe that the vast majority of literate mankind is of the opinion that the assumptions of the marginal utility school are correct. 'Everyone' believes that we are born with a certain quota of wants independent of social conditions: that wants are naturally insatiable.

The theory assumes that man is a calculator and that some will have an advantage over other due to monopoly. It is the duty of the government therefore to abolish monopoly.

The theory is a rationalization of free enterprise, which may explain the persistence of the theory.

ALFRED MARSHALL

Marshall's Principles of Economics

From your reading of the first chapters of Marshall's *Principles of Economics* did you find any differences between the thinking of the classical school and the Jevons-Austrian school on the one hand and Marshall's ideas with respect to the scope and nature of political economy (or economics as Marshall calls it) on the other hand?

Mill defined economics as the study of wealth, i.e., the study of production, distribution and consumption of wealth.

In the opening paragraph in chapter 1, book I, Marshall gives his first definition.

> Political economy or economics is a study of mankind in the ordinary business of life; it examines that part of individual and social action which is most closely connected with the attainment and with the use of the material requisites of wellbeing (p. 1).

A bit later he says:

> Economics is a study of men as they live and move and think in the ordinary business of life. But it concerns itself chiefly with those motives which affect, most powerfully and most steadily, man's conduct in the business part of his life (p. 14).

Here we see that the subject with which economics is concerned is the *behavior* of man in connection with the attainment of material wealth, not simply with wealth. Economics is the study of human behavior, or a part of human behavior in society. It is not simply individual behavior; it is, as in modern economics, man's *social* behavior.

According to Marshall there are many studies of man, and of human behavior; studies which are carried on in the different social sciences. To Marshall the study with which economics is concerned is the study of behavior in the production and consumption of goods. Notice the word 'material'; it is the study of *material* requisites of wellbeing, not spiritual, not psychological, but material wellbeing.

Marshall finds that economics enjoys certain advantages over other social sciences. This advantage, or one of the advantages, is that the phenomena with which economics deals can be measured. Economics concerns itself with human motives, and the effects of these motives can be measured (not the motives themselves, but the effects).

Marshall takes man as he is. Man is influenced by all sorts of motives, but the economist is not concerned with the motives, only with the effects of these motives; and the economist measures the effects of the motives; he measures the strength of the motives by the use of money; the economist uses money as the means to measure the strength of human motives.

Why, according to Marshall, is the economist concerned with the effect of motive, and why does he think it is an advantage to the economist that he can measure these motives of man?

The fact that economics can measure the effects of human motives makes it more scientific (more scientific according to the 19th century concept, not according to the 20th century concept of science). The 19th century concept was that a discipline can be a science only if it is able to measure the phenomena with which it deals and if it is able to discover regularities in these phenomena. Only that part of economics is scientific which deals with human motives that are measurable in terms of money and which is able to disclose regularities in human motives that are measurable in terms of money.

> ... the steadiest motive to ordinary business work is the desire for the pay which is the material reward of work. The pay may be on its way to be spent selfishly or unselfishly, for noble or base ends; and here the variety of human nature comes into play. But the motive is supplied by a definite amount of money; and it is this definite and exact money measurement of the steadiest motives in business life, which has enabled economics far to outrun every other branch of social science. But of course economics cannot be compared with the exact physical sciences; for it deals with the ever changing and subtle forces of human nature (*Principles*, p. 14).

Marshall disavows hedonism in the beginning of his book (although he does not strictly maintain this disavowal throughout). He states the advantages of economics more specifically:

> ... The advantages which economics has over other branches of social science appear then to arise from the fact that its special field of work gives rather larger opportunities from exact methods than any other branch. It concerns itself chiefly with those desires, aspirations and other affections of human nature, the outward manifestation of which appear as incentives to action in such a form that the force or quantity of the incentive can be estimated and measured with some approach to accuracy; and which therefore are in some degree amenable to treatment by scientific machinery. An opening is made for the methods and the tests of science as soon as the force of a person's motives – not the motives themselves – can be approximately measured by the sum of money, which he will just give up in order to secure a desired satisfaction; or again by the sum which is just required to induce him to undergo a certain fatigue (*Principles*, p. 15).

This differs from Jevons, who thought it was possible to measure the motives themselves. The problem encountered by Jevons was to take the step from subjective individual value to the objective market value. Marshall's first step from subjective to objective value is that he uses money as a means of measure of the force or strength of human motives.

> It is essential to note that the economist does not claim to measure any affection of the mind in itself, or directly; but only indirectly through its effect. No one can compare and measure accurately against one another even his own mental states at different times; and no one can measure the mental states of another at all except indirectly and conjecturally by their effects. Of course various affections belong to man's higher nature and others to his lower, and are thus different in kind. But even if we confine our attention to mere physical pleasures and pains of the same kind, we find that they can only be compared indirectly by their effects. In fact, even this comparison is necessarily to some extent conjectural, unless they occur to the same person at the same time.
>
> For instance, the pleasures which two persons derive from smoking cannot be directly compared: nor even those which the same person derives from it at different times. But if we find a man in doubt whether to spend a few pence on a cigar, or a cup of tea, or on riding home instead of walking home, then we may follow ordinary usage, and say that he expects from them equal pleasures (Ibid).

Marshall realizes that man acts under different motives; there are family affections, sense of responsibility, etc., but even if Marshall realized that, what he is interested in is the 'study of man as he lives and moves and thinks in the ordinary business of life, . . . the steadiest motive to ordinary business work is the desire for the pay which is the material reward of work'. But, according to Marshall, economics is not concerned with the motives but with the type of behavior which results from these motives, so he measures the strength of the motives from the action, and he measures this action by the use of money. We are not concerned, according to Marshall, with the motive but with the fact that people enter the market, not with the reason they entered the market. So Marshall limits economics to the study of value and distribution, to price phenomena.

Economics is the study of *normal* behavior, behavior expected in any given situation of normal conditions.

Marshall has a solution of the problem of transition from subjective value to objective market value. He does it by measuring the strength of motives by the use of money. There is another problem, however, because of the fact that when money is used as a measure, the fact is encountered that equal amounts of money mean different things to different people. A shilling may mean more pleasure to one person than to another, due to the different incomes these people have. Furthermore, a shilling may give different amounts of pleasure to one person at one time than at another.[10] Marshall solves this problem by the use of the law of large numbers.[11]

Marshall assumes that one universe (the inhabitants of Sheffield) is equal to another universe (the inhabitants of Leeds); then there will be the same variation in the character of different individuals and the same distribution of income. What we have are two samples, which are similar, so that anything which affects one universe will affect the other in the same way, because Marshall assumes the two samples to be identical.

Marshall is not very concerned with the psychology of individuals; he is concerned with the group, with groups of people. According to Marshall, it is impossible to use money to compare the amount of pleasure of two individuals, but you can compare the effects on two groups, when the groups are sufficiently large. When the two samples (Sheffield and Leeds) are sufficiently large, you will cut across different individuals. The two samples are sufficiently identical to be treated as identities, and the marginal utility of a commodity to the two groups may be considered as approximately the same.[12]

To Marshall, economics is a social science. Large numbers give him the answer to the problem of transition from the individual subjective value to objective market value. This is the same answer large numbers give an insurance company when it estimates the probabilities involved in life insurance.

Marshall points out the evils of society in his work; *laissez faire* has failed to maximize wellbeing. As an economist Marshall does not pass judgment; he passes value judgments as a social and moral philosopher.

He criticizes Jevons for burdening economics with hedonistic values. We shall see, later on, how successful Marshall is in divesting himself of this concept.

To Marshall economics is the study of certain aspects of human behavior in the society in which man lives, with its social and institutional framework. He "hates to think what will be the fate of his own principles in 50 years;" he says it is impossible to discover universal laws, because laws are only statements of how human beings are expected to act under certain given circumstances. When these circumstances change, human behavior may change too.

We cannot do much with the individual. One dollar does not measure the same pleasure in two different persons. "It would . . . not be safe to say that any two men with the same income derive equal benefit from its use." His solution is to take a sufficiently large number. "If we take averages sufficiently broad to cause the personal peculiarities of individuals to counterbalance one another, the money which people of equal income will give to obtain a benefit or avoid an injury is a good measure of benefit or injury."

. . . Perhaps the earlier English economists confined their attention too much to the motives of individual action. But in fact economists, like all other student of social science, are concerned with individuals chiefly as members of the social organism . . . life of society is something more than the sum of the lives of its individual members. It is true that the action of the whole is made up of that of its constituent parts; and that in most economic problems the best starting point is to be found in the motives that affect the individual, regarded not indeed as an isolated atom, but as a member of some particular trade or industrial group but it is also true ... that economics has a great and an increasing concern in motives connected with the collective ownership of property, and the collective pursuit of important aims (*Ibid.*, p. 25).

Marshall disavows the concept of 'economic man', the concept of completely rational behavior. "... they [economists of Marshall's type] deal with man as he is: not with an abstract or 'economic' man; but a man of flesh an blood." (pp. 26–27)

Since economics for Marshall has no function unless it throws light on problems, it certainly cannot do that unless it is fairly realistic. The economic man is too great an abstraction. A discipline which departs too much from reality becomes merely a philosophical exercise. We must determine later whether or not Marshall really rids himself of the economic man; but so far, Marshall maintains that economics is not a study of psychology; it is a purely descriptive science to Marshall.

Economics as a Science

As we mentioned last time, Alfred Marshall was concerned with economics as a science. His concept of science was, however, that of the 19th century not of the 20th. According to Marshall two things are necessary in order to make a discipline scientific:

(1) The phenomena with which it deals must be measurable
(2) The phenomena which is measured must exhibit regularities in lesser or greater degree.

Only that part of economics is scientific, according to Marshall, which deals with human motives that are measurable in terms of money, and which is able to disclose regularities in human motives that are measurable. It measures the strength of the motives at work in the process of making a living by measuring their effects. With this idea of science and that part of economics which is truly scientific, what would be included in economics?

It limits economics to *price and distribution theory.* The core of economics for Marshall is the theory of value and distribution as it has been for orthodox economics since the time of Ricardo.

Marshall's general criticism of classical theory (albeit a sympathetic one, see p. 47 in *Principles*) is that it focused its attention on conditions of supply. This condition was corrected by the marginal utility school, but this school went to the opposite extreme. For example, Jevons fell into deeper error by concentrating his attention on the demand side in terms of individual feelings of pleasure-pain relations. What Marshall is trying to do is to synthesize the older classical approach with marginal utility.

The great difficulty that confronts the investigator seeking regularity in economic phenomena is the dynamic character of the economy. Society is highly dynamic, highly volatile and fluid. Things never remain the same for any length of time. Population increases, technological innovations occur, capital is accumulated, new resources are discovered either in a geographic sense or as the result of advance of knowledge. These factors alter the situation from one day to the next. The result is that behavior which would result from a given set of circumstances is not the same as behavior from a different set of circumstances. The question is: do these things ever stand still long enough to allow the discovery of uniformities and permit predictions?

The older classical economists solved the problem by ignoring it; they assumed the economy to be static. Marshall believes this assumption departs too much from reality; yet taking the economy as it is – highly dynamic – will render it impossible to detect any regularity. Marshall then permits the economy to be dynamic, but it is *controlled dynamics*: in his scheme capital accumulation occurs, but at a regular rate of increase; he leaves out innovations, not completely but almost; and he assumes population to increase at a stable rate. By this quasi-static analysis, he reaches the regularity he investigates.

Bear in mind that economics has a very practical function to perform for Marshall; it can perform this function only if knowledge is scientific in character, so Marshall cannot allow himself to abstract too much from reality, which is highly dynamic; still some abstractions must be made in order to proceed at all. Marshall then uses two techniques to take care of this problem: (1) the technique of *ceteris paribus* or as he says: ". . . economics undertakes to study the effects which will be produced by certain causes, not absolutely, but subject to the condition that *other things are equal,* and that the causes are able to work out their effects undisturbed." (p. 36) He assumes all variables to remain constant except the one to be measured. (2) the technique of *quasi-static analysis*. He is unwilling to assume a completely static situation because this involves too high a degree of abstraction; but nevertheless, he cannot deal with changing phenomena in all their 'changefullness', so he permits population and capital to increase, but at a steady rate so that the ratio between them does not change. This is only to say that he permits *quantitative* change, but rules out *qualitative* change. He then rules out (almost) changes in technology, techniques of production, advances of scientific knowledge, or changes in the quality of the labor force. He also rules out institutional change. Marshall examines economic behavior within the limits of the existing institutional order. This is what all his predecessors had done.

There is a big difference, however; almost without exception the earlier orthodox economists had assumed the existing order to exist forever. They were aware of the fact that changes had occurred in the past, but assumed no change in the future. Now Marshall makes no such assumption. He is not only aware for the fact that institutional change will occur, hence the economic principles which he derives will have only temporary value, only within the existing institutional framework without substantial modifications. He is under no illusion that he is discovering universal laws or universal truths, as Jevons and others. Truths are valid at a given time under given circumstances.

Marshall seeks economic laws which are descriptions of regularity. First he defines laws in general:

> ... The term 'law' means nothing more than a general proposition or statement of tendencies, more or less certain, more or less definite ... Many such statements are made in every science but we do not, indeed we cannot, give to all of them a formal character and call them laws. We must select; and the selection is directed less by purely scientific considerations than by practical convenience. If there is any general statement which we want to bring to bear so often, that the trouble of quoting it at length, when needed, is greater than that of burdening the discussion with an additional formal statement and an additional technical name, then it receives a special name, otherwise not (*Ibid.*, p. 33).

He derives 'economic' law from 'social' law which he defines as:

> ... a statement of social tendencies; that is, a statement that a certain course of action may be expected under certain conditions from the members of a social group (Ibid.).

> ... Economic laws, or statements of economic tendencies, are those social laws which relate to branches of conduct in which the strength of the motives chiefly concerned can be measured by money price (Ibid.).

Marshall's economic law is a *law of production and distribution.*

Two observations should be made here. (1) It would not be correct to say that Marshall is not concerned with human motives; he is. But human motives cannot be directly observed and compared; these motives cannot be treated scientifically (according to Marshall) therefore Marshall confines his attention to the measure of the strength of the motives as they come into action. The economist is focusing his attention on economic behavior, and measures the effect of the strength of the motives, by the use of money prices. (2) Marshall is of the opinion that there is knowledge to be gained from that particular aspect of human behavior which he calls economic behavior; and the reason why he singles out this particular feature of behavior is that these motives, which are among the most constant, can be measured by the use of money; a measurement which cannot be made in other aspects of human behavior.

Marshall does not assume that man is an economic animal; he realizes that man has all sorts of motives, based on such things as family affection, etc. The economist can never obtain final answers; he cannot give final answers in terms of economics. Nevertheless, knowledge can be gained from the study of economic behavior, a behavior for which we are so fortunate to have a measure – money.[13]

Marshall next attempts to define what is 'normal' in economic behavior:

> . . . following our definition of an economic law, we may say that the course of action which may be expected *under certain conditions* from the members of an industrial group is the *normal action* of the members of that group relatively to those conditions (p. 34).

Normal is what is expected under certain conditions; that is group behavior. Marshall attempts to rid the term 'normal' of all ethical and supernatural connotations so prevalent in classical economics. Normal behavior is just the behavior expected with the group under certain circumstances. He says that competition is not necessarily the 'normal' condition.

> Another misunderstanding to be guarded against arises from the notion that only those economic results are normal which are due to the undisturbed action of free competition. But the term has often to be applied to conditions in which perfectly free competition does not exist, and can hardly ever be supposed to exist; and even where free competition is most dominant, the normal conditions of every fact and tendency will include vital elements that are not a part of competition nor even akin to it (*Principles,* p. 35).

He continues:

> Lastly it is sometimes erroneously supposed that normal action in economics is that which is right morally. But that is to be understood only when the context implies that the action is being judged from the ethical point of view. When we are considering the facts of the world, *as they are,* and *not as they ought to be,* we shall have to regard as 'normal' to the circumstances in view, *much action which we should use our utmost efforts to stop.*

'Normal' then is not that which is ethically 'good' but any action which can be expected from the social group under certain circumstances.

Marshall lists the sort of things with which the economist is concerned; by this list he limits the scope of economics. Note that this list set up by Marshall are the problems dealt with in most elementary economics textbooks. Marshall limits himself to theory, because theory throws light on the problems.

> . . . the special business of the economist is to study and interpret facts and to find out what are the effects of different causes acting singly and in combination (p. 40).

> . . . This may be illustrated by enumerating some of the chief questions to which the economist addresses himself.

... What are the causes which, especially in the modern world, affect the consumption and production, the distribution and exchange of wealth; the organization of industry and trade; the money market; wholesale and retail dealing; foreign trade; and the relations between employers and employed? How do all these movements act and react upon one another? How do their ultimate effect differ from their immediate tendencies?

Subject to what limitations is the price of anything a measure of its desirability? What increase of wellbeing is *prima facie* likely to result from a given increase in the wealth of any class of society? How far is the industrial efficiency of any class impaired by the insufficiency of its income? How far would an increase of the income of any class, if once affected, be likely to sustain itself through its effects in increasing their efficiency and earning power?

How far does, as a matter of fact, the influence of economic freedom reach (or how far has it reached at any particular time) in any place, in any rank of society, or in any particular branch of industry? What other influences are most powerful there; and how is the action of all these influences combined? In particular, how far does economic freedom tend of its own action to build up combinations and monopolies, and what are their effects? How are the various classes of society likely to be affected by its action in the long run; what will be the intermediate effects while its ultimate results are being worked out; and, account being taken of the time over which they will be spread, what is the relative importance of these two classes of ultimate and intermediate effects? What will be the incidence of any system of taxes? What burdens will it impose on the community, and what revenue will it afford to the State? (p. 40).

Marshall is going to study *what is;* he is not concerned, as an economist, with *what ought to be*. The economist has no peculiar knowledge which enables him to answer questions with respect to ethical or social policy; but economics does throw light on these problems:

... Economics has then as its purpose firstly to acquire knowledge for its own sake, and secondly to throw light on practical issues (p. 39).

Knowledge should be acquired for its own sake, but Marshall does not stop here; he was not just interested in 'idle curiosity' (a la Veblen). Marshall wanted to use knowledge to throw light on practical problems and issues. Economics deals with human motives, but only that part of man's action which lends itself to measurement and analysis. This is the narrow 19th century concept of science – dealing with quantity – not the modern concept of science – dealing with quality. Marshall was interested in value judgments, but not as an economist. According to Marshall an economist cannot, as an economist, pass value judgments; but economics will throw light on the right means to reach a given end (the end determined by value judgments). Marshall would say, I believe, that social ends are determined by the democratic process, and the economist can tell the lawmakers how to reach the goals or ends they have set themselves by value judgments; but the economist is no better equipped than anyone else to pass value judgments with respect to what ends should be realized.

Marshall admits that he himself has certain views, but he has not reached a conclusion with respect to these ends as an economist, but as an ordinary citizen. He knows, as an economist, which means can be used to reach these preconceived goals.

Marshall criticizes the widely held opinion that the older classical economists pictured man as a selfish beast.

> ... The fact is that nearly all the founders of modern economics were men of gentle and sympathetic temper, touched with the enthusiasm of humanity. They cared little for wealth for themselves; they cared much for its wide diffusion among the masses of the people. They opposed antisocial monopolies however powerful. In their several generations they supported the movement against the class legislation which denied to trade unions privileges that were open to associations of employers ... (p. 39).

This characterization of the older economists depends on the selection. He is correct in regard to the 'great economists'; but they differed with respect to the means to bring about these ends – a fact of great importance.

Marshall says that he, as an economist, does not make value judgments. But, a student asks, does he not rely on value judgments when he selects the problems with which economists should be concerned?[14]

Marshall says that he has selected the problems which beset England; but of course he does not list all the problems, and in making this selection, he must use value judgments. But no one can avoid this sort of value judgments, because the scope of inquiry must be limited. This is not, however, exactly the sort of judgments involved in determining the goal of public policy. Marshall is interested in knowledge for its own sake, but to stop here is insufficient for Marshall. 'Idle curiosity' has never been the sole motivation for Marshall's inquiry or that of most people.

All the great theories of economics have been reactions to problems of their times. In the absence of economic problems, there would be no economic theory. (This thesis is rather thin, as noted, in the case of Jevons, but it applies.) Marshall is deeply concerned with the problems of Great Britain of his day; but he would no doubt say that when he passes value judgments, he does it in his capacity as a member of society, not in his capacity as an economist. Of all the predecessors Marshall was most influenced by Mill, who himself was deeply concerned with social conditions. Both Mill and Marshall were concerned with the evils of society.

What is Marshall's position with respect to the thesis that economics is primarily concerned with the allocation of scarce resources for the satisfaction of unlimited wants, as against the idea that economics is mainly concerned with consumption?

Marshall says that wants are not given, that they can be and are being changed. On p. 72 of the *Principles* he says: "Human wants and desires are countless in number and very various in kind: *but they are generally limited and capable of being satisfied.*" So wants are *not* unlimited.

... in dress conventional wants overshadow those which are natural (natural in the sense that they result from climate and the season of the year etc.) (p. 74).

... It is not true therefore that the Theory of Consumption is the scientific basis of economics. For much that is of chief interest in the science of wants is borrowed from the science of efforts and activities. These two supplement one another; neither is incomplete without the other. But if either, more than the other, may claim to be the interpreter of the history of man, whether on the economic side or any other, it is the science of activities and not that of wants (p. 76).

According to Marshall, except for certain very primitive wants, such as food and clothing, all wants grow out of human activities. Of course, many of these activities are those involved in the production of goods; productive activities themselves give rise to wants. Marshall thus rejects the marginal utility school's thesis that wants are given. It is activity which gives rise to wants, not wants which give rise to activity – the very opposite of the marginal utility thesis.

Marshall also thought that the older classical economists over-stressed supply, but they were more nearly correct than the marginal utility stress on demand.

Marshall denies the possibility of comparing one want with another; the utility of any given goods are greater for a poor man than for a rich man. This is the reason why *laissez faire* cannot maximize satisfaction; income is unequally distributed under such a system.

The science of activities is the theory of production, from which wants result. The older classical theory was a theory of production; it was more nearly on the right track with its emphasis on supply and the process of production than the marginal utility school with its emphasis on wants and the utility of goods.

In the modern marginal utility school, hedonistic psychology has become the object of such criticism that economists have become very sensitive and realize the danger of having economics tied to any psychological theory. Generally modern orthodox economists make no open acceptance of hedonistic psychology or of any other. They take the position that economists are not interested in why people prefer one thing to another, but only in the fact that they do. They substitute, for the analytical tools of diminishing utility and marginal utility, *indifference curves.*[15]

Marshall explicitly rejects hedonistic psychology and regards man as an active animal. This means of course that he cannot say much about demand; in fact, demand itself becomes in some part the result of the production. We do not want to overemphasize this point. Demand and supply are both important in determining price, according to Marshall. He does not rule out demand, but says that economists cannot throw much light on it. Of course there are other reasons in terms of Marshall's concept of the nature of economics as a science. Demand is too variable, too shifting. We can find out from a study of statistical data what amounts have been sold, but we cannot know what quantities could have been sold at other prices, nor can we assume that the same schedule will obtain in the future.

In Book III of *Principles* Marshall sums up the elements of marginal utility theory: the law of diminishing utility, marginal utility determining the price an individual offers; marginal utility determining the price an individual offers in the market, from which we get a demand schedule for the individual; by adding up the individual demand schedules, we get an aggregate demand schedule.[16]

Marshall is under no compulsion to assume that decisions on the part of individuals are based on rationality; but he does say that as more is supplied of a given commodity, it will only be purchased at lower and lower prices. This is what is expressed in the familiar demand curve sloping downward toward the right. Marshall does not hold that the price at which a commodity sells in the market is an accurate measure of its utility, because price depends not only on the want-satisfying power of the commodity but also on the purchasing power of the buyers, which will vary. Though all buyers pay the same price it does not follow that the utility is the same for all of them, nor does it follow that the utility to society as a whole of one commodity is greater than that of another commodity at a lower price. The first may be purchased mainly by the rich, the second, by the poor. He does not accept value to society as an organism, which again means that he does assume that the utility of a given good for which all buyers pay the same price differs among the buyers and will be greater for the poorer buyer.

This is one reason why, for Marshall, a theory of demand could never be made into a complete theory of prices. The price of a commodity, Marshall thinks, is a pretty accurate index of its utility – not to an individual buyer, but to the buyers generally in the market. He uses the concept of the group in his analysis. Marshall assumes that inequality will be about the same in different groups (such as two different towns or cities) of buyers and sellers. His general law of demand is that a greater quantity can only be sold at a lower price in a given market at a given time. It is the same conclusion at which the marginal utility school arrived.

> ... The price will measure the marginal utility of the commodity to each purchaser individually: we cannot speak about price as measuring marginal utility in general, because the wants and circumstances of different people are different (p. 84).

> ... In large markets, then – where rich and poor, old and young, men and women, persons of all varieties of tastes, temperaments and occupations are all mingled together, – the peculiarities in the wants of individuals will compensate one another in a comparatively regular

gradation to total demand. Every fall, however slight in the price of a commodity in general use, will, other things being equal, increase the total sales of it (p. 83).

In the case of an individual, we will have the familiar demand schedule. For an individual, the demand curve is determined by decreasing marginal utility. There are, according to Marshall, three reasons why the curve slopes down to the right: (1) the law of diminishing utility; the more of a commodity one buys, the smaller the utility of an additional unit; (2) Difference in taste among purchasers. Some buyers place higher value on the good than others do because of the fact that their want for it is greater. It necessarily must fall to the right (the curve) because any one buyer would buy more at a lower price; and (3) Difference in purchasing power. Marshall points to the fact, or the exception that with some few articles, the demand increases with an increase in price (pp. 79–80).

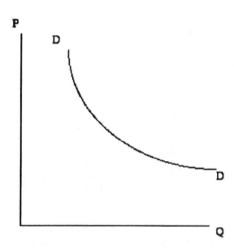

On p. 80 of *Principles:* "... A greater utility will be required to induce him (the individual) to buy a thing if he is poor than if he is rich." For both a rich man and a poor man the utility of a bus ride is measured by a twopence; but the marginal utility is greater in the case of the poorer man than in the case of the richer. Marshall uses the example (Ibid.) of a man with an income of £100 per year, who may use a bus 20 times in a year; and a man with an income of £300 per year who may use the bus 100 times a year; both paying twopence a trip.

> ... the utility of the hundredth ride which the richer man is only just induced to take is measured to him by the twopence; and the utility of the twentieth ride which the poorer man is only just induced to take is measure to him by twopence. For each of them the

marginal utility is measured by twopence; but this marginal utility is greater in the case of
the poorer man than in that of the richer (p. 81).

More units can be sold at a lower price, because the purchasing power of individuals is limited; one individual has different tastes than another. However, as
the price goes down more and more people will be willing to purchase the
given commodity, because now the lower price may induce people with a lower
degree of taste than others to be willing to purchase the commodity, their taste
or desire for the commodity not being strong enough for them to purchase it
at a higher price, with income unchanged.

More regarding Marshall's use of the term 'willingness'. 'Willingness to buy'
for Marshall means *desire plus purchasing power*. There are many things people
can purchase if they so choose. There are of course many who do not purchase
a Cadillac because they simply cannot; on the other hand, there are many who
can, but do not do so, they are simply not willing to. There are many people
who are able to buy butter, but who are nevertheless are not willing to buy it;
they prefer margarine.

All that Marshall is saying is that when prices fall, the amount of goods sold
will increase. The slope of the demand curve may differ for different products,
because of different elasticities.[17]

> ... The price will measure the marginal utility of the commodity to each purchaser individu-
> ally: we cannot speak of price as measuring marginal utility in general, because of the wants
> and circumstances of different people are different.

> The demand prices in our list (demand schedule) are those at which various quantities of a
> thing can be sold in a market *during a given time and under given conditions.* If these condi-
> tions change; the price will probably require to be changed, and this has constantly to be
> done when the desire for anything is materially altered by a variation of custom, by the
> cheapening of the supply of a rival commodity, or by the invention of a new one (p. 84).

Up to this point Marshall's analysis has not differed much from that of the marginal
utility school. He does introduce a concept which may not have been unknown to
the marginal utility school, mainly the concept of elasticity of demand. This is the
degree in which the quantity demanded changes with a change in price.

> We have seen that the only universal law as to a person's desire for a commodity is that
> it diminishes, other things being equal, with every increase in the supply of that commodity.
> But the diminution may be slow or rapid. If it is slow the price that he will give for the
> commodity will not fall much in consequence of a considerable increase in his supply of
> it; and a small fall in price will cause a comparatively large increase in his purchase ...
> his willingness to purchase the thing stretches itself out a great deal under the action of a
> small inducement: the elasticity of his want is great (p. 86).

> ... But if it is rapid (the diminution in desire as the quantity of the commodity increases),
> a small fall in the price will cause only a very small increase in his purchase. The extra

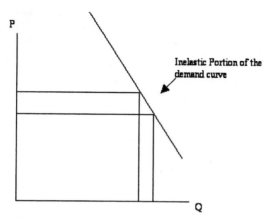

Inelastic Portion of the
demand curve

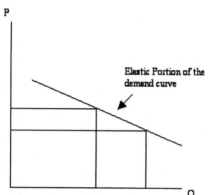

Elastic Portion of the
demand curve

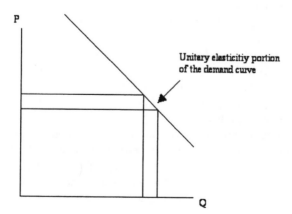

Unitary elasticitiy portion
of the demand curve

inducement given by the fall in price causes hardly any extension of his desire to purchase: the elasticity of his demand is small ... And as with the demand of one person so with that of the whole market; and we may say generally: – *The elasticity of demand* (or responsiveness of demand) in a market is great or small according as the amount demanded increases much or little for a given fall in price, and diminishes much or little for a given rise in price. (footnote 1: We may say that the elasticity is one, if a small fall in price will cause an equal proportionate increase in the amount demanded ...) (p. 86).

A fall of one percent in price will increase the sales by one percent: unit elasticity.

If demand were infinitely elastic, the curve would be a horizontal line; this is obviously the highest degree of elasticity of demand. Any commodity whose quantity demanded varies in greater degree than the variation in price is elastic; i.e., the demand for a commodity is elastic if the total amount of money spent on its purchase varies inversely with its price. An inelastic demand is one in which a given change in price produces a less than proportionate change in quantity. The dividing line is unit elasticity, when the total spent in buying a commodity remains constant regardless of price – a curve so drawn that a rectangle made by joining any point on the curve to the two axes always has the same area. (I do not believe Marshall used the term unit elasticity.)

Elasticity varies among different goods because of: (1) the existence or non-existence of substitutes, and (2) the different fractions of income spent on different commodities. For example, if a commodity is one on which only a small proportion of income is spent, the demand for the commodity will be inelastic. On the other hand, in the case of a commodity on which a large fraction of income is spent, demand will tend to be elastic. Salt is an example of the former (inelastic demand) and automobiles will tend to belong to the latter category (elastic demand). Habitual goods (beer, coffee, cigarettes) tend to have an inelastic demand. Also, 'necessities' will have an inelastic demand. Necessities cannot be defined in technological terms, except perhaps for such goods as water, air, salt, etc. Food is a technological necessity, but food is available in many different forms.

We might reverse the definition and say that necessities are goods for which the demand is inelastic. The individual determines what is a necessity for him. If he continues to purchase a commodity when its price increases, it is a necessity.

Now, does the concept of demand elasticity have any practical value, significance? Or is it just a toy?

I believe considerable use may be made of the concept. It is of value, for example, for a seller to know the elasticity of the demand for his product. Tax authorities are very interested in the concept; they will tend to place a sales tax on commodities which have a relatively inelastic demand – whiskey, beer, cigarettes – the sales of which will continue in spite of the tax. It is also important in the field of public utilities; the demand for such services tends to be inelastic; the profit will be the greater where there are decreasing costs.

The degree of elasticity may not be the same in all price ranges. It may be that demand for a commodity is inelastic in customary price ranges, but may become highly elastic in a higher range. This might be the case for whiskey, where a slight rise in price may have no affect on sales, but an extremely high tax might cause sales to drop significantly.

While the concept of elasticity was not entirely new in Marshall, he did introduce a new concept – *consumers' surplus.*

> . . . We have already seen that the price which a person pays for a thing can never exceed, and seldom comes up to that which he would be willing to pay rather than go without it: so that the satisfaction which he gets from its purchase generally exceeds that which he gives up in paying away its price; and he thus derives from the purchase a surplus of satisfaction. *The excess of the price which he would be willing to pay rather than go without the thing, over that which he actually does pay, is the economic measure of this surplus satisfaction.* It may be called *consumers' surplus* (p. 103).

If a person is willing to buy:

1	unit when the price is	$0.20
2	units when the price is	$0.14
3	units when the price is	$0.10
4	units when the price is	$0.08
		$0.52

and if he actually purchases 4 units @ $0.08, he spends altogether $0.32, and his consumer's surplus is $0.52 less $0.32 or $0.20.

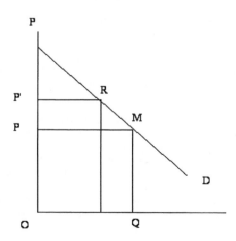

Consumer's Surplus (continued)

To continue our discussion of the Marshallian concept of 'consumers' surplus', let us examine Marshall's exposition:

> ... In order to give definiteness to our notions, let us consider the case of tea purchased for domestic consumption ... (p. 104).

Marshall here gives an illustration which we may express in a table:

A consumer would buy 1 lb. of tea when the price is 20s.

$$
\begin{array}{ll}
2 \text{ lbs.} & 14s. \\
3 & 10s. \\
4 & 6s. \\
5 & 4s. \\
6 & 3s. \\
7 & 2s.
\end{array}
$$

Marshall continues:

> ... The fact that he would just be induced to purchase one pound of tea if the price were 20s proves that the total enjoyment of satisfaction which he derives from that pound is as great as that which he could obtain by spending 20s. on other things. When the price falls to 14s., he could, if he chose, continue to buy only one pound. He would then get for 14s., what was worth to him at least 20s.; and he will obtain a surplus satisfaction of 6s. at least; or in other words a consumers' surplus of 6s. But in fact he buys a second pound of his own free choice, thus showing that he regards it as worth to him at least 14s, and that this represents the *additional* utility of the second pound to him. He obtains for 28s. (two pounds @14s.) what is worth to him at least 20s. plus 14s., i.e., 34s. His surplus satisfaction is at all events not diminished by buying it, but remains at least 6s. to him. The total utility of the two pounds is worth at least 34s., his consumer's surplus is at least 6s.

> The fact that each additional purchase reacts upon the utility of the purchases which he had previously decided to make has already been allowed for in making out the schedule and must not be counted a second time.

> When the price falls to 10s., he might, if he chose, continue to buy only two pounds; and obtain for 20s. what was worth to him at least 34s. and derive a surplus satisfaction worth at least 14s. But in fact he prefers to buy a third pound: and as he does this freely, we know that he does not diminish his surplus satisfaction by doing it. He now gets for 30s. three pounds, of which the first is worth at least 20s. the second at least 14s. and so on. When at last the price has fallen to 2s. he buys seven pounds, which are severally worth to him not less than 20, 14, 10, 6, 4, 3 and 2s. or 59s. in all. This sum measures their total utility to him; his consumer's surplus is (at least) the excess of this sum over 14 (2×7), he actually pays for them, i.e., consumer's surplus is 45s. (59–14).

This is the excess value of the satisfaction he gets from buying the tea over that which he could have got by other commodities, of which he had just not thought it worth the while to buy more at their current prices; and any further purchases of which at those prices would not yield him any consumer's surplus. In other words, he derives this 45s. worth of surplus enjoyment from his conjecture, from the adaptation of the environment to his wants in the particular matter of tea (p. 104–106).

Marshall is not necessarily concerned with the forces which lower prices.

This concept of consumers' surplus is rather strange. For one thing, it seems that Marshall has relaxed his earlier thesis that it is impossible to measure human motives themselves. He is using here price as an *index of motive*.

Marshall's measure of total utility is the same as Jevons'.

If the consumers' surplus concept is used in connection with absolute necessities, then the consumers' surplus would be infinite. Marshall does not count consumers' surplus until the individual has a sufficient real income to account for biological necessities. The whole thing will tend to be hypothetical, as you never know what an individual would have bought at various prices, you only know what he actually did buy at market prices.

The concept may, nevertheless, have some sense. What does an individual mean, e.g., when he (or she) says: 'I bought this thing at a real bargain'? Normally people mean that they got something at below the price they usually pay. Pressed further the individual may say that he bought the article at the bargain price – below what other people pay – but that he would have been willing to pay a higher price. In this case the buyer ends with a surplus, but a *surplus of purchasing power*.

At any rate I do not think that Marshall uses the concept except in one connection. I do not believe that he uses it for the purpose of proving that everybody gains in exchange, as the marginal utility school assumes. The specific purpose for which Marshall later on uses the concept (consumers' surplus) is pointing out that government intervention in the form of regulating public utility rates can maximize satisfaction.

By setting the rates below marginal cost, and then paying a subsidy out of general taxation (progressive), the consumers will gain more as consumers than they pay as taxpayers. Consumers will gain because of the fact that the public utilities are decreasing cost industries, marginal cost decreases as production increases; a part of the gain to consumers would result from the lower unit cost made possible by the subsidy, which will increase consumption of the products, and thereby increase total production and lower cost per unit (because of decreasing cost). A part of the gain to consumers would result from the lower cost per unit, and this reduction in cost would be greater than the subsidy.[18]

Here Marshall finds one of his exceptions to the thesis that the policy of *laissez faire* will maximize human satisfactions.

This is about all that Marshall has to say about demand. We skip Book IV, where Marshall discusses the theory of diminishing returns, of which not much is left when Marshall is finished, even though he himself thinks that he has not completely invalidated the thesis.

Marshall accepts Ricardo's theory of rent, as the payment for the 'undestructable forces of land', but includes in the undestructable forces such things as air, sunshine, rainfall: his land is land in area only, as in the Ricardian sense.

> ... By land is meant the material and the forces which Nature gives freely for man's aid, in land and water, in air and light and heat ... (p. 115) ... The right to use a piece of land gives command over a certain space – a certain part of the earth's surface (p. 120).

His definition does not apply to mineral deposits, which are exhausted in the process of production, so rent cannot be applied to mineral deposits. But it is applied to land in space on the earth's surface, and it might also be applied to the depths of the ocean, because the stock of fish is generally not depleted by the activities of commercial fishing.

Regarding the law of diminishing return, Marshall says that it is impossible to define fertility, because one plant may grow under some set of conditions, another not; so what is fertile for one is not fertile for another. Furthermore there is no standard for a good system of cultivation. What may be good in England – intensive cultivation – may be bad in the United States, where more extensive cultivation gives better results.[19]

According to Marshall, Ricardo was careless in his definitions, because you cannot define what is 'best' land. The settlers of the Rockies cultivated stoned and hilled land; whereas the Indians had the fertile land of the plains. What land is the best under the given situation? By getting rid of the Indians, more land would be obtained.

> ... He (Ricardo) states that the first settlers in a new country invariably chose the richest lands, and as population increased, poorer and poorer soils were gradually brought under cultivation, speaking carelessly as though there were an absolute standard of fertility. But as we have already seen, where land is free, everyone chooses that which is best adapted for his own purpose, and which will give him, all things considered, the best return for his capital and labour. He looks out, therefore, for the land that can be cultivated at once, and passes by land that has any weak links in the chain of its elements of fertility, however strong it may be in other links. But besides having to avoid malaria, he must think of his communication with his markets, and the base of his resources; and in some cases the need for security against the attacks of enemies and wild beasts outweighs all other consideration. It is therefore not to be expected that the lands which were first chosen, should turn out always to be those which ultimately come to be regarded as the most fertile. Ricardo did not consider this and laid himself open to attack. The fact that, in new countries, soils

which an English farmer would regard as poor, are sometimes cultivated before neighboring soils which he would regard as rich, is not inconsistent, as some foreign writers have supposed, with the general tenor of Ricardo's doctrines. Its practical importance is in relation to the conditions under which the growth of population tends to cause increased pressure on the means of subsistence: it shifts the centre of interest from the mere amount of the farmer's produce to its exchange *value* in terms of the things which the industrial population in his neighborhood will offer for it. (pp. 136–137).

In any given situation, at any given time, with a given labor force, people will take the land which gives the best return. If this is what Ricardo meant, he was correct; but Ricardo was careless, Marshall says, so if he takes it as a universal law that the best land will always be taken into use first; Ricardo is not correct.

In his definition of diminishing return, Marshall says: "In general (i.e., a statement of a tendency) the law (of diminishing return) is a statement of a tendency which may indeed be held in check for a time by improvements in the arts of agriculture and by the fitful course of the development of the full powers of the soil". (p. 153) ". . . but (he continues) which must ultimately become irresistible if the demand for produce should increase without limit" (Ibid.).

Marshall's point[20] is that even in the absence of technological development, the produce per unit of capital and labor may increase through an increase in demand, or increase in population. Farmers may become more efficient so they turn out more units of capital, and furthermore the produce may be of higher value, as markets expand, so that there will be an increase in both physical produce and value per unit of capital and labor.

Marshall thinks he retains the law of diminishing return, but not much is left of it when he is through with Book IV.

I believe that modern technology makes it impossible for the individual to determine his needs. How can you determine, e.g., your need for a particular brand of cigarettes? Can you determine which brand is better than the rest? You would have to be equipped with a testing laboratory in order to determine what utility you would get out of each of the many commodities available today. So, orthodox theory of consumer demand as the determining factor in the allocation of resources breaks down.

In the United States today we do not rely on the demand in the market for the allocation of resources. Government expenditures for goods and services are not determined by an impersonal market. In 1944, 50% of the national income originated from government activity: so 50% (at least) of the allocation of resources was not determined by the market mechanism.

The goal (winning the war) was predetermined, and experts were called in to determine how resources should be allocated. The individual relies to a large extent on experts also; he calls on a doctor when he is ill.

If we could agree on the social policy, we could let experts, not the market mechanism, allocate resources. It is believed however that the market mechanism does the better job in peace time, *but not in war*. Why is this so? How can a system be superior when it is incapable in an emergency? If it were superior, it should be relied upon under all conditions. Of course, during a war we all agree on the objective – victory – but in peacetime, there are conflicting objectives.

When the common man speaks of 'the law of supply and demand' he thinks it is a law of the physical universe, and that man is powerless in the face of such a law. Therefore, no interference; the law of the universe creates conditions. To Marshall, the 'law' of supply and demand is simply a statement of tendencies under given conditions, conditions determined by the institutional framework of society. If an institutional feature is changed – say by the introduction of a progressive income tax – then the conditions are changes, and supply and demand may be vastly changed.

The law tells us nothing unless we know the conditions. The market simply reflects the conditions created by the institutional framework. The statement of tendencies – the law – applies only to a given group under given conditions; when conditions change, behavior changes.

When people talk of the 'immutable' law of supply and demand, they do not know what they are talking about. The law of gravity is immutable because the conditions from which it results are immutable; supply and demand are not immutable. What people really mean when they speak of the 'immutable' law of supply and demand, is that they do not want any change; they do not want any interference which may work to their disadvantage. They may want interference with the law of supply and demand if it works to their advantage, e.g., protective tariff.

Marshall talks about 'normal' behavior as one expects the behavior to be under a certain condition. This normal behavior is the regularities he wants to establish. In his price theory he is concerned with discovering such regularities. but runs into difficulties because the world is highly dynamic, and conditions change rapidly. We shall look at his solution a little later.

Marshall's demand schedule is the schedule of prices under a series of conditions. It is on the conditions of supply that Marshall devotes his most careful and fullest analysis. This is because supply is much more amenable to scientific handling, as Marshall conceives science. Demand gets you into consideration of wants and psychology and other unmeasureable magnitudes; supply takes you into money cost. You can have an exact measure for that.

Marshall seeks to establish the thesis that normal prices or equilibrium prices equal cost of production; i.e. supply is determined by cost of production. Given competitive markets, output will be pushed to the point at which the price equals cost of production. *Note:* Price is not determined by cost of production; price is determined by the forces of supply and demand. Supply is only one blade of the scissors; the forces of the competitive market would result in a rate of output at which unit cost equals price. This is his thesis.

To establish his thesis, he has to solve certain problems:

(1) Supply is determined by cost of production, but what cost? Marshall's theory is a partial equilibrium theory, and the market is constituted of several firms, whose cost determines supply. With whose cost does price equate? Is it the cost of the lowest-cost firm? The average firm? the highest cost firm? Or what?

(2) The second problem results from the range of cost. The cost the entrepreneur takes into account varies over the period of time taken into consideration. So a different range of cost would be considered in a short period of time from that taken into consideration during a longer period of time. What are the particular costs then which determine the normal supply schedule? This element of time confronts Marshall with some of his greatest difficulties.

Before we consider how Marshall solves these problems, we will look at the assumptions he makes as a basis for the solutions. Marshall does not list all of his assumptions in the same place; but the most important of these is – competition.

> ... The position then is this: we are investigating the equilibrium of normal demand and normal supply in their most general form; we are neglecting those features which are special to particular parts of economic science, and are confining our attention to those broad relations which are common to nearly the whole of it. Thus we assume that the forces of demand and supply have free play; that there is no close combination among dealers on either side, but each acts for himself, *and there is much free competition;* that is, buyers generally compete freely with buyers, and sellers compete freely with sellers. But though everyone acts for himself, his knowledge of what others are doing is supposed to be *generally sufficient* to prevent him from taking a lower or paying a higher price than others are doing. This is assumed provisionally to be true both of finished goods and of the factors of production, of the hire of labor and of the borrowing of capital. We have already inquired to some extent, and we shall have to inquire further, how far these assumptions are in accordance with the actual facts of life; but meanwhile this *is the supposition* on which we proceed; we assume that there is only one price in the market at one and the same time; it is being understood that separate allowance is made, when necessary for differences in the expense of delivering goods to dealers in different parts of the market; including allowances for the special expenses of retailing, if it is a retail market (pp. 270–271).

So, included in the assumption of free competition is the conception of a market in which people are so close to each other that they know *sufficiently* well enough the conditions of the market so that they do not pay too much or ask too low a price. This is the concept of ' pure competition', which only requires sufficient knowledge, sufficient mobility of capital and labor and other factors of production so that the factors will move to more profitable employment if sufficient time is allowed (to make the supply price equal to equilibrium price). As we shall see later, according to Marshall a situation of increasing costs is present in the short run. There may also be situations of decreasing cost, but such a situation cannot be solved with his analytical tools.

Marshall's concept of *pure competition* may be distinguished from another concept – *perfect competition*. Perfect competition implies complete knowledge on behalf of individuals with respect to all prices and conditions in the market, complete mobility of all factors of production. All conditions are such that the market price is always in equilibrium. Perfect competition involves absence of all frictions and barriers.

Marshall does not go so far as to assume perfect competition, but he does assume that people have *sufficient* knowledge and that factors of production have *sufficient* mobility.

> ... Thus the more nearly perfect a market is, the stronger is the tendency for the same price to be paid for the same thing at the same time in all parts of the market: but of course if the market is large, allowance must be made for the expense of delivering the goods to different purchasers; each of whom must be supposed to pay in addition to the market price a special charge on account of delivery (p. 325).

As a corollary of this assumption of pure competition, Marshall also assumes one price in the market for each commodity.

Furthermore, there is the assumption of the existing institutional framework of society. Although Marshall says nothing about Say's Law, it is present in the *Principles*. The conditions of supply would depend on the length of time under; we will note his four periods of time later.

Marshall never gives any very exact definition of competition. In fact, in analyzing the determination of price in the short period, he assumes that the sellers have some degree of *control* over price, which runs contrary to what we now think of as a competitive market. Orthodox economists generally did not take the trouble of defining these terms.

We have competition for markets solely on quality of products rather than price competition. The concepts were never clarified (if they are now) until the development of the theory of monopolistic competition. I assume you know how economists now define it – homogeneous product, no individual producer or group of producers can affect price. Sellers must be homogenous. There is only one reason why a buyer would prefer one seller to another – that is price. This used to be true, I think, of the cotton market. The demand for the supply of any one seller is infinitely elastic. No seller attempts to enlarge his market by lowering his price – no price competition what so ever. There is no advertising, no attempt to induce customers to buy. In a purely competitive market, there is, in a sense, no competition at all! The futures market is an example of the purely competitive market. All producers can sell at the market price, but none can sell at a higher price. Now, we will note that that concept of a competitive market is a little different from that of Marshall. His sellers, in the short period, will not sell at a lower price, for fear of spoiling the market.

What conditions make a market monopolistically competitive? Although the terminology is not standard, I think generally of this existing where there is more than one seller of a differentiated product; the product of one seller is a fairly good substitute for that of another seller. I had better say – a sufficient number of sellers that no one seller takes account of the effect that his policies will have on the others and hence back on himself. In oligopoly you have sellers taking account of the back-lash on themselves.

Now monopoly receives a more intelligible and applicable definition. You have only one seller of a product for which there are no accessible substitutes, with the consequence that the seller takes no account of the effect that his price or production policy will have on anybody and, hence, on himself. It would differ from oligopoly in two respects: (1) the number of sellers, and (2) consideration of the effects on one's policy of actions. AT&T has a monopoly; CocaCola does not.

Back to Marshall – what we have listed above (exclusive of the discussion of monopolistic competition) is an incomplete list of Marshallian assumption.

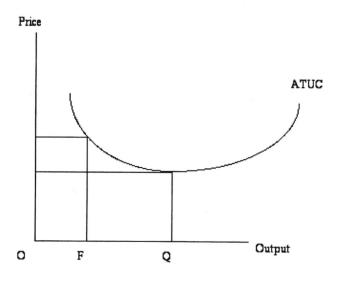

According to Marshall, the supply would depend on the length of time under consideration. He has four time periods.

In the short run the cost curve will slope up to the right, except in the so-called decreasing cost industries. The orthodox economists were not clear in their definitions (this includes Marshall) of increasing, constant and decreasing cost industries.

One thing influencing unit cost with change in output will be the effect of overhead cost resulting from utilization of capacity. If a plant is operating below capacity, the increase in production will result in a decrease in overhead cost per unit of output. So, if the increase in variable cost resulting from increased production is less than the decrease in overhead cost (both measured per unit of output), total average cost will decrease. Later on, if variable costs increase more than overhead cost decreases, the total average cost will be increasing.

Assuming competition, each plant would operate at capacity, determining the product OQ. This is Marshall's short run period, in which you cannot increase plant and equipment, only hire more workers, or let them work longer hours, if you want to expand production; and you have increasing cost (beyond Q). Supply would only be increased if demand increased (demand schedule shifted). Under monopoly, you would have decreasing cost. The monopolist would offer the output OF, because he would be able to fix a higher price at lower output which would give him optimum profit. Most of the decreasing cost industries would be public utility monopolies.

Allowing time for increase in productive capacity (enlargement of plant, building of new plants, introduction of additional machinery, etc.) we are in Marshall's long-run period. This raises the question – what would be the effect on cost in this long-run period, where all costs of production become variable?

Marshall's Long Run

Last time I mentioned that in Book V the thesis is that equilibrium price is the cost of production price. Marshall has certain problems to solve in order to establish this thesis. Before we go into a discussion of these problems we will have to note how Marshall defines cost of production, which determines supply. (Cost of production does not determine equilibrium price, which is determined by the interplay of supply and demand.)

In discussing cost of production, Marshall distinguishes between 'cost of production' and 'expenses of production'.

> ... the price required to call forth the exertion necessary for producing any given amount of a commodity may be called the *supply price* for that amount, with reference of course to a given unit of time.

> ... The exertions of all the different kinds of labour that are directly or indirectly involved in making it; together with the abstinence or rather the waiting required for saving the capital used in making it; all these efforts and sacrifices together will be called the *real cost of production* of the commodity. The sums of money that have to be paid for these efforts and sacrifices will be called either its *money cost of production*, or for shortness, its *expenses of production* (p. 282).

The real cost then is the sacrifice involved in production; this sacrifice consists of two elements – sacrifice of working and sacrifice of waiting. The amount of money necessary to induce people to undergo the sacrifice of working and to induce the capitalist to undergo the sacrifice of waiting (necessary for capital accumulation) is the money cost of expenses of production. Money cost is the relative measure of sacrifice in the short run.

The money cost of production then will determine the supply and the supply price of output. But cost of production does not alone determine the equilibrium price. Demand is equally important for the determination of price, according to Marshall. He illustrates this by the use of his famous scissors analogy.[21]

> ... Thus we may conclude that, *as a general rule*, the shorter the period which we are considering, the greater must be the share of our attention which is given to the influence of demand on value; and the longer the period, the more important will be the influence of cost of production on value. For the influence of changes in cost of production takes as a rule a longer time to work itself out than does the influence of changes in demand (p. 291).

All prices then are determined by demand and supply, but cost only determines supply.

For Marshall, under competition, the equilibrium price will coincide with the money price necessary to induce the workers and capitalists to undertake the production. It is the *real* cost which determines the *money* cost or expenses of production. Real cost is the disutility of working and the disutility of waiting – the sacrifices of the laborer and the capitalist. Disutility on the supply side offsets the utility on the demand side and the equilibrium will be between the utility or satisfaction derived from a commodity in use and the disutility of producing the commodity. The supply price is the money-pain cost of production.

As we have mentioned, Marshall encounters two major problems in his cost analysis: (1) the problem of determining whose cost determines supply – high-cost producer, low-cost producer, or average producer cost; and (2) the problem relating to the range of cost. This is the tough problem due to the fact that the range of cost varies according to the length of time involved. Time always gives Marshall trouble in his search for regularity in economic phenomena in a world which is dynamic and changing.

Let us consider the first problem. To Marshall the solution of this problem is fairly simple. It may be, however, that the problem is not as simple as he assumes.

Marshall says that the cost determining supply is the cost of the *representative firm*. Is the representative firm cost the average cost of all firms of producers in a given industry? Is it the cost of the typical firm in a model sense; i.e. the cost of the greatest number of producers in the industry? The answer in Marshall is not very clear.

> ... our representative firm must be one which has had a fairly long life, and fair success, which is managed with normal ability, and which has normal access to the economies, external and internal, which belong to that aggregate volume of production; accounting being taken of the class of goods produced, the conditions of marketing them and the economic environment generally (p. 265).

> ... we can see (how far the economies, internal and external, of production have extended generally in the industry and country) ... fairly well by selecting, after a broad survey, a firm, whether in private or joint-stock management (or better still, more than one), that represents, to the best of our judgement, this particular average (p. 265).

> ... Let us call to mind the 'representative firm', whose economies of production, internal and external, are dependent on the aggregate volume of production of the commodity that it makes; and, postponing all further study of the nature of this dependence, let us assume that the normal supply price of any amount of that commodity may be taken to be its normal expenses of production (including *gross* earnings of management) by that firm. That is, let us assume that this is the price the expectation of which will just suffice to maintain the existing aggregate amount of production; some firms meanwhile rising and increasing their output, and others falling and diminishing theirs; but the aggregate production remaining unchanged. A price higher than this would increase the growth of the rising firms, and slacken, though it might not arrest, the decay of the falling firms; with the net result of an increase in the aggregate production. On the other hand, a price lower than this would hasten the decay of the falling firms, and slacken the growth of the rising firms; and on the whole diminish production; and a rise or fall of price would affect in like manner though perhaps not in an equal degree those great joint-stock companies which often stagnate, but seldom die (p. 285–286).

I do not think that the cost of the representative firm means simply an arithmetic average of all cost in the industry. If Marshall had meant this, he would have said so. What Marshall seems to mean is that at any given time in any given industry, there are enterprises in all stages of development, some rising, some falling, some neither falling nor rising; these firms which are neither rising nor falling may be the representative firms. In a stationary state, every firm would be representative.[22]

Marshall does not assume a stationary state, but he controls the rate of growth in order to discover regularities in a dynamic world. In the real world, some firms rise and some decline; it is the cost of the 'representative firm' that determines long run supply. We are, however, still in doubt as to what the 'representative firm' is. The representative firm represents the industry in question; this price analysis is industry-price analysis; equilibrium price is industry-price equilibrium not firm-price equilibrium. In the stationary state, as Marshall conceives it, there is a static situation, no change occurs and economic forces are allowed to work out their full effects; all producers would produce at the same marginal and average cost. (Marshall removes the 'gloom' from the stationary state as Ricardo visualized it; for Marshall the stationary state may be a pleasant one.)

But Marshall does not assume a stationary state. In a stationary state there would be no problems because no change occurs; but in the real world we have change and we have problems.[23]

To Marshall 'normal' does not mean 'natural'.[24] Normal price is the price which can be expected during a given period under a given set of conditions or circumstances. It is a tendency.

Marshall, as a theorist, had to abstract from reality. Any theory must be an abstraction from reality because theory cannot handle the raw multitude of reality. All theories are abstractions. The only relevant criticism which can be leveled against a theory is that the abstraction is so great that it cannot solve the problems it is intended to solve. If a theorist abstracts to this degree, then his theory has no relevance; he has defeated himself.

This is exactly what Marshall tries to avoid. He wants to abstract, but not too much.

Marshall states again and again that economics has to be scientific. His concept of science is the 19th century concept, which means that he attempts to establish regularities. This is a difficult task because of the dynamic nature of the economy. He compares the conditions in the economy with a stone hanging in the troubled waters of a mill-race, when the person holding the string to which the stone is attached swings his hand with movements partly rhythmical and partly arbitrary.

Marshall lets the stone hang in the mill-race, but the stream is moving at a constant rate, and the hand that moves the stone moves rhythmically.

The representative firm, as we have seen, is 'one which has normal access to the economies, external and internal, which belong to that aggregate volume of production'; i.e. the internal and external economies of production 'are dependent on the aggregate volume of production of the commodity that it (the representative firm) makes'.

Internal and external economies are economies of scale. The firm will enjoy all the advantages of external economy, that is, it will enjoy the advantages provided by the size of the industry to which it belongs. Specialized firms are external to the representative firm, but it will enjoy the advantages developed in these external firms in various ways (when it obtains services and products from them, etc.).

It also enjoys the advantages of internal economies, which are derived from the growth of the firm itself, and which results in large scale internal production in the representative firm itself.

Since the cost of production in any industry varies with the size of the firm, then Marshall's representative firm enjoys all the advantages of the external and internal economies. It is, therefore, of optimum size internally, so that it utilizes all the internal advantages of scale. If it grows, the growth will be disadvantageous.

The representative firm is not actually defined; but if there were such a firm, the cost of such a firm would determine supply.

How does Marshall handle time? He has four time periods, and analyzes price formation in each period:

(1) *The market period* (the shortest period); the market price in any given market at any given time – day, week or month. It is a period so short that the quantities of commodities available are fixed at maximum. No increase in stock is permitted in the market period, because of the shortness of time.

> ... the period is short, the supply is limited to the stores which happen to be at hand (p. 274).

> ... In such a market there is a demand price for each amount of the commodity, that is, a price at which each particular amount of the commodity can find purchasers in a day, or week or year. The circumstances which govern this price for any given commodity vary in character from one problem to another; but in every case the more of a thing is offered for sale in a market the lower the price at which it finds purchasers, or in other words, the demand price for each bushel or yard diminishes with every increase in the amount offered (p. 285).

(2) *The short run period.* In this period equipment, plant, and machinery are fixed even if the number of workers is fixed, because the workers can work faster or longer hours.) The short period of supply is a period in which the rate of output may be increased by increasing the *variable* factors of production.

> ... To sum up then as regards short periods. The supply of specialized skill and ability, of suitable machinery and other material capital, and of the appropriate industrial organization has not time to be fully adopted to demand; but the producers have to adjust their supply to the demand as best they can with the appliances already at their disposal (pp. 312–313).

(3) *The long run period.* This is a period where all the factors of production can be varied. Increase in plant and numbers of plants, machinery, equipment, land, labor, raw materials: all the factors of production can be expanded. But population, taste, technology are all assumed to be unchanged during the long run.

... In long run periods on the other hand all investments of capital and effort in providing the material plant and the organization of business, and in acquiring trade knowledge and specialized ability, have time to be adjusted to the incomes which are expected to be earned by them: and the estimates of these incomes, therefore directly govern supply are the true long-period normal supply price of the commodities produced (p. 313).

(4) The secular run. This is the longest period; change in technology, taste, and population is permitted as well as change in the factors of production. Marshall says very little about the secular run, as he cannot predict the future.

Marshall's analysis is quasi-static;

(1) In the market period everything is static.
(2) In the short run plant, equipment, machinery are static.
(3) In the long run factors of production may be varied, but population, technology, and taste are static.
(4) Everything is dynamic in the secular run.

In Book V Chapter 2 gives the market situation, Chapters 3 and 4 set the stage, and in Chapter 5 the short and long run are discussed.

... Four classes stand out. In each, price is governed by the relations between demand and supply. As regards *market* price, supply is taken to mean the stock of the commodity in question which is on hand, or at all events 'in sight'. As regards *normal* prices, when the term *normal* is taken to relate to *short* periods of a few months or a year, supply means broadly what can be produced for the price in question with the existing stock of plant, personal and impersonal, in the given time. As regards *normal* prices when the term normal is to refer to long periods of several years, supply means what can be produced by plant, which itself can be remuneratively produced and applied within the given time; while lastly, there are very gradual or *secular* movements of normal price, caused by the gradual growth of knowledge, population and capital, and the changing conditions of supply and demand from one generation to another (pp. 314–315).

Marshall's Analytical Tools

We have been looking at some of Marshall's analytical tools:

1. The representative firm.
2. Time period analysis; the four periods. What are some of his other tools?
3. Marshall permits change to occur but only at a regular rate and in an 'orderly fashion'. Marshall is unwilling to use a static method, but as he wants to discover regularities, he must rule out certain of the changes which occur in

the real world. So Marshall employs a quasi-static analysis. He assumes that no sudden changes or shifts occur. Capital and population increase, but at a regular rate 'controlled' by Marshall. This is the third tool.

4. The *ceteris paribus* assumption. He takes one factor at a time and keeps all other factors constant; then he analyzes the effect resulting from the change in the varied factor. After analyzing the effect from change in one factor, he takes another, keeps all other factors constant, and analyzes the effect of the change in this varied factor, and so on.

This is the only method he finds available in the social sciences, where you cannot use a laboratory technique as in the physical sciences. The *ceteris paribus* technique then corresponds to laboratory technique.[25]

Keynes uses a 'moving equilibrium' analysis which is not too different from Marshall's approach. Keynes' instantaneous effect of the multiplier, e.g., is a logical, timeless device; whereas in the real world, things do not happen instantaneously, and effects may change. Keynes takes the situation after the effects of the multiplier has worked itself out; he passes from one stage to another, it is timeless analysis.

Marshall's analysis, on the other hand, is not timeless. He attempts to use four time periods, and the device is fairly satisfactory for Marshall (as he sees it) except in decreasing cost industries, in which case the static analysis is not applicable.

The older classical economists assumed that the only increasing cost industry was the extractive industries, that all manufacturing industries were decreasing cost industries, and that the handicraft industries were constant cost industries. But, in fact, the older classical economists never understood clearly the meaning of increasing, decreasing, and constant cost industry.

Marshall's difficulty in applying a static analysis to a decreasing cost industry is due to the fact that a supply schedule cannot be drawn for any given time, because this would assume that any given increase in demand would result in lower prices. (See picture on next page.)

As output increases unit cost decreases. Then assume an increase in demand (buyers willing to purchase a greater quantity at each price); such an increase in demand (shift in curve to $D'D'$) will result in lower prices than before. But in the real world, an increase in demand will, at least temporarily, result in increased prices, because it takes time for industry to adjust the production to the increased demand, resulting in lower cost per unit. But over time, the increased demand would not result in higher prices.

It is marginal cost which determines supply price.

... This leads to the consideration of some difficulties of a technical character connected with the marginal expenses of production of a commodity that obeys the law of increasing

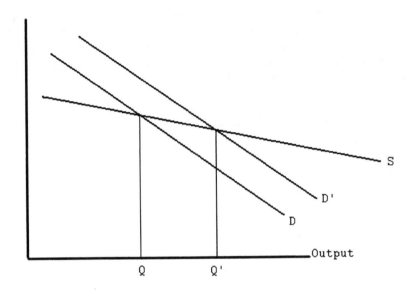

return. The difficulties arise from the temptation to represent supply price as dependent on the amount produced, without allowing for the length of time that is necessarily occupied by each individual business in extending its internal, and still more its external organization; and in consequence they have been most conspicuous in mathematical and semi-mathematical discussions of the theory of value. For when changes of supply price and amount produced are regarded as dependent exclusively on one another without any reference to gradual growth, it appears reasonable to argue that the marginal supply price for each individual producer is the addition to his aggregate expenses of production made by producing his last element; that this marginal price is likely in many cases to be diminished by an increase in his output much more than the demand price in the general market would be by the same cause. The statical theory of equilibrium is therefore not wholly applicable to commodities which obey the law of increasing return (pp. 414–415).

The supply curve represents conditions of supply not at any given time, but over a period of time.

In the short run analysis Marshall has no difficulty because he assumes marginal cost to increase as output increases; in the long run, on the other hand, marginal cost may decrease as supply increases (in the so-called decreasing cost industries).

In decreasing cost industries, when price falls, the marginal cost will also decrease, so it becomes a question of whether you can talk about equilibrium price in decreasing cost industries. Therefore, the equilibrium theory is not applicable to these industries in the long run, according to Marshall.

But in the short run, all cost is increasing. Let us get a clearer picture of this. We have to make two distinctions: (1) We have to distinguish the supply situation of a given producer from the supply situation of the industry to which he belongs; and (2) We have to distinguish between conditions of supply in the short run and conditions in the long run.

Take the individual firm. There are several factors affecting its cost situation for various outputs. First there is the influence of overhead cost. Optimum level of output for the individual firm is that output which results in minimum average unit cost. If the firm is producing less than optimum output then an increase in output will result in a decrease in average total unit cost (ATUC):

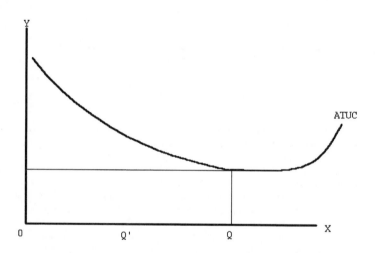

For a plant of any size the average total unit cost (ATUC) curve will be U-shaped. OQ represents the optimum output. The amount which results in minimum ATUC. If the plant has an actual production of OQ' then an increase in production up to OQ will result in a decrease in ATUC. This is because of the fact that the fixed cost is spread over more units of output; and the increase in variable cost is less than the decrease per unit of fixed cost. After OQ the per unit increase in variable cost is greater than the per unit decrease in fixed cost, resulting in an increase in ATUC. This is the situation for the firm.

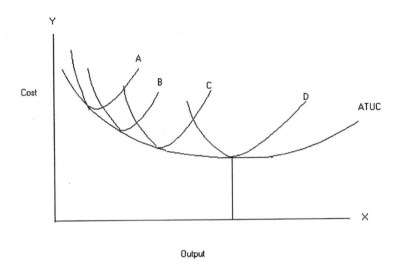

Now take a plant or firm in a competitive industry. Under Marshall's theory, the plant's position of equilibrium will be the point where ATUC is at a minimum, and this will be the optimum size of the plant. The same firm, let us call it firm "X", will have different optimum outputs, but these different optima will result from the economies of large-scale production.

The plant curve "A" is the cost curve for the firm "X" of size "A", curve "B" the cost curve for plant "X" of size "B" and so on; for each size of the plant, the cost curve is U-shaped, but the ATUC is lower for each larger plant. The plant cost curve "D" is the cost curve for the optimum-size "D" of plant "X".

The "planning curve" – the curve underlying the plant curves – shows that there is decreasing cost resulting from the economy of scale, different from the decreasing cost resulting from diminishing ATUC which results from the spread of overhead over greater number of units of output (which determines the optimum production of each size of plant "X" as shown by plant curves A, B, C, etc.). The planning curve shows the decreasing cost resulting from the expansion of the individual plant. Beyond OQ you run into diseconomies of the scale of production. Plant size "D" would be the optimum size, which is, by definition, that one which produces at its most economic output, and therefore enjoys the fullest economies. This analysis applies to the long run, which permits an increase in productive facilities.

The question arises – what size plant should be constructed? It will depend on the anticipated demand for power within a period during which it will not pay to enlarge the plant. Let us assume that the plant built has size "A" above, because the demand is such that it will not yield a proceed which would cover the minimum cost of plant "B"; then if and when the demand increases it will pay to enlarge the plant to size "B" which may then be economically constructed, and so on until the optimum size "D" is reached.

Here we assume a decreasing cost industry and a decreasing cost firm, because there is only the one firm in the industry.

The result or effect from change in scale of production is different from the effect of change in overhead. The effect of large scale is due to the fact that the firm, when it increases its scale will obtain advantages from internal economies.

This graph below illustrates the case of the power plant. D^1D^1 represents a demand which will bring equilibrium at minimum ATUC for size "A" It will not pay to increase the size of the firm to "B" until demand increases to D^2D^2. The optimum scale will be, as before, size "D" The "basic" curve is the long run cost curve.

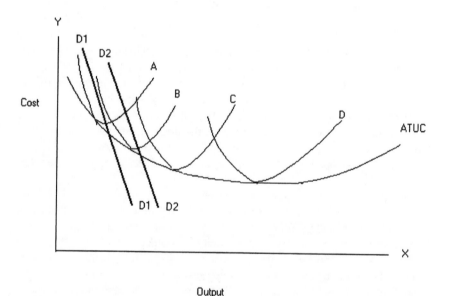

Output

As mentioned before, Marshall distinguishes between internal and external economies. Internal economies result from internal growth of scale. External economies result from developments in the industry, and are external to the individual firm. For example, when the automobile industry grows, special plants are developed for the production of parts – tires, batteries, etc. These economies are external to the firm, but internal to the industry.

As the industry expands, the ATUC will tend to decrease due to the fact that expansion of the *industry* permits specialization of plants and firms. Another thing is specialized – transportation facilities, such as car-trailers, which will increase mobility of labor; special labor supplies develop – all reducing the ATUC in any firm and thereby in the industry.

Marshall talks of decreasing cost because of the internal and external economies of scale.

But this can only be true in monopolistic industries; only monopolies can be operated at such an output that increase in output will result in a reduction of ATUC. In a competitive industry, the output of each firm is such an insignificant part of total production that it has no influence on price or on total volume of production. In a competitive situation, therefore, each firm must be of optimum size and producing at optimum level of output. So under competition there will be no advantage from internal economies. The force of competition will force each firm to operate at optimum size and produce at minimum ATUC.

From the graph we see that, under competition, only those firms operating at size "G" will be able to stay in the industry; all others will be forced either to close or expand to this size. There will be no advantage from internal economies, as all the firms will be of size "G" and cannot expand further.

So in a competitive industry, you can have decreasing cost only if an expanding industry results in external economies.

In a monopoly situation, where firm and industry are synonymous, you can have effects from both internal and external economies, or even from overhead cost (because of operation below optimum). In a monopoly, you can increase internal economies as you increase scale. The monopolist will be able to expand his output and reduce cost, because he typically operates below optimum capacity.

In a competitive industry expansion takes place only as a result of the entry of new firms, because all the existing firms are operating at optimum capacity and optimum size. And decreasing cost can only result from expansion of the industry, which may take place as a result of specialization. It is only external economies which can decrease the ATUC under competition.

Marshall does not even have a theory of pure competition; his theory is, in fact, a theory of monopolistic competition.

If a buyer does not care from whom he purchases and if the customer can value quality, then you may have pure competition. But this is not the case in the real world; people purchase brands. Each producer has a "little" monopoly on his own brand of the commodity; and certain buyers have a preference for certain brands, the real quality of which he cannot grade. So, we have monopolistic competition.

Cost of Production

What part, if any, does cost of production play in determining supply in the *market period* in any given day's transactions?

Marshall defines supply as a supply schedule. Would the supply be infinitely inelastic?

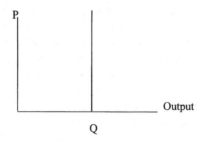

That is, will the supply be fixed irrespective of changes in price?

Take a dealer, in a given market, selling a perishable product, will the supply curve then be inelastic? Take the case of Christmas trees at 7 o'clock p.m. on December 24? This is a tricky question.

What will generally be the objective of the seller? His objective will normally be to maximize sales proceeds; and the sales proceeds will depend on the price realized per unit sold. A price of zero will not contribute to the maximization of sales proceeds; on the other hand, the price may be so high that no sale will occur. This will be the maximum price. The price will be somewhere between this maximum and zero. The dealer will figure that he can sell more at a lower price than at a higher one; so he will sell Christmas trees at decreasing prices as time goes on, the price becoming gradually lower as 7 p.m., Dec. 24 approaches.

Normally, in the case of non-perishable commodities, the period shortest period) will be longer than a single day.

In order to stay in business, the dealer will have to replenish his stock; so he will have to take into account the cost of replenishing his stock; so even if *past cost* will not directly determine the supply, the anticipation of future cost (which are the costs involved in replenishment), together with certain other factors, will determine the supply. In this process, past cost may indirectly influence supply, as the expectations with respect to future cost may be based on past cost. But past cost will only in this *indirect* manner determine supply, not directly. (Storage is an important part of future cost.)

So even in the market period (Marshall's shortest period) cost, at least anticipated future cost, may play some part in determining supply (together with certain other factors). But in the case of holiday commodities and perishable commodities cost will not play any role in determining supply.

However, supply plays a role in determining price even in Marshall's shortest run; even if demand is the more active factor in this market period. Supply and demand always determine price together, according to Marshall. But in perishable commodities, cost does not determine supply; in non-perishable commodities, the expected future cost (storage cost, replenishment, etc.) will determine the price at which the goods will be offered, and future cost will therefore determine supply of non-perishable commodities in the shortest run. (With respect to replenishment, the dealer will take into consideration when he is offering his goods today, what he will have to, or what he expects to pay for replenishment.)

When the dealer gives away Christmas trees at 7 p.m. on Dec. 24 he does this in order to get rid of his stock, but he is not motivated by the desire to maximize sales proceeds. When the planters in Brazil destroyed stocks of coffee and coffee trees in the 1930s, they did so, not in order to maximize proceeds in the shortest run, but in order to get rid of the stock. They were, however, influenced by the desire to maximize proceeds in the long run.

The factors determining supply are different in the shortest run (the market period) and in the short run. We will next consider Marshall's short run.

As you remember, Marshall's short run is the period during which output can be changed by changing the variable factors of production used in connection with a fixed plant (plant, machinery, land, etc. unchanged). What, according to Marshall, determines supply in the short run? When the plant cannot be increased, supply will be determined by prime cost (marginal).

According to Marshall[26] the *normal* price is that price which will result when (and if) the economic forces have sufficient time to work out their full effect. It is an equilibrium price, also, at which the quantity offered and demanded are equal.

But the forces at work are different in the different periods; so you will have normal prices which will be different for different periods. These forces at work are different in the different periods, and these forces are mainly related to supply, because of the fact that the conditions of demand are the same in all periods; conditions of demand are the same irrespective of the length of the period. Demand is simply determined by the amount of money buyers are able and willing to use in the purchase of goods and services. Then the demand conditions are the same in all periods; but the supply conditions are different in each of the four periods.

Back to the short run. In his analysis of the short run period, Marshall drops one of his basic assumptions – pure competition. He talks about the producers' "fear of spoiling the market."[27]

According to Marshall, in the short run, producers will reduce production at a cost level very much above the price necessary to cover the marginal prime cost, because of the "fear of spoiling the market."

Could any one producer in a competitive market have much fear of spoiling the market, which would lead him to curtail production, even when price was more than sufficient to cover marginal variable cost? Of course not. The only producer who can spoil the market is one who has some degree of control over the supply of the market. But in pure competition nobody produces sufficiently to influence the market. When a producer has a fear of spoiling the market, you have a presentation of the concept of monopolistic competition. Furthermore, his assumption of "formal or informal agreement with other producers" is not compatible with pure competition. So you have some sort of monopolistic competition. However, Marshall did not have the concept of marginal revenue. Marshall can draw a supply curve, but does not have anything definite at which to fix it; that is, he does not have the marginal revenue curve, which when intersected by the marginal cost curve will determine the level of output of each "monopolistic competitor."

However, Marshall is close to the concepts of Chamberlin and Joan Robinson. According to Marshall, *the producers do not sell at their marginal cost* for fear of spoiling the market. But he cannot determine the level of production in the case of each monopolistic competitor, because he does not have the marginal revenue concept. But he is close to it. Of course Chamberlin's and Joan Robinson's contributions are just an extension of Marshall's concepts, a filling in of the gap Marshall did not close himself in his theoretical analysis.

> ... On the other side of the line of division are periods of time long enough to enable producers to adapt their production to changes in demand, insofar as that can be done with the existing provision of specialized skill, specialized capital, and industrial organization; but not long enough to enable them to make important changes in the supplies of these factors of production. For such periods the stock of material and personal appliances of production has to be taken in a great measure for granted; and the marginal increment of supply is determined by estimates of producers as the amount of production it is worth their while to get out of those appliances. If trade is brisk all energies are strained to their utmost, overtime is worked, and then *the limit to production is given by want of will* to go further or faster. But if trade is slack every producer has to make up his

mind how near to prime cost it is worth his while to take fresh orders. And here there is *no definite law*; and that *chief operative force is the fear of spoiling the market*; and that acts in different ways and with different strengths on different individuals and different industrial groups. For *the chief motive of all open combinations and of all informal silent and "customary" understanding whether among employers or employed is the need for preventing individuals from spoiling the common market by action that may bring them immediate gains, but at the cost of a greater aggregate loss to the trade* (p. 412).

So Marshall says there is no definite law stating when production will be slowed down, but he is sure that it will happen at prices higher than those necessary to cover the marginal prime cost, because of the fear of spoiling the market. He cannot state what the level of production will be, because he lacks the concept of marginal revenue.

This quotation indicates explicitly that Marshall has dropped his concept of pure competition. Such agreements among producers are not in accordance with a concept of pure competition.

Why is it that Marshall drops his concept of pure competition in the short run? It may be that he simply was influenced by the real world around him, in which the monopolistic practices were prevalent.

... A man is likely to be a better economist if he trusts to his common sense, and practical instincts, than if he professes to study the theory of value and is resolved to find it easy (p. 305).

However we must remember that Marshall has never committed himself to the concept of competition. A normal price is not a competitive force (price) to Marshall, but simply the price resulting from the fact that the forces in the economy have had time to work themselves out. As these forces are different in the different time periods, we will have different normal prices in each period. Marshall states specifically that:

... Of course Normal does not mean competitive. Market prices and Normal prices are alike brought about by a multitude of influences, of which some rest on a moral basis and some on physical; of which some are competitive and some are not. It is to the persistence of the influences considered, and the time allowed for them to work out their effects that we refer when contrasting Market and Normal price, and again when contrasting the narrower and broader use of the term Normal price (p. 289).

A normal price then is not necessarily a competitive price, but only the price which results when the economic forces have had time to work themselves out.

But on the other hand, when Marshall states that supply is determined by cost, as he does in several places, he must assume competition.

When you have only two sellers (duopoly) and each takes account of all the effects on himself resulting from the other fellow's actions, you would have a monopoly, because there will be no difference in their behavior. On the other hand, if you have a duopoly ("A" and "B") and "A" does not take account of his own actions on "B", then the price will not be determinable. Of course no one party will assume that his action has no influence on the other fellow's policy; if one changes, both will change.

Now let us consider Marshall's long run.

This is the period during which all the factors of production are variable; not only may the "variable" factors – labor, raw materials, etc. – be changed, but the fixed plant and machinery itself will have time to be expanded.

What determines, according to Marshall, supply in the long run?

Total marginal cost determines supply in the long run, taking into consideration both prime cost and supplementary cost. They will all influence supply in the long run, because the supplementary cost also becomes variable in the long run. All cost is variable in the long run, and therefore price must cover *total cost of any addition to production* (as this cost of additional production may result from both additional workers and additional amounts of raw material, as well as additions to plant and facilities). That is, price must cover total marginal cost, made up of both prime and supplementary cost.

According to Marshall, there are four factors of production: (1) labor, (2) capital, (3) land, and (4) organization of business or entrepreneurship. All these factors have a supply price; the reward paid to the entrepreneur is profit; so "normal" profit will enter into the supply price. Or in other words, total money cost includes "normal" profit.

You do not necessarily have to cover supplementary cost in the *short run*, as entrepreneurs may be willing to produce for some time, if marginal cost (which only includes prime cost in the short run) is covered by the price realized. In the *long run* supplementary cost has to be covered, that is, all cost has to be covered in the long run, according to Marshall.

Assumptions

We have mentioned earlier some of the assumptions Marshall makes as a basis of his theory of value (or prices). The major assumptions are:

1. Competition (which he abandons in the short run).
2. Given institutional framework of society.
3. Given technology (in his theory of Normal value).
4. Unchanged consumer taste (over considerable length of time).
5. Changes which do occur are purely quantitative.

6. Such changes occur in a regular, uniform manner. (Population and capital increase at a uniform and regular rate.)
7. Everyone wants to maximize his gain. (By the principle of substitution; all entrepreneurs want to obtain production at least cost, and try to combine the factors of production in such a way that this goal is achieved.) This assumption is a hangover from hedonism, which Marshall tries to escape.
8. Marshall permits a change in the demand schedule resulting from a change in the distribution of income.

This is not a complete list of the Marshallian assumptions.

Marshall states that the duty of the economist is to seek knowledge for its own sake, but also to apply this knowledge in the solving of problems. Marshall would not be content with gaining knowledge simply for its own sake; this is part of the function of the economist; but still more important, the economist has to utilize his knowledge in order to solve problems.

Marshall was deeply influenced by J. S. Mill, who, like Marshall, was deeply concerned with the social problems created by modern industrialization.[28]

In the secular run, Marshall allows qualitative changes to occur – increase and change in technology, change in institutions, etc., therefore Marshall cannot say much about this period.

This is important: Marshall allows population and capital to increase in all his time periods, but at a regular rate, "controlled" by Marshall. To Marshall, the four time periods are *analytical tools*, used in order to isolate the effects of time, and to discover the forces determining normal value (the value which will result when the forces have the time to work themselves out). As these forces are different in his various time periods, he must use these four periods. These periods are not to be found in the real world; they are only analytical tools. Therefore when he considers other problems, such as quasi-rent, he does not consider any specific run of time, and he can talk of technological change, etc., which will have influence on the specific problem under consideration.

Even if marginal cost may coincide with price, Marshall does not hold that marginal cost determines price in any time period. He differs in this respect from J. E. Clark.

> ... The part played by the net product at the margin of production in the modern doctrine of Distribution is apt to be misunderstood. In particular many able writers have supposed that it represents the marginal use of a thing as *governing* the value of the whole. It is not so; the doctrine says we must *go to the margin to study the action of those forces which govern* the value of the whole; and that is a very different affair....
>
> ... with regard to machinery and other appliances of production made by man, there is a margin through which additional supplies come in after overcoming the resistance of a spring, called "cost of production." For when supply of those appliances is so small relatively

to the demand that the earnings expected from new supplies are more than sufficient to yield normal interest (or profits, if earnings of management are reckoned in) on their cost of production, besides allowing for depreciation, etc., then the valve opens, and the new supplies come in. When the earnings are less than this, the valve remains shut: and as anyhow the existing supply is always in process of slow destruction by use and the lapse of time, the supply is always shrinking when the valve is closed. The valve is that part of the machinery by which the general relations of demand and supply govern value. But marginal uses do not govern value; because they, together with value, are themselves governed by those general relations (p. 340).

According to Marshall, then, you have to go to the margin to see the forces operating in order to determine price. It is only on the margin that the additional factors are brought in, or withdrawn. Cost determines the margin, not the other way round.

Quasi-Rent. – Marshall distinguishes between interest and "quasi-rent:

... that which is rightly regarded as interest on "free" or "floating" capital, or on new investments of capital, is more properly treated as a sort of rent, a quasi-rent – on old investments of capital (p. 341).

... the payment made by a borrower for the use of a loan for, say, a year is expressed as the ratio which that payment bears to the loan, and is called *interest*. And this term is also used more broadly to represent *the money equivalent of the whole income which is derived from capital*. It is commonly expressed as a certain percentage on the "capital', sum of the loan. Whenever this is done the capital must not be regarded as a stock of things in general. It must be regarded as a stock of one particular thing, money, which is taken to represent them.

... the balance of advantage seems to lie in favor of reserving the term *rent* for the income derived from the free gifts of nature, whenever the discussion of business passes from the point of view of the individual to that of society *at large*.

... the term *quasi-rent* will be used in the present volume for the income derived from machines and other appliances for production made by man.

... we cannot properly speak of the interest yielded by a machine. If we use the term "interest" at all, it must be in relation not to the machine itself, but to its money value (pp. 61–63).

... the supplementary costs, which the owner of a factory expects to be able to add to the prime costs of its products, are the source of the quasi-rents which it will yield to him. If they come up to his expectations, then his business so far yields good profits; if they fall much short of it, his business tends to go to the bad. But this statement bears only on long-run period problems of value; and in that connection the difference between prime and supplementary cost has no special significance. The importance of the distinction between them is confined to short-period problems (p. 301n).

... It is of course just as essential in the long run that the price obtained should cover general or supplementary costs as that it should cover prime costs. An industry will be driven out of existence in the long run as certainly by failing to return even a moderate interest on capital invested in steam engines, as by failing to replace the price of the coal or the raw material used up from day to day (prime cost) . . . So an industry may, and often does, keep tolerably active during a whole year or even more, in which very little is earned beyond prime costs, and the fixed plant has "to work for nothing." But when the price falls so low that it does not pay for out-of-pocket expenses during the years for wages and raw materials, for coal and for lighting, etc., then the production is likely to come to a sharp stop.

This is the fundamental difference between those incomes yielded by agents of production which are to be regarded as rents or *quasi-rents* and those which (after allowing for the replacement of wear-and-tear and other destruction) may be regarded as interest (or profits on current investment). The difference is fundamental, but only one of degree (p. 349).

What does all this mean? Let us see.

First, what were the peculiar characteristics of the Ricardian rent, peculiarities which were not shared by any other factor incomes (such as wages and interest)?

1. The Ricardian rent is a result of price, and not a cause of price. 2. Ricardian rent was the result of the use of a non-reproducible, fixed factor. (This is the reason why rent is the *result* of price.) 3. The rent on any given piece of land will depend on the relationship between the demand for the product of the land and the fixed quantity of that quality of land.

What similarities will a machine (and income from a machine) have to some of these three peculiarities. If it is similar to all three, income from a machine would be rent; but it is, according to Marshall, only quasi-rent. It must have some similarity, at least.

Before we consider similarities, let us consider what differences there are between land and machines, if any.

One major difference would be that land is fixed in amount, while machines are reproducible.

Once the investment has been made it is beyond recall. For the life of the machine, when the machine has been created, the return the owner will obtain from the use of the machine will depend on demand for the products turned out by the machine. The cost incurred in the creation of the machine will have nothing to do with the return. Assume that the return on a machine should greatly increase, because of increase in price. This will stimulate the building of other, similar machines. Part of the return on machines already in existence will partly be quasi-rent during the period the new machinery is being built What part will be quasi-rent? That part of the return which is above the return on "free" or "floating" capital.[29]

Assume, on the other hand, that demand for the product turned out by our machine falls, and as a result prices fall close to prime cost. Then quasi-rent is reduced, and the return obtained by the entrepreneur will be dependent on the demand for the products produced by the machine; the return will not be determined by the cost of production (incurred in the production of the machine). Any return on any and all investments is quasi-rent once the investment has been made, because the return will depend, not only on cost of the investment, but on demand.

The marginal cost that equals normal price is the marginal cost of the "representative firm." Of course, those that are more efficient than the representative firm will realize a surplus. That surplus is not rent, but profit. Marshall's quasi-rent concept relates to the return or income derived by the owner of capital equipment from the time that the investment is made until such as time as that investment could be withdrawn (but investments can rarely be withdrawn). During that time, for that entrepreneur, it is a fixed factor of production. The return becomes of the nature of a quasi-rent.

For instance, let us suppose that a firm has purchased a machine costing $5,000. The interest rate is 5%, so that this $5,000 would cost $250 per year. *Total cost* would be $1,000 per year. At the time of the investment, Marshall says, the entrepreneur, in making it, did so because of the expectation that his gross income would be increased by more than $1,000. In determining his production policy, he would take into account the cost incurred in this machine. Now he has made it, and he cannot do anything about it, at least during the 10 years the machine may be assumed to last. The return actually obtained will depend on the price at which the output is actually sold. Let us assume that in fact the gross addition to the value of the output imputed to the machine should be $1,500 a year; the entrepreneur would receive $500 in rent. If the gross addition to value should fall to $500 a year, then the entrepreneur will suffer a loss of $500. The income derived by the owner of the machine becomes determined by the price during that period of time. It is quasi-rent because machinery does not last forever. By not using the machine at all, some costs could be avoided, but not all. The only part of the cost that could enter into supply price would be those that could be avoided if the machine was not used at all (prime variable cost). The quasi-rent then would be the difference between the income and the costs which could not be avoided. If the proceeds derived from the use of the machine should fall below a figure which could compensate for the cost incurred for the use of the machine, it would pay the entrepreneur not to use the machine. If the proceeds are sufficient to more than recover the cost incurred in using the machine, it would pay the entrepreneur to use it. The difference would be quasi-rent; i.e. gross returns less the cost of using the machine.

In the short run the only cost that necessarily determines price would be the marginal prime cost. Prime cost would be only a minimum in a competitive market; but Marshall drops the idea of competition in the short run. In a non-competitive market in the short run, price would be determined by prime cost plus something considered necessary to prevent spoiling the market.

Utility and purchasing power determine conditions of the demand. Marginal cost determines conditions of supply. Together they determine the price of the commodity.

Fear of spoiling the market is the entrepreneurs' opinion that if he maintains a certain price he will receive over a period of time under consideration a maximum gain or minimum loss. It is simply monopoly price.

What would seem to be the effect of the concept of quasi-rent on Marshall's theory of normal value, if any? Normal value always results from both supply and demand, but price will tend to coincide with cost of production. In the long run there would be no quasi-rent, when there is time enough for all forces to work themselves out. Normal price, as mentioned, will tend to coincide with marginal cost. Quasi-rents are not costs that enter into normal price. When normal price is obtained, there is no quasi-rent. I think it would be correct to say that if and when price is normal, quasi-rent will not exist in any period.

Once investment is made in durable equipment it cannot be withdrawn in the short term (which is contained in the term "durable"). To enable quasi-rent to disappear in Marshall's long run would require a period so long and so stable that the forces at work could work out their effect completely. But it is highly unrealistic to assume such stability in the long run. So, because of the continuity of change, the forces are not free to work out their full effects, you have a new set of conditions, and quasi-rent would never disappear. It would only disappear under conditions of *perfect* competition. Quasi-rents result from the immobility of investment.

Take the investment in the interurban line between Dallas and Fort Worth. Since the investment was made changes have occurred, mainly due to the introduction of automobiles and city buses. Result: decline in transportation of freight, passengers and mail on the line. What did the cost of the investment have to do with price? Nothing at all.

If those who made the investment in the interurban could have withdrawn their investment through depreciation, they would have been delighted to do so, but they simply could not. Marshall assumes that people cannot fix their price (except in the short run); even if an individual can determine his minimum price, he cannot determine his income, as his income depends on the willingness and ability of people to purchase his goods or services at the price charged. So the owners of the Dallas-Fort Worth interurban were prevented from withdrawing their investment by depreciation. Quasi-rent results from lack of mobility of the factors of production.

Some parts of some factors are mobile in fairly short periods; other parts only in long periods; others in still longer periods. Durability means immobility in fairly long periods. So investment in durable equipment is immobile, and thereby gives rise to quasi-rent. Investment in raw materials is mobile in comparison with plant and equipment.

> ... Thus, so long as the resources of an individual producer are in the form of general purchasing power, he will push every investment up to the margin at which he no longer expects from it a higher net return than he could get by investing in some other material, or machine, or advertisement, or in the hire of some additional labor; every investment will, as it were, be driven up to a value which offers to it a resistance equal to its own expanding force. If he invests in material or in labor, that is soon embodied in some saleable product; the sale replenishes his fluid capital, and that again is invested up to the margin at which any further investment would yield a return so diminished as not to be profitable.

But if he invests in land, or in a *durable building or machine*, the return which he gets from his investment may vary widely from his expectation. It will be governed by the *market* for his products, which may change character largely through new inventions, changes in fashion, etc. during the life of the machine, to say nothing of the perpetual life of land. The incomes which he thus may derive from investments in land and in machinery differ from his individual point of view mainly in the longer life of the land. But in regard to production in general, (that is, from the social point of view) a dominant difference between the two lies in the fact that the supply of land is fixed (though in a new country, the supply of land utilized in man's service may be increased); while the supply of machines may be increased without limit. And this difference reacts on the individual producer. For if no great invention renders his machines obsolete, while there is a steady demand for the things made by them, they will be constantly on sale at about their cost of production; and this machine will generally yield him normal profits on that cost of production, with deductions corresponding to their wear and tear.

Thus the rate of interest is a ratio; and the two things which it connects are both sums of money, or general purchasing power. So long as capital is "free," and the sum of money or general purchasing power over which it gives command is known, the net money income, expected to be derived from it, can be represented at once as bearing a given ratio (four or five or ten percent) to that sum. But when the free capital has been invested in a particular thing, its money value cannot as a rule be ascertained except by capitalizing the net income it will yield; and therefore the causes which govern it are likely to be akin in a greater or lesser degree to those which govern rents.

We are thus brought to the central doctrine of this part of economics, *viz.*;
– That which is rightly regarded as *interest* on "free" or "floating" capital, or

on new investments of capital, is more rightly treated as a sort of *rent – quasi-rent –* on old investment of capital. And there is no sharp line of distinction between floating capital and that which has been "sunk" for a special branch of production, nor between new and old investments of capital; each group shades into the other gradually. And thus even the rent of land is seen, not as a thing by itself, but as the leading species of a large genus; though indeed it has peculiarities of its own which are of vital importance from the point of view of theory as well as of practice (pp. 340–341).

When you have old equipment producing supplies this production will not be governed by cost of production as long as the durable equipment lasts.[30]

Once a railroad has been built, there is no way to get out of the business. Therefore, as long a time as the loss from operation is less than the loss incurred in abandoning the railroad, operation will be continued. The return will depend on additional investments – luxury trains, etc. – which represents floating capital. Bankrupt railroads still make additional investments; this is the only way they can reduce their losses below what the loss would be otherwise if the railroads were abandoned. Interest is, according to Marshall, return on free or floating capital (liquid assets or money funds). The return on investment, when it has been made in durable equipment, represents quasi-rent.

Marshall's Concept of Demand and Supply

Points of clarification with respect to Marshall's concept of demand and supply.

Demand – Marshall says that whatever the conditions determining demand may be, those forces determine demand irrespective of periods of time. The conditions determining demand are the same during all time periods. So, according to Marshall, we do not have to analyze demand in the various time periods. Demand is the quantity of goods or services people will be willing and able to buy; which again will be determined by the purchasers' preference and purchasing power. According to Marshall, wants are *not* innate in man. As demand will be based to a certain degree on psychological factors Marshall does not say very much about demand. Let us next consider cost in the Marshallian system.

Marginal cost – We have to be careful with respect to marginal cost in Marshall's system. When modern theorists talk about marginal cost, it is the marginal cost of the firm. It is common for modern theorists to define marginal cost of the firm as:

> ... the amount which is added to the total cost when the output is increased by one unit. Over a range of output, the marginal cost may be defined as the increase in the total cost divided by the corresponding increase in output.[31]

This is not Marshall's concept of marginal cost. Marshall's marginal cost is the marginal cost of the industry, not of the firm. Marshall's marginal cost of the industry is close to Ricardo's concept of the margin of land utilization. To Marshall, marginal cost is a cost resulting from the adding to the output of the *industry*. The cost that governs the margin depends on the length of time under consideration. In the long run all costs, according to Marshall, are variable (both prime cost – wages, price of raw materials, etc. – and supplementary cost – cost of equipment, plant, etc.). Production is pushed to the point at which price equals marginal cost so defined.

Theoretically, within the Marshallian framework, supply should be governed by marginal cost in the short run. But it is obvious to Marshall that we do not have pure competition. So he drops the assumption of pure competition in the short run, and supply will be determined by the marginal cost of the industry plus something else based on the fear of spoiling the market (that is, the supply price will be above the marginal cost from fear of spoiling the market).

In the long run, supply will be determined by cost, except when you have monopoly (as defined by Marshall). In the long run price will coincide with *average total cost*, according to Marshall (the average total cost of the industry).

But in the long run, the market cannot be spoiled. It is already spoiled!

According to Marshall, it is only on the margin that factors of production are added or withdrawn (similar to the Ricardian concept of margin).

In the short run, according to Marshall, certain costs are fixed, therefore the only cost the entrepreneur can take account of are the variable costs. So under competition the fixed cost will not be taken into consideration in the short run. So in the short run price will coincide with marginal cost, if there were no fear of spoiling the market. But there is this fear, so price will be above marginal cost (industry).

According to Marshall, all the forces at work are mutually interdependent, just as three balls in a bowl determine each other's position. There is mutual interaction between price demand and supply.

When analyzing equilibrium in the industry, you have to take all other prices in the economy as given. Unless this is assumed, you cannot determine the industry-equilibrium price, because the industry price is influenced by all other prices. Therefore Marshall makes his *ceteris paribus* assumption. By this device he allows the forces (determining the industry price) to work themselves out. Marshall's equilibrium price is the industry price. As the modern price theorists, to whom the equilibrium price is the price of the firm, Marshall has to take all other prices as given. To Marshall the "normal" price is the price which results in any run, when the forces determining the price in that run have had sufficient time to work out their full effect.

In Marshall's long run, *average total cost* will be covered by normal price. So what is normal in one period is not normal in another, because the forces may be different in the different periods.

However, it is not given that the actual market price will correspond to the normal price. Over long periods of time the market price may fluctuate around the normal price. Prices in the long run will tend to equal total average unit cost. This is not to say that in fact in the real world in which we live price will actually cover average total unit cost, but if the price-determining forces are given time to work themselves out in full effect, price will correspond to ATUC, and thereby be normal price.

But in the real world, these forces are not given time to work themselves out fully, so Marshall impounds in his *ceteris paribus* all other changes; he keeps all other forces and conditions unchanged, so the forces which determine "normal" price are allowed to work themselves out fully.

With respect to normal value:

> ... the value of a thing tends in the long run to correspond to its cost of production (see pp. 289–290).

> ... we may emphasize the distinction already made between average price and normal price. An average may be taken of the prices of any set of sales extending over a day or a week or a year or any other time; or it may be the average of sales at any time in many markets; or it may be the average of many such variables. But the conditions which are normal to any one set of sales are not likely to be exactly those which are normal to the others; and therefore it is only by accident that an average price will be a *normal price: that is, the price which any one set of conditions tends to produce*. In a stationary state alone, the term normal always means the same thing: there, but only there, "average price" and "normal price" are convertible terms.

> ... The general drift of the term normal supply price is always the same whether the period to which it refers is short or long; but there are great differences in detail. In every case reference is made to a certain given rate of aggregate production; that is, to the production of a certain aggregate amount daily or annually. In every case the price is that the expectation of which is sufficient and only just sufficient to make it worth while for people to set themselves to produce that aggregate amount; in every case the cost of production is *marginal; that is, it is the cost of production of those goods which are on the margin of not being produced* if the price to be got for them were expected to be lower. But the causes which determine this margin vary with the length of the period under consideration (p. 309).

The fact that the conditions in the real world are ever-changing gives Marshall great trouble. The dynamic economy is the source of all his trouble. He is unwilling to assume a stationary state; on the other hand, he maintains that economics must discover regularities and uniformity. How can you find regularity in a dynamic world? What is there to be done? Marshall will not assume change away, but on the other hand, he handles the phenomena of dynamic change in such a way as to discover regularities. His compromise includes these methods:

(1) the representative firm
(2) time periods
(3) *ceteris paribus*
(4) predictable and regular change.

Even Keynes' assumptions are more unrealistic than Marshall's. The multiplier, e.g., is an instantaneous phenomenon; you do not find such a thing in the real world, because the multiplying effect of investment takes time to work itself out. Keynes disregards that. Furthermore, when he analyzes variable cost, he assumes that labor is the only variable factor, which is unrealistic. *Nevertheless*, Keynes has given us a set of tools for the solution of problems in the real world.

Marshall does not want to depart from reality so much that he cannot see the real world. His assumptions are not so unrealistic as, e.g., those of Jevons.

According to Marshall, in order to be scientific economics must deal with measurable and regular phenomena. It is the 19th century concept of science as performing the task of discovering regularities and uniformity. Modern scientific concepts do not assume it necessary to be able to find regularities in order to be scientific.

If you should take a competitive industry and it should be selling its product at this moment at a certain price, there are then certain factors determining the normal price in that industry. If every one of these factors have time to work out their full effect, and no new factors come in, and none of the old factors drop out, then the normal price would be established. This normal price will coincide with cost of production. And you have different costs in different periods of time. However, Marshall does not say that old forces do not drop out and that new forces do not come in. All that he is saying is that the price will be normal if the forces have time to work out their full effect; so he makes the ceteris paribus assumption, in order to permit the forces to have their full effect. He admits that in the real world, the market price will coincide with normal price only by accident.

To Marshall, marginal cost is the cost on the margin where new factors come in. It is the cost of the representative firm which is, perhaps, a model firm.

When is a price abnormally low, according to Marshall? When the existing, actual price is below the normal price; a price is abnormally high when it is above normal price:

> ... when it is said that the price of wool on a certain day was abnormally high though the
> average price for the year was abnormally low, that the wages of coal-miners were abnor-

mally high in 1872 and abnormally low in 1879, that the (real) wages of labor were abnormally high at the end of the 14th century and abnormally low in the middle of the 16th; everyone understands that the scope of the term normal is not the same in these various cases.

The best illustration of this comes from manufacturers where the plant is long-lived, and the products short-lived (p. 301).

... The element of time is a chief cause of all those difficulties in economic investigations which make it necessary for man with his limited powers to go step by step; breaking up a complex question, studying one bit at a time, and at last combining his partial solutions into a more or less complete solution of the whole riddle. In breaking it up, he segregates those disturbing causes whose wanderings happen to be inconvenient, for the time in a pound called *Ceteris Paribus.* The study of some groups of tendencies is isolated by the assumption *other things being equal*; the existence of other tendencies is not denied, but their disturbing effect is neglected for a time. The more the issue is thus narrowed, the more exactly it can be handled; but also the less closely does it correspond to real life.

You can only handle the problems of a dynamic world by narrowing the scope of the investigation. Marshall does not want to abstract too much from reality, but he goes as far as he can without becoming wholly unrealistic.

MARSHALLIAN THEORY OF DISTRIBUTION

This morning we are ready for the discussion of Marshall's theory of distribution. It is not an entirely new subject to Marshall. He is still concerned with value in his discussion of distribution; he is here occupied with the determination of the price or value of the factors of production – capital, land, labor and enterprise. Why does Marshall treat the distribution theory in a separate book, when his analysis is similar to the analysis of the determination of value in the case of the commodities produced by the use of the factors of production? He gives only one reason – that in the case of commodities produced through the use of the factors of production, they are, in a free enterprise economy, produced for the market, whereas labor is not.

The first point to which we have to direct our attention is the fact that human agents of production are not bought and sold as machinery and other material agents of production are. The worker sells his work, but he himself remains his own property: those who bear the expenses of rearing and educating him receive but very little of the price that is paid for his services in later years (p. 466).

So, because of the fact that labor is not produced for the market (that is, the workers as agents in the productive process), this would be true not only of workers, but also of entrepreneurs and businessmen. In the case of capital goods, the principles are the same as in the case of commodities. Land differs because it is fixed in amount; it would be in the same category as any non-reproducible good or commodity. The value of land cannot have any effect on its supply.

> ... The keynote of this Book (Book VI) is in the fact that free human beings are not brought up to their work on the same principle as a machine, a horse, or a slave. If it were, there would be very little difference between the distribution and the exchange side of value; for every agent of production would reap a return adequate to cover its own expenses of production with wear-and-tear, etc.; at all events after allowance had been made for causal failures to adjust supply to demand (p. 418).

Note that the classical economists made exactly that assumption – that labor was just a commodity. With the exception of land, they assumed that in fact normal or natural wages were determined by the cost of producing labor and capital. If that were true, then for Marshall there would be no distinction between distribution and exchange, but:

> ... as it is, our growing power over nature makes her yield an ever larger surplus above necessaries; and this is not absorbed by an unlimited increase of the population. There remain therefore the question: What are the general causes which govern the distribution of this surplus among the people? (p. 418).

The output is more than enough to cover the cost of producing the factors of production and this is not limited by the increase of population. There remains therefore the problem of determining what governs the distribution of this surplus of wealth among the people. There are a number of similarities between Marshall's theory of distribution and that of commodities. He is merely calling attention to the fact that as a result of technological improvements, output has increased by so much over the decades that the national dividend is more than sufficient to meet the costs of producing the reproducible factors of production. Something is left over. Hence, in the theory of distribution, Marshall says we have to inquire into the distribution of the surplus. The classical economists also noted that the productive process results in a surplus and they argued that it could not go to labor because to the extent that wages rose above the standard of living level, population would increase and consequently the supply of labor would increase, forcing wages down again. It could not go to the capitalists, because the capitalists assumed some minimum rate of profit; if the rate of profit increased above this level, capital accumulation would increase and profit would fall again because of a resort to lower margins of land utilization, and the surplus would then go to the landowners in the form of rent.

Marshall could not accept this because it was contrary to fact. He notes that since the time of Adam Smith and Ricardo the standard of living had increased in Britain. Great numbers of the laboring population in fact command an income in excess of the amount necessary to meet their purely physical and biological needs.[32]

Now what is the principle, according to Marshall, which determines the value per unit of any given factor of production? As in Marshall's theory of commodities and their value, the value of any unit of the factors of production is determined by supply and demand.

> The production of *everything*, whether an agent of production or a commodity ready for immediate consumption, is carried forward up to that limit or margin at which there is an equilibrium between the forces of *demand* and *supply*. The amount of the thing and its price, the amounts of the several factors or agents of production used in making it, and their prices – all these elements mutually govern one another, and if an external cause should alter any one of them the effect of the disturbance extends to all the others (p. 437).

In his discussion of wages:

> ... again we see that demand and supply exert coordinate influences on wages; neither has a claim on predominance... Wages tend to equal the net product of labor; its marginal productivity rules the *demand-price* for it; and, on the other side, wages tend to retain a close though indirect and intricate relation with the cost of rearing, training and sustaining the energy of efficient labor. The various elements of the problem mutually determine (in the sense of governing) one another; and incidentally this secures that supply-price and demand-price tend to equality: *wages are not governed by demand-price nor by supply-price, but by the whole set of causes which govern demand and supply.*

Let us, in continuation of this line of thought, first discuss the determination of the price of labor.

> ... We have seen how the alert businessman is ever seeking for the most profitable application of his resources, and endeavoring to make use of each several agent of production up to that margin, or limit, at which he would gain by transferring a small part of his expenditure to some other agent; and how he is thus, so far as his influence goes, the medium through which the principle of substitution so adjusts the employment of each agent that, in its marginal application, its cost is proportionate to the additional net product resulting from its use. We have to apply this general reasoning to the case of the hire of labor...

> ... sometimes it is heard that somebody says that a certain farmer starves his land for labor. Perhaps he has enough horse and plant; but "if he took on another man, he would get his money back; and a good deal more;" that is *the net product of an additional man would more than cover his wages.* Let us suppose that a farmer is raising a question as to the number of his shepherds. For simplicity, we may suppose that an additional man would not require any further expenditure on plant or stock; that he would save the farmer himself just as much trouble in some ways as he gives in others; so that nothing has to be allowed for earnings of management (even when these are interpreted broadly so as to include insurance against risk, etc.); and lastly that the farmer reckons that he would do just so much in preventing the wastage of lambs, and in other ways *as will increase by twenty his annual output of sheep* in good condition. That is to say, he reckons that *the net product of an additional man will be twenty sheep.* If he can be got for much less than the equivalent of their price, the alert farmer will certainly hire him; *but, if only for about that price,* the farmer will be on the *margin* of doubt; and the man may then be called a *marginal shepherd,* because his employment is marginal (pp. 426–429).

This illustration has been chosen from a simple industry; but, though the form may be different, the substance of the problem is the same in every industry. . . . the wages of every class of labor tend to be equal to the net product due to the additional labor of the marginal laborer of that class.

This doctrine has sometimes been put forward as the theory of wages. (J. B. Clark and others) But there is no valid ground for any such pretension. The doctrine that the earnings of a worker tend to be equal to the net product of his work, has by *itself* no real meaning; since in order to estimate net product, we have to take for granted all the expenses of production of the commodity on which he works, others than his own wages.

> But though this objection is valid against the claim that it contains a theory of wages; it is not valid against a claim that the doctrine throws into clear light the action of one of the causes that govern (pp. 429–430).

See Marshall's footnote No. 1, p. 428, where he has a table showing the traditional increase in marginal productivity from the hiring of an extra man, when the wages of a man is corresponding to 20 sheep.

(1)	(2)	(3)	(4)	(5)	(6)
No. of Shepherds	No. of Sheep	Product Due to Last Man	Average Product Per Man	Wages Bill (at a price of 20 sheep per man)	Excess of (2) over (5)
8	580	—	72.50	160	420
9	615	35	68.33	180	435
10	640	25	64.	200	440
11	660	20	60.	220	440
12	676	16	56.33	240	436

This table indicates that the farmer's interests are equally well served by hiring 10 or 11 men, but that they are less well served by hiring 8, 9, or 12. The 11th man (supposed to be of normal efficiency) is the marginal man – when the markets for labor and sheep are such that one man can be hired for a year for the price of 20 sheep.

To repeat, demand and supply govern all prices. So we have to find out what determines supply and demand. As we have already partly seen from the foregoing, what determines *demand*, we will continue the analysis of the factors which determine the demand for labor, namely marginal productivity.

The *one* cause determining the value of labor mentioned by Marshall is demand; and demand for labor is determined by the marginal productivity of labor:

> . . . The wages of every class of labor tend to be equal to the net product due to the additional labor of the marginal laborer of that class (p. 429).

The exact way in which Marshall defines the marginal product is seen in the table (p. 428). The marginal product is the net increase in the value of the total output resulting from the employment of one additional unit of labor. It is determined by taking the total value of the product of any given quantity of labor (e.g. 9 workers on the table) – 615 sheep, adding an additional unit of labor (the 10th worker), ascertaining the value of the product of 10 workers – 640 sheep, subtracting the value of output before the addition of the 10th worker – 615 sheep – from the total output resulting from the hiring of 10 workers – 640 sheep. The difference – 25 sheep – is the *marginal net product.*

If the rate of wages for labor of this kind and grade were equal in value to 20 sheep per annum, the farmer would employ all laborers who would add 20 (or more) sheep to the output. If the supply of labor were fixed, Marshall assumes that all laborers would be employed who would be willing to work for the going wage rate. So long as an entrepreneur is adding laborers at less wages than his net marginal product, the entrepreneur can gain up to the point at which the wages and the net product are equal.

The marginal productivity tells us what one entrepreneur will be willing to pay for one additional worker, which will determine his demand for labor.

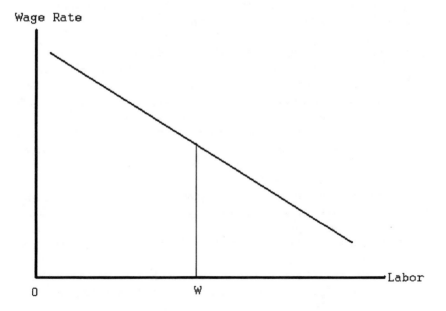

OW equals the wage equals marginal productivity. The demand curve shows how many units of labor would be hired at any given wage rate of a series, and that demand schedule is determined by the marginal productivity of labor.

Each entrepreneur in determining what wage he will be willing to pay for each additional unit of labor will determine how much each additional unit of labor will add to the entrepreneur's total product, and thus be willing to hire workers at a wage corresponding to the marginal product.

Additional employment will be offered up to the point where the wage is equal to the net addition to total production resulting from the hiring of the additional (marginal) worker.

If the productivity of labor should increase, the demand curve would shift upward, indicating that the entrepreneur would be willing to pay a higher wage for each quantity of labor. This increase in productivity may result from change in technology.

At any given time, however, there will be a certain demand curve for labor.

As more and more workers are hired, the marginal productivity of labor will decrease; i.e. there will be diminishing returns. Therefore the demand schedule is just like the demand schedule for a commodity. As in the case of the demand for commodities, the conditions of demand for labor is similar in all the Marshallian time periods. In considering conditions of demand, we do not have to take into account the various runs, as in the conditions of supply. Conditions of demand are the same in all the time periods.

The same holds true in the case of capital goods. The demand for capital goods is determined by the marginal productivity of capital. However, marginal productivity of labor and marginal productivity of capital are *not independent* of each other; because each can, within limits, be substituted for the other. So we cannot draw a demand schedule for either unless we know the price at which the other is available. All the various prices mutually determine one another.[33]

How would an entrepreneur combine workers and capital in order to get the best net result? He would combine the two factors in such a way that he will maximize his profit. But how will he do this? How will he be able to ascertain the best possible combination?

The knowledge of marginal productivity of labor and the marginal productivity of capital does not help him, *unless he knows the price of an additional unit of capital and the price of an additional unit of labor*. If he knows this he will be in a position to make a decision. But will he make it? What combination will maximize his profit?

If, e.g., the marginal productivity of capital results in a marginal product at a value of $50; and the marginal productivity of labor in a marginal product at a value of $10; what factors of production would the capitalist use, or what would the combination of these two factors be? You cannot tell from the mere knowledge of the marginal productivity of the two factors; you must know the price, or cost of each factor.

The entrepreneur will employ each factor up to the point where the value of the marginal product of each factor is equal to the price the entrepreneur must pay for that factor (for a unit of the factor). The entrepreneur will substitute one factor for another up to the point at which he can realize a greater net return from adding to one and not adding to the other. The substitution will stop at the point where the gain obtainable from adding to one factor will not be greater than from adding to the other. At that point it will be a matter of indifference to the entrepreneur which factor he uses. This point is where the marginal product of both factors is equal to their price or cost.[34]

> ... The nominal value of everything, whether it be a particular kind of labor or capital or anything else, rests, like the keystone of an arch, balanced in equilibrium between the contending pressures of its two opposing sides; the forces of demand press on the one side, and those of supply on the other (pp. 436–437).

Marshall on Laissez Faire

I discover that we have omitted the discussion of the problems stated by Marshall in Book V, Chapters 12 and 13. It is extremely important that we take up Marshall's points as presented in these two chapters, because they are points which have never been made by the exponents of classical theory.

Marshall's points simply undermine the economic defense of *laissez faire* or the contention that *laissez faire* will automatically result in maximum want satisfaction.

Adam Smith and his followers of the classical school all made the claim that *laissez faire* would maximize income and production. The marginal utility school said that *laissez faire* would maximize want satisfaction, because the individual knows better than anyone else what will benefit him; so if you let the individual alone, he, and he alone, will know what serves him best; the individual alone will know how to maximize his want satisfaction.

Marshall notes two qualifications to this thesis, he mentions two reasons why it is not true that *laissez faire* will accomplish the goals the classical school and the marginal utility school imputed to *laissez faire*. These two reasons are:

1. The unequal distribution of income; and
2. The existence of decreasing cost industries. (Marshall calls them increasing return industries.) His argument in this connection runs in terms of his

concept of "consumers' surplus." In the case of increasing return industries, maximum want satisfaction is impossible under *laissez faire*, because
government intervention will tend to increase want satisfaction of
consumers utilizing the production of increasing return industries, as
government intervention will increase the consumers' surplus above what
it would be under *laissez faire*.

We will first consider the second point. You remember Marshall's concept of
"consumers' surplus:"

> ... The excess of the price which he would be willing to pay rather than go without the
> thing, over that which he actually does pay, is the economic measure of this surplus satis-
> faction. It may be called consumer's surplus.

Marshall's concept of consumers' surplus may be shown on a curve such as this:

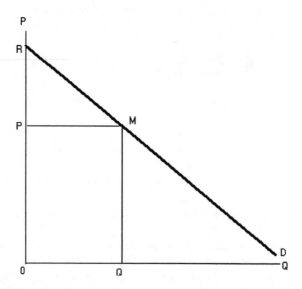

Total price paid by the consumer is OPMQ; consumer's surplus is PMR.
Consumer's surplus is the difference between the price the consumer would be
willing to pay and the price he actually pays. Though he pays the same price
for all units, the utility of the first units purchased is greater than that of the
later units. Consumer's surplus, according to Marshall, is an expression of satisfaction, and the excess of the price he would be willing to pay, is the measure
of this satisfaction.

As mentioned before, the concept raises some questions. It will be valid only if you can measure the satisfaction which an individual can derive from the use of a commodity; and Marshall has earlier in his work denied that satisfaction can be directly measured, because no two individuals will obtain the same intensities of satisfaction.[35] You cannot, I think, measure the total satisfaction derived in relation to the total satisfaction given up in the price paid for the commodity; and this determination is necessary in order to discover how much consumer's surplus is obtained in the form of surplus satisfaction.

Now back to Marshall's problem in connection with decreasing cost industries. On pp. 383–390, Marshall discusses the effect of a tax and a bounty (subsidy) on consumer's surplus under three conditions: constant return industries; diminishing return industries; and increasing return industries. We will confine ourselves here to the discussion of the effect of a bounty in connection with the latter – increasing return industries.

> . . . a bounty on such a commodity (a commodity which obeys the law of increasing return) causes so great a fall in its price to the consumer, that the consequent increase of consumers' surplus may exceed the total payment by the State to the producers; and certainly will do so in case the law of increasing return acts at all sharply (p. 389).

Marshall illustrates this proposition in the following manner in footnote No. 2, p. 389:

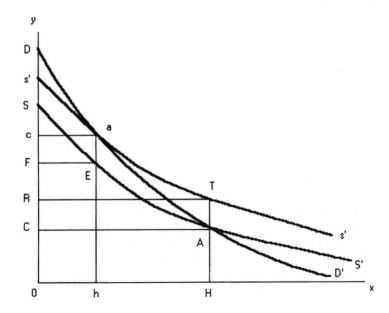

In the diagram, ss' is the position of the supply curve before the granting of the bounty, and SS' is the position of the supply curve after granting of the bounty. DD^1 is the demand curve. Thus "a" is the old equilibrium point, and "A" is the point to which the equilibrium moves when the bounty is given. The *increase* of the consumers' surplus (originally Dca) is represented by cCAa, while the direct payments made by the State under the subsidy (bounty) are represented by RCAT.

The increase in consumers' surplus is greater than the subsidy paid by the government. The granting of the bounty results in an increase in consumption from Oh to OH, at lower prices; because of the fact that the bounty makes greater production possible, and per unit total cost decreases as production increases.

Marshall's analysis of normalcy is not applicable here because of the instability of the equilibrium point.

If the government fixes the price below that currently charged by a decreasing cost industry, such as public utilities, and then gives the utilities a subsidy from a tax, the subsidy would be smaller than the increase in consumers' surplus because of the fact that the resulting expansion of production decreases the ATUC; i.e. the gain in the form of increase in consumers' surplus is greater than the loss of taxes.

The principle involved is that the new cost per unit will be lower, so the difference between the old price and the new price will partly be made up for by the lower unit cost.

What type of a tax should be used for the financing of the subsidy? What about a tax on the consumers themselves? That is, a sales tax on electricity produced by the public utility? This will not work because that would reduce the demand for the product and the situation would not be improved. The tax would have to be levied elsewhere.

> . . . One simple plan would be the levying of a tax by the community on their own incomes, or on the production of goods which obey the law of diminishing return, and devoting the tax to a bounty on the production of those goods with regard to which the law of increasing return acts sharply (p. 392).

The total satisfaction will be increased then by taxing the increasing cost industries – where the decrease in consumers' surplus will be less than the tax – and using the tax for a subsidy to the decreasing cost industries – where the increase in the consumers' surplus will be greater than the tax used for the subsidy.[36]

When government interferes in this way the total cost would not be so great as the increase in total satisfaction of consumers.

The principle of consumers' surplus overlooks the fact that in purchasing one commodity, the consumer foregoes the purchase of another; so in equilibrium there would be no consumers' surplus. I think that the surplus obtained is not so much a surplus of satisfaction, as Marshall assumes, as a surplus of purchasing power.

In any event, Marshall certainly undermines the whole rationale of *laissez faire*. Adam Smith's simple system of natural liberties with automatic regulation could no longer be rationalized on economic grounds.

Now we come to the first of Marshall's reasons which undermine the *laissez faire* theory of the best method of maximizing income, or want satisfaction.

> . . . Enough has been said to indicate the character of the second great limitation which has to be introduced into the doctrine that the maximum satisfaction is *generally* to be attained by encouraging each individual to spend his own resources in that way which suits him best. It is clear that if he spends his income in such a way as to increase the demand for the services of the poor and to increase their incomes, he adds something more to the total happiness than if he adds an equal amount to the incomes of the rich, because the happiness which an additional shilling brings to a poor man is greater than that which it brings to a rich one.

> . . . But further, even if we assume that a shilling's worth of happiness is of equal importance to whomsoever it comes, and that every shilling's worth of consumers' surplus is of equal importance from whatever commodity it is derived, we have to admit that the manner in which a person spends his income is a matter of direct economic concern to the community. For so far as he spends it on things which obey the law of diminishing return, he makes these things more difficult to be obtained by his neighbors, and thus lowered the real purchasing power of their incomes; while insofar as he spends it on things which obey the law of increasing return, he makes those things more easily obtainable to others, and thus increases the real purchasing power of their incomes.

These conclusions. . . do not by themselves afford a valid ground for government interference; but they show that much remains to be done, by a careful collection of statistics of demand and supply and interpretation of these data, in order to discover what are the limits of the work that society can with advantage do towards turning the economic actions of individuals into those channels in which they will add the most to the sum total of happiness (p. 393).[37]

Marshall states specifically that, because of the unequal distribution of wealth and because of the existence of increasing return industries, *laissez faire* policy may not result in maximum satisfaction of wants in the economy as a whole – a break with the classical and marginal utility economics.

What does equal distribution mean in Marshall's terms? Does it mean the same amount of money income to each individual or to each economic unit? Or is it equal real income per individual or economic unit. Only if you assume that the needs of all individuals are equal, will equal distribution of money income result in equal distribution of real income.

If needs of individuals are different, then equal satisfaction of different needs would require an unequal distribution of money income.

We have to distinguish between the effect of an increase in production on the ATUC in a firm and in an industry. People are convinced that what businessmen think is true, is true; that is, manufacturing enterprises are operating at constant cost on a long range of output. There seems no reason to doubt that in many industries, there is a long range of output where ATUC is constant.

In the case of monopolies and public utilities there is a difference, because of the fact that the firm is the industry. We have here the effect of overhead cost; i.e., total overhead is spread over a greater number of units as production increases, which means decreasing total cost, as long as the variable cost per unit does not increase more than the fixed cost per unit decreases. When the plant is installed and the distribution set up in order to produce a maximum output per unit of time and distribute this output; as long as the public utility is producing at less than full capacity, an increase in production will result in decreased per unit total cost, because overhead is spread over more units.

But this is not what Marshall means when he talks of increasing returns. In his system, you could only have decreasing cost due to external economies; and this could be in almost any industry.

Modern price theorists, and people in general, think in terms of the former proposition; i.e., they apply the principle of decreasing cost to water plants, electric power, city transportation, railroads, and other forms of public utilities and public transportation.

Laissez Faire continued

Classical economists would argue that unequal distribution of income is advantageous, because it would mean an increase in total saving, which means increase in capital accumulation, because they assumed all savings to be automatically invested.

Capital accumulation would, according to classical theory, result in increased well being.

Does Marshall accept Say's Law? Keynes says that he can find no specific place in Marshall's *Principles* where Marshall states his acceptance of Say's Law, but that it seems to be implied.

> ... in this broad sense it is true that all production is for consumption; that the national dividend is convertible with the aggregate of net production, and also with the aggregate of consumption.

Under ordinary conditions of industry, production and consumption move together; there is no consumption except that for which the way has been prepared by appropriate production: and all production is followed by the consumption for which it is designed. There may be indeed some miscalculation in particular branches of production; and a collapse of commercial credit may fill nearly all warehouses for a time with unsold goods. But such conditions are exceptional, and are not within our present view.

This statement seems to indicate an acceptance of Say's Law, where supply creates its own demand, money and goods are not hoarded, and the market is cleared of all goods.

Under *laissez faire* it is assumed that each will be rewarded according to his contributions. We have to distinguish between *laissez faire* and competition. *Laissez faire* will, in the real world, normally result in monopoly. The more *laissez faire*, the more monopoly. This is, of course, not what Smith meant. Smith assumed that when government withdrew its support from the existing monopolies, the competing forces of, selfish, calculating, and lazy individuals would prevent the creation of monopolies. The actual development has not been in this direction. When we justify certain government interferences today, it is in order to maintain competition. Antitrust legislation and measures are designed to preserve that competition, which will disappear under *laissez faire*. But government intervention for the preservation of competition means less *laissez faire*. We must sacrifice *laissez faire* in order to maintain competition.

As long as we have property income, we will have unequal distribution of income. If property were equally distributed, we would not have capitalism; so to the extent that measures taken towards the equalization of income are successful, to that extent we will have a reduction of capitalism.

Does Marshall tell us where to set the price in the decreasing cost industries? He is not certain whether government should control some part of the economy; it may result in greater evils from administration, etc., even if there are evils, it is not true, as some people maintain, that

> ... a position of equilibrium of demand and supply is one of maximum satisfaction in the aggregate: that is, that an increase of production beyond the equilibrium level would directly diminish the aggregate satisfaction of both parties. *The doctrine so interpreted is not true.*

> In the first place it assumes that all differences in wealth between the different parties concerned may be neglected, and that the satisfaction which is rated at a shilling by any one of them, may be taken as equal to one that is rated at a shilling by any other. Now it is obvious that, if the producers were as a class very much poorer than the consumers, aggregate satisfaction might be increased by a stinting of supply when it would cause a

great rise in demand price (elastic demand); and that if the consumers were the poorer as
a class, the aggregate satisfaction might be increased by extending the production beyond
the equilibrium amount and selling the commodity at a loss (pp. 390–391).

This means that Marshall, if we disregard his remark about the evils of government regulation because of the interest of the ones making the regulations,
assumes government regulation to be beneficial. Furthermore it seems to be
indicated that his concept of equal distribution of income is not equal distribution of money income, because of the different needs of individuals. The
unequal distribution of income then, according to Marshall, prevents the maximization of satisfaction. These are serious blows to the doctrine of *laissez faire*.

Where would Marshall set the price in the decreasing cost industries? He
does not say it specifically, but the logical conclusion of his remarks would be
that the price would be fixed at a level of production where the cost starts to
become increasing per unit of output. It would be the price which would just
cover variable cost, but not fixed or overhead cost.

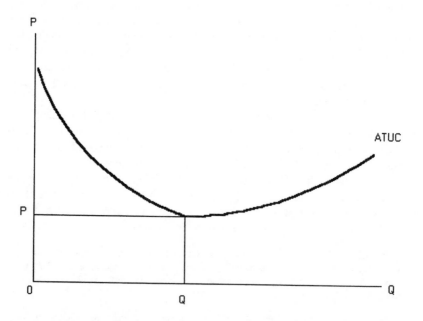

On the above diagram, the price would be P and the output Q. The price
would be the point before which the decrease in overhead cost per unit is greater

than the increase in variable unit cost, and therefore total unit cost decreasing. At an output OQ we have minimum total cost because from now on, the increase in variable cost per unit more than counteracts the decrease in fixed cost per unit. So we may assume that price P would be the price at which Marshall would logically arrive.

I would go much further. I would set the price at zero, and let the production of water, gas, electricity, personal transportation, and the use of other household services be free of charge; and then let the operations of the public utilities be paid out of general taxation. The rationale of this would be that it would result in better economic conditions in the area as a whole. What is the difference between the free services of the streets and highways and the city bus service on the streets? What is the difference between the free service of education, police and fire departments, and the service of public utilities? Waste? You would not have any substantial waste, as people would have to use household appliances, just as they have to use automobiles in order to use the highways. From a purely economic viewpoint, there is much to be said for it. The TVA put in very low rates, and the effect on consumption was tremendous. Free local transportation would solve traffic problems, decentralize the cities, etc.

Let us return to Marshall's labor theory.

In his wage theory, which is analyzed in terms of supply and demand, just as with normal value in the theory of commodities, Marshall must have the supply of labor determined by cost of production. If this is not the case, then he cannot establish a *normal* wage. This presents problems.

1. The parents bear the cost of production; it is not borne by those who receive the rewards. Costs are borne by the parents and by society at large, but the reward is received by the individual.

    ... The first point to which we have to direct our attention is the fact that human agents of production are not bought and sold as machinery and other material agents of production are. The worker sells his work, but he himself remains his own property; those who bear the expenses of rearing and educating him receive but very little of the price that is paid for his services in later years (p. 466).

How then is it possible to relate cost of production of labor to the price of labor?

2. The second great difference in kind (from other things sold and bought) is the fact that labor is not produced for sale in the market. People do not "produce" children in order to sell the children's labor power in the market.

These are the two major factors, or peculiarities, which distinguish labor from the other factors of production, and from commodities in general. There are other minor problems, such as less mobility of labor, etc., but they are differences in degree, not in kind.

If you accept Malthus's theory of population, the problems are solved. Then the supply of labor will always be such that the wages of labor will be around the standard of living level. But Marshall was unwilling to accept the Malthusian doctrine in its extreme form. Marshall notes that in the time of Malthus, wages were so low in England that they just covered the minimum necessities; but in Marshall's own time, the standard of living had increased very much; so he would not accept the Malthusian theory.

On the other hand, if the supply of labor is independent of its cost of production, then he could not assume any forces which would work themselves out and if given sufficient time, result in the "normal" wage.

One way in which Marshall solves his problem is by his definition of supply of labor and his definition of labor power; he defines these in such terms that the quantity of labor power should be measured in money terms.

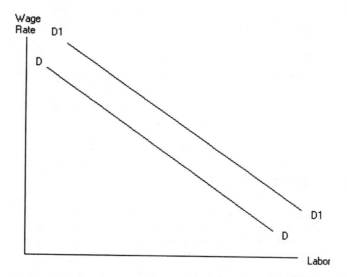

According to Marshall, marginal productivity will determine the wages offered. As more and more workers are added, the marginal productivity will decrease (diminishing return); therefore, lower wages will be offered – a demand curve sloping downward to the right, DD.

If there should be an increase in marginal productivity, higher wages will be offered for such additional worker; the demand curve will shift upward,

D¹D¹. When this happens, according to Marshall, more labor will be forth-coming.

Why does the supply curve for labor slope upward to the right? For a commodity, the supply curve slopes upward because of increasing per unit cost, as production increases. But the labor supply curve slopes upward because of the increasing *disutility of working*. The pain involved in working or the disu-tility of working is the real cost of labor, which is measured by the money offered in order to offset that disutility.

The supply curve then is determined by the disutility of working. On the assumption that disutility increases as longer hours are worked, an individual will be willing to work longer hours only when wages increase; his maximum length of working time will be governed by the relationship of his marginal disutility of working and the wage offered.

But in terms of the availability of labor in the long run, Marshall must say that it will be determined by the cost of rearing and educating labor:

> We conclude then that the increase of wages, unless earned under unwholesome conditions, almost always increases the strength, physical, mental and even moral of the coming generation; and that, other things being equal, an increase in the earnings that are to be got by labor increases its rate of growth; or, in other words, a rise in its demand-price increases its supply. If the state of knowledge, and of social and domestic habits be given; then the vigor of the people as a whole if not their number, and both the numbers and vigor of any trade in particular may be said to have a *supply price in this sense, that there is a certain level of demand-price which will keep them stationary; that a higher price would cause them to increase, and that a lower price would cause them to decrease* (pp. 441–442).

> ... Wages tend to equal the net product of labor; its marginal productivity rules the demand price for it; and, on the other side, wages tend to retain a close though indirect and intri-cate relation with the cost of rearing, training and sustaining the energy of efficient labor (p. 442).

Marshall then, defines labor as the ability to work; so cost of labor production is not only the cost of producing the number of workers, but also the cost of creating their efficiency, that is, the cost of creating their physical, mental and sustaining abilities, which determine the efficiency of labor. (He mentions *earning efficiency* on p. 456.)

If at any time wages are higher than the cost of creating, or increasing effi-ciency, more labor will be forthcoming, without any necessary increase in number of workers; simply because the workers may be willing to increase the working; that is, increase the disutility of working, now justified by the higher wage.

Marshall has to assume that even if workers increase their real wage, they do not increase their efficiency so much that it cannot be increased still further.

In Marshall's terms, labor supply is not merely in terms of the number of workers, but the efficiency of workers. He uses a unit of work to measure labor supply. In the long run the cost of rearing, educating and training children must be considered.

The Marshallian supply of labor is the amount of work that will be performed; i.e., the amount of labor forthcoming at any given level of real wages. In order to substantiate his concept of normality Marshall must prove:

1. that demand for labor has influence on supply of labor;
2. that the supply of labor forthcoming is controlled by the cost of producing labor power.

Labor Supply

Marshall is of the opinion that in the eastern countries the number of the members of the labor force, or the laboring class *as a whole* is independent of the level of real wages, except insofar as it is related to the death rate. Generally, however, the number of the labor class would, according to Marshall, be independent of the real wage level. In any given trade or industry, however, the supply of labor (in terms of number) will be dependent on the wage level, but not with respect to the labor force as a whole.

There is a direct correlation between efficiency of the labor force and the real wage, however. In the days of Marshall, even, the wages of the labor force were so low (that is for laborers as a class) in relation to the standard of living that increase in skill, strength, and vigor, that is, in efficiency of the workers, will result from an increase in real wages. So Marshall assumes that an increase in real wages will increase efficiency of workers – an important part of his concept of the supply of labor.

Marshall distinguishes between "strict necessities" and "conventional necessities." Strict necessities may be considered to be the level of consumption necessary to maintain physical health; and conventional necessities, the consumption goods which are not strictly necessary in a biological sense. These are necessities in the sense that the workers will be willing to give up some of the strict necessities in order to obtain the conventional necessities.

> ... This, the question how closely the supply of labor responds to the demand for it, is in a great measure resolved into the question how great a part of the present consumption of the people *at large* consists of necessaries, strictly so called, for the life and efficiency of young and old; how much consists of conventional necessaries which theoretically could be dispensed with, but *practically* would be preferred by the majority of the people to some of those things that were really necessary for efficiency; and how much is really

superfluous regarded as a means towards production, though of course part of it may be of supreme importance regarded as an end in itself (p. 440).

An increase in the real wage which enters into strict necessities "more than pays its way," according to Marshall:

> ... Any increase in consumption that is strictly necessary to efficiently pays its own way and adds to, as much as draws from, the national dividend. But an increase in consumption, that is not thus necessary, can be afforded only through an increase in man's command over nature; and that can come about through advance in knowledge and the arts of production, through improved organization and access to larger and richer sources of raw material, and lastly through the growth of capital and the material means of attaining desired ends in any form (p. 440).

So any increase in wages which results in increase in consumption of strict necessaries more than pays its way; it increases the labor supply in terms of efficiency by increasing the health and vigor of the workers. The increase in real wages which results in increased consumption of conventional necessaries, also pays its way by increasing the morale of the working force, and thereby increasing efficiency.

Even in the England of Marshall's time, the wages were not so high that they covered both strict and conventional necessities, Marshall assumed, so an increase in real wages would, according to Marshall, increase the labor supply in Marshall's terms.

For a given worker, during any given period of time, the amount of work he will perform will depend on the real wage he will obtain, because of the disutility resulting from an increase in the working time from 7 to 8 or from 8 to 9 hours, according to Marshall.

In the long run, however, although Marshall notes that the workers are not produced for the market, the supply of labor is determined by cost of production; in the long run an increase in real wages will call forth more labor, because of the fact that an increase in the real wage increases the efficiency of the workers.

As long as you are ready to accept the Malthusian theory of population, there is a direct relationship between real wages and labor supply in terms of numbers. Marshall did not accept the Malthusian theory of population; but he maintained that the workers did not yet have so high a living standard that an increase in real wages would not have any influence on the supply of labor. So the increase in real wages, to Marshall, will result in an increase in labor supply, but mostly in terms of increased efficiency of the working class, not so much in terms of numbers of workers.[38]

If I were a classical economist, which I am not, I think I would assume that the supply of labor is determined by non-economic factors, so that they would have to be taken as given.

There is, however, something to be said for Marshall's point, that is, given low real wages, there will be some increase in efficiency resulting from increase in real wages. It will, of course, depend on what country you are talking about. In Marshall's days this proposition might have been correct to some extent, but whether or not it would be correct in the Great Britain or the United States of today, we do not know. When we are considering the real world of today, we will have to take into consideration the level of real wages, health and death rate. So, possibly, for the lowest paid workers today Marshall's proposition may be correct. But for the great mass of American workers today, no essential increase in efficiency will result from increase in real wages, because the real wage is above the level which gives sufficiency in terms of health, vigor, etc.

Today we have strong labor unions which have increased the real wage level above the level Marshall considered necessary to cover the "strict necessaries."

What determines the national wage bill (that is that part of the national dividend – as Marshall calls it – or of the net national product – the modern equivalent? – which accrues to labor)? With respect to the distribution of aggregate national dividend, it is distributed among the factors of production according to the need for their services – that is determined by demand.

> . . . the uses of each agent of production are governed by the general conditions of demand in relation to supply; that is, on the one hand, by the urgency of all the uses to which the agent can be put, taken together with the means at the command of those who need it; and on the other hand, by the available stocks of it (p. 432).

Workers get the net product of their labor, but this proposition may not mean very much because that depends on the supply of labor. All the various elements mutually determine each other.

According to Marshall, there is no such thing as technological unemployment. Labor in general is not in competition with machinery; increase in capital goods will increase the marginal productivity of labor – more labor will be demanded at any given wage rate.

To return to the distribution of income. The factors which increase rapidly will find their proportion of national dividend decreasing, because,

> . . . an increase in the proportionate share or rate of remuneration of any agent is likely to bring into play forces, that will reduce that share and leave a larger proportionate share of the dividend to be shared among others. That is because the initial increase will do some-thing towards filling up the more urgent needs for that agent; and will thus lessen the marginal need for it, and lower the price at which it can find a market (p. 445).

Marshall would say that the alternative is not between labor and capital, but between labor "with little waiting" and labor "with more waiting." The national dividend or aggregate net product:

... is distributed among (the agents of production), speaking generally, in proportion to the need which people have for their several services – i.e. not the total need, but the marginal need. By this is meant the need at that point, at which people are indifferent whether they purchase a little more of the services (or the fruits of the services) of one agent, or devote their further resources to purchasing the services (or the fruits) of the services) of other agents. Other things being equal, each agent is likely to increase the faster, the larger the share which it gets, unless indeed it is not capable of being increased at all. But every such increase will do something towards filling up the more urgent needs for that agent; and will thus lessen the marginal need for it, and lower the price at which it can find a market. That is to say, an increase in the proportionate share, or rate of remuneration, of an agent is likely to bring into play forces, that will reduce that share, and leave a larger proportionate share of the dividend to be shared among others. This reflex may be slow. But, if there is no violent change in the arts of production or in the general economic condition of society, the supply of each agent will be closely governed by its cost of production; account being taken of those conventional necessaries, which constantly expand as the growing richness of the national income yields to one class after another an increasing surplus above the mere necessaries for efficiency (p. 445).

Marshall does not say that labor "should" receive a certain proportion of national dividend. He could not say either that labor receives the net product of labor (as a measure of labor's total share of national dividend) because the net product depends on the amount of labor; it does not tell us how much labor gets out of the total income (that is, its share of total dividend). What the worker earns depends on all other prices; so the ethical concept of J. B. Clark – that wages are determined by marginal productivity, means nothing; it merely says that labor gets what labor gets.

CONCLUDING REMARKS

I would not classify Marshall as a positive economist.

When you approach economic problems from the supply side, you make a social approach; when you approach from the demand side, you abstract from society, and economics ceases to be occupied with social phenomena. In conducting his supply analysis the economist looks at economics as a matter in relation to human behavior in society; production is going on as a process in society. Production is a cooperative process, in which several people are involved.

Under demand analysis, you consider that the problems and solutions of Robinson Crusoe on his island are applicable to the United States in the 20th century.

As long as you consider the individual as a self-determining unit, you abstract from society. Wants must therefore be considered as determined by nature (a la the marginal utility school). But, when you place man in society, you discover that his wants are socially determined almost 100%; the individual is no longer a unit, he is a social product.

The positivist say that they do not pass value judgements, and then go ahead and pass them right and left.

Public policy in the United States has been "what is good for General Motors is good for the United States." A business-oriented economy bases its policy on the principles which will benefit business. In Marx's terms – M–C–M^1. That is, production is organized for profit, even if the technological logic is production for consumption.

What Marshall tried was to make a synthesis of the older classical (cost of production) theory and the modern demand (marginal utility) theory. Marshall is a man of great ability, he tried to take all factors into account and "leaves always the back door open."

NOTES

1. Paul M. Sweezy, "Economics and the Crisis of Capitalism," *The Economic Forum*, III (Spring 1935): 70. Murray E. Polakoff (of The University of Texas) has recently received a letter from Dr. Sweezy in which he stated that he has long ago ceased to believe that capitalist economics can be of much use to a socialist society. But he apparently still holds that Marxian economics, "is essentially the economics of capitalism."

2. According to the Winston Dictionary, "teleology" is the "idea or doctrine that the existence of everything in nature can be explained in terms of purpose." As C. E. Ayres expresses it in the *Theory of Economic Progress*, "This way of thinking has been aptly characterized as that of people who think it very wonderful that fishes which after all can live in nothing else should *be provided with so much water*" (Chapel Hill: University of North Carolina Press, 1944), p. 63.

3. In addition to assuming, with the classicists, perfect competition, Marx also assumes that commodities exchange at their Value – one coat equals ten yards of linen because they contain the same amount of embodied labor.

4. Marx's theory is the inverse of neo-classical theory, which assumes that the worker obtains the marginal additional value resulting from hiring of *marginal workers*.

5. Marx denies the Malthusian theory of population, because Marx considers the laws of population determined by cultural factors, not by any primitive "natural" propensity in man to reproduce.

6. In the third edition of his *Principles*, Ricardo agrees that labor can be displaced by machinery, although he had denied it in the first and second *editions*.

7. The reason why the people of India had a tendency to hoard precious metals, which amounts to storing up highly liquid commodities, was that they wanted to store potential use-value. The purpose was not to obtain surplus value. Commodities were exchanged for other commodities (precious metals); it was the classical process, ending in commodities. This could not cause interruption in the functioning of a simple commodity producing economy, which the Indian economy was formerly.

8. The reason why Keynes has lately been set up in mathematical formulae is that his theory is also a theory of comparative statistics, which lends itself to mathematics. This, I think, is unfortunate.

9. It is interesting to note that all the influential economic theories took as their unit of investigation the economy as a whole; this is true of Smith, Ricardo, Marx and Keynes. But the marginal utility analysis, although it had considerable influence in academic circles, had no influence on policy nor on the thinking of the man in the street. This for pretty obvious reasons. When the individual is abstracted from society, the theory obviously *can have no application to any* particular economic system or economic order.

10. See Marshall's *Principles of Economics: An Introductory Volume*, (London: Macmillan) 8th ed., p. 15.

11. *Ibid.*, pp. 15–16.

12. Ibid., p. 16.

13. *Principles*, p. 28.

14. See *Principles*, p. 33.

15. You take two commodities and draw a curve so that at any point on it would be a matter of indifference whether any further exchange took place at that point. Economists do not inquire as to why this is true, but simply accept it as a fact. I have never been convinced that utility and want *satisfaction is not the* background of determining wants.

16. A student complained of Marshall's use of the term "willingness" to buy. Marshall fully realized that the term was purely academic in the case of a *lack of purchasing power*.

17. See again *Principles*, pp. 82–83.

18. This is the basis for Professor Robert H. Montgomery's public utility theory.

19. See *Principles*, pp. 135–136.

20. See *Principles*, pp. 130–131, 133, 137–138.

21. *Principles*, pp. 289–290.

22. *Principles*, pp. 366–367 for discussion of the stationary state, and Marshall's modification of the concept.

23. See *Principles*, pp. 304–305.

24. *Ibid.*, p. 289.

25. *Principles*, p. 304.

26. *Principles*, pp. 314–315.

27. See *Principles*, pp. 310–311.

28. The "historical" school in Germany – Gustav Schmoller, Friedrich List – may be considered forerunners of the American institutionalist school.

29. For definition, see *Principles*, p. 61.

30. Marshall has a no-rent part on the intensive margin of land; labor and capital would be pushed so far that the return will cover only wages and costs. And in the same way, you can have no-rent machines, when the return covers only marginal cost.

31. Kenneth E. Boulding, *Economic Analysis* (New York: Harpers, 1948) p. 432.

32. Marshall notes that the standard of living of many workers at his time is greater than the standard of living of a Medieval prince, pp. 574–575.

33. *Principles*, pp. 436–437.

34. *Principles*, pp. 431–433.

35. *Principles*, pp. 12–14.

36. *Principles*, pp. 387–388.

37. See also *Principles*, pp. 415–416.

38. *Principles*, pp. 441–442.